IMAGES
of Modern America

KENOSHA

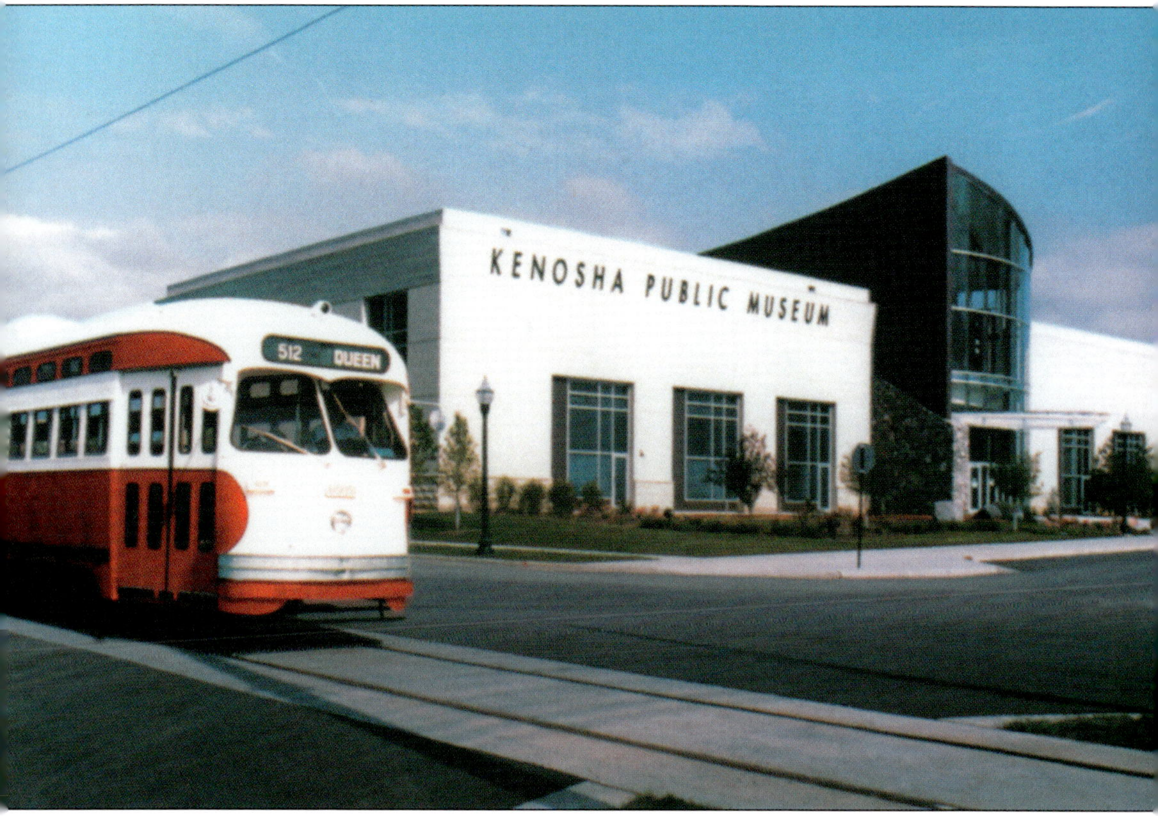

This postcard from 2002 shows two of Kenosha's most well-known landmarks: the Kenosha Public Museum and the downtown trolley heading to one of its 18 stops. Oddly enough, both of these constructions are fairly new, although they are modern iterations of historical establishments in Kenosha. (Courtesy of the Kenosha Public Museum.)

On the Front Cover: Clockwise from top left:
Harbor Park after the factory was torn down (courtesy of the Kenosha Public Museum), the streetcar's first day in service (courtesy of the Kenosha Public Museum), the Kenosha Kingfish mascot King Elvis the First (courtesy of the Kenosha Kingfish Baseball Club), Herbert's Jewelers at its original downtown location in 1950 (courtesy of Herbert's Jewelers), a 4-H float from the 1970 Memorial Day Parade (courtesy of the Kenosha County University of Wisconsin-Extension).

On the Back Cover: From left to right:
The 1971 Kenosha 4-H State Congress (courtesy of the Kenosha County University of Wisconsin-Extension), students building a snowman at Carthage College (courtesy of the Carthage College Archives), the original building for the Kenosha Public Museum (courtesy of the Kenosha Public Museum).

IMAGES
of Modern America

KENOSHA

Jennifer Billock

ARCADIA
PUBLISHING

ISBN 978-1-4671-1412-7

Published by Arcadia Publishing
Charleston, South Carolina

Printed in the United States of America

Library of Congress Control Number: 2014958530

For all general information, please contact Arcadia Publishing:
Telephone 843-853-2070
Fax 843-853-0044
E-mail sales@arcadiapublishing.com
For customer service and orders:
Toll-Free 1-888-313-2665

Visit us on the Internet at www.arcadiapublishing.com

Dedicated to my family and friends who support me and my writing, no matter what. You all mean the world to me.

Contents

Acknowledgments

A very heartfelt thank-you goes out to the Kenosha Kingfish, Herbert's Jewelers, the Kenosha Public Museum, the Kenosha County Extension, and the Bristol Renaissance Faire for your generosity in freely sharing your private photograph collections. Thanks go to the staff of the archives at Carthage College for helping me in every way possible; it is because of all of you that this book exists. And thanks also to the team at 1050AM WLIP for allowing me on the *Happenings Magazine* radio show to promote this book.

Thanks so much to my title manager at Arcadia, Jesse Darland, for all your thoughts and assistance, and to Emilia Monell for seeing me through the proposal stages.

As always, thanks to my spectacular husband, wonderful family, and great friends for supporting me, pushing me, dealing with my wacky schedule, and helping me along in every way possible to pursue my dreams. I love you all.

INTRODUCTION

In spring 1835, early explorers came to Kenosha on a whim, after a disagreement with landowners farther north—the city was meant to be where Racine is now. A failed business deal sparked an argument that forced the potential landowners out of town, and they headed south to Pike Creek on June 6, 1835.

The exploration party settled there, taking on the name given to the area by fur traders. Pike Creek did not stay Pike Creek though. The next year, a post office was established under the name Pike, and the settlement name changed with it. In 1837, it changed yet again. Townspeople held a meeting to rename the area and decided on Southport, as it was located at the southernmost Wisconsin port on Lake Michigan. The town was officially incorporated in 1850, and with that came another name change. Finally, one stuck. Locals decided to name the town Kenosha, a mixture of place and history. At that point, Pike Creek had grown to become Pike River, and it bisected downtown, forming a little peninsula with the Pike on two sides and the lake on one. Native Ojibwa Indians noticed that pike and trout reproduced at this meeting place of lake and river, and labeled the land Masu-kinoja, or "place where fish spawn." Kinoja became Kenosha, and the city has been named such ever since.

Kenosha has grown up around that little peninsula in the Pike River. From humble beginnings of just a few people, the city now sprawls out over roughly 27 square miles with a population of more than 100,000. The peninsula is still there, still surrounded by the Pike, but now it is called Simmons Island and has a sprawling park and beach, a beach house listed in the National Register of Historic Places, and two lighthouses. During 1837, about 141 boats came calling on Kenosha, and the town decided to put a lighthouse on Simmons Island. The early incarnation was a thing of beauty—a 10-foot-tall oak stump topped with a wooden platform lined with rocks. Every night, the "lighthouse" keeper would light a fire on the rocks so boats would know where to go. The current light, the Southport Lighthouse, did not arrive until 1866. The other lighthouse in Kenosha, the North Pier Light, arrived 40 years later, in 1906. It was painted red, typical of lighthouses that dotted the Lake Michigan coast, and built to match a twin lighthouse in Milwaukee. In 2011, the North Pier Light was deemed excess by the Coast Guard and auctioned off to the highest bidder. John Burhani, a local artist, bought the light for $5,000 and transformed it into his art studio. The light is located on the north pier of Simmons Island.

Simmons Island has a unique history all its own. For a year, beginning in 1835, it was the site of a miniature war: the Resique War. Samuel Resique and John Noble were two explorers from Chicago. In July 1835, they left the city and came north to Kenosha. They noticed right away that the land had been claimed, but decided to stay a while and enjoy the scenery. Then they happened upon Simmons Island. The land was still wild, although owned by the Pike Creek settlement, and had no buildings or residents on it. Resique and Noble decided to claim the island as their own and set to work building a cabin. Once construction was complete, Resique left for Chicago to obtain supplies and bring them back "home." While he was gone, Pike Creek residents realized the two were basically squatters on the island, attempting to keep it, and ordered Noble off the land. Noble, of course, refused, and then the real battle began. Early morning on July 25, six men armed with axes quietly boated over to the island. They did not come for a fight though—once they set foot on the island, the men began chopping down trees and building a fence. They enclosed a one-acre parcel in the fence, with Resique and Noble's cabin at the center. Noble held his position. When Resique returned a few days later with provisions, they set to work. Every night, a little bit of the fence would mysteriously disappear, until it was completely missing. It was the official declaration of war. From then through the summer of 1836, armed skirmishes would pop up around the island, with hostility increasing with every fight. Eventually, when the warring became a serious threat to the townspeople, a compromise was reached: Resique and Noble were allowed to take a portion of the land, and Pike Creek got the rest.

Kenosha's history does not end there; it carries on with historic downtown areas, refurbished buildings from the 1800s, and life-long residents. Kenosha was even an active stop on the Underground Railroad in the 1850s. Reuben Deming, whose home was located near the site of current-day Library Square, came to Kenosha in 1836. He was a Methodist preacher and despised slavery. He would often let runaway slaves hide in his attic. Deming and his wife stayed in Kenosha their entire lives and are buried in Green Ridge Cemetery in the city. The former location of his house is now marked with a historical marker.

Residents today hold fast to that sense of freedom, both of person and of creativity. Art and music play a huge role in the city, even attracting the likes of Duke Ellington, who played several concerts at Carthage College. Sports are big news as well; Carthage's teams are some of the top in their division. Kenosha almost always has its own baseball team playing at historic Simmons Field, the home stadium of the Kenosha Comets from the era of the All-American Girls Professional Baseball League (made famous by the movie *A League of their Own*).

Overall, it is not just location that makes Kenosha one of the top tourist destinations in the Midwest. Residents and visitors alike thrive on the city's scenery, culture, recreation, and excitement. There is nowhere else many would rather be.

One

Downtown and the Harbor Park

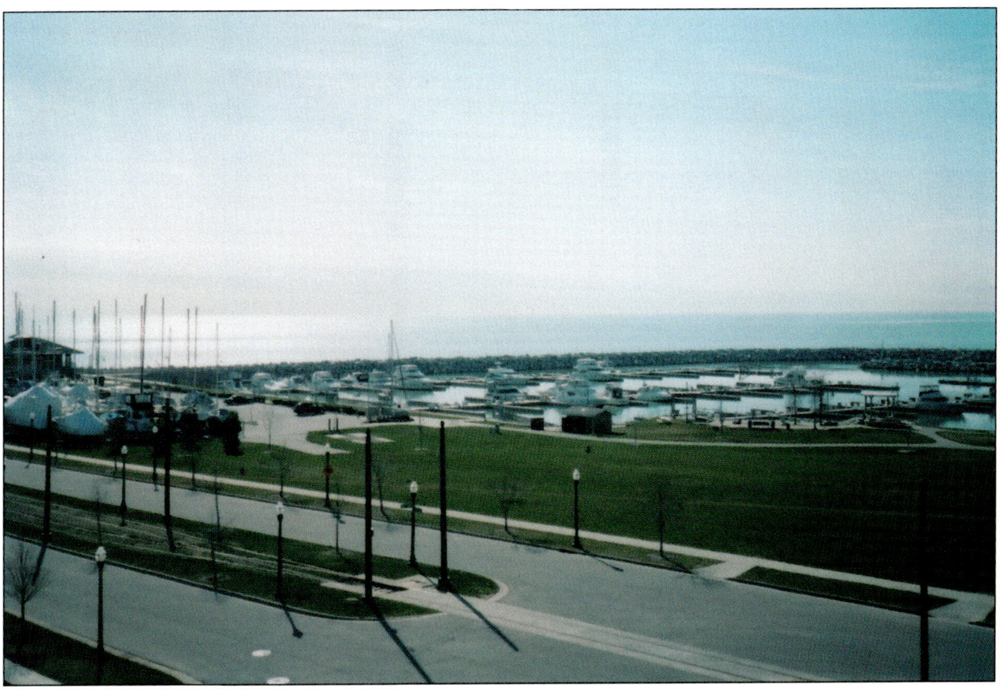

Kenosha sits on the shores of Lake Michigan, roughly halfway between Milwaukee and Chicago. This picture shows Southport Marina and the southeast end of Harbor Park before any development occurred. Southport prides itself on being a public marina with the feel of a private club. (Courtesy of the Kenosha Public Museum.)

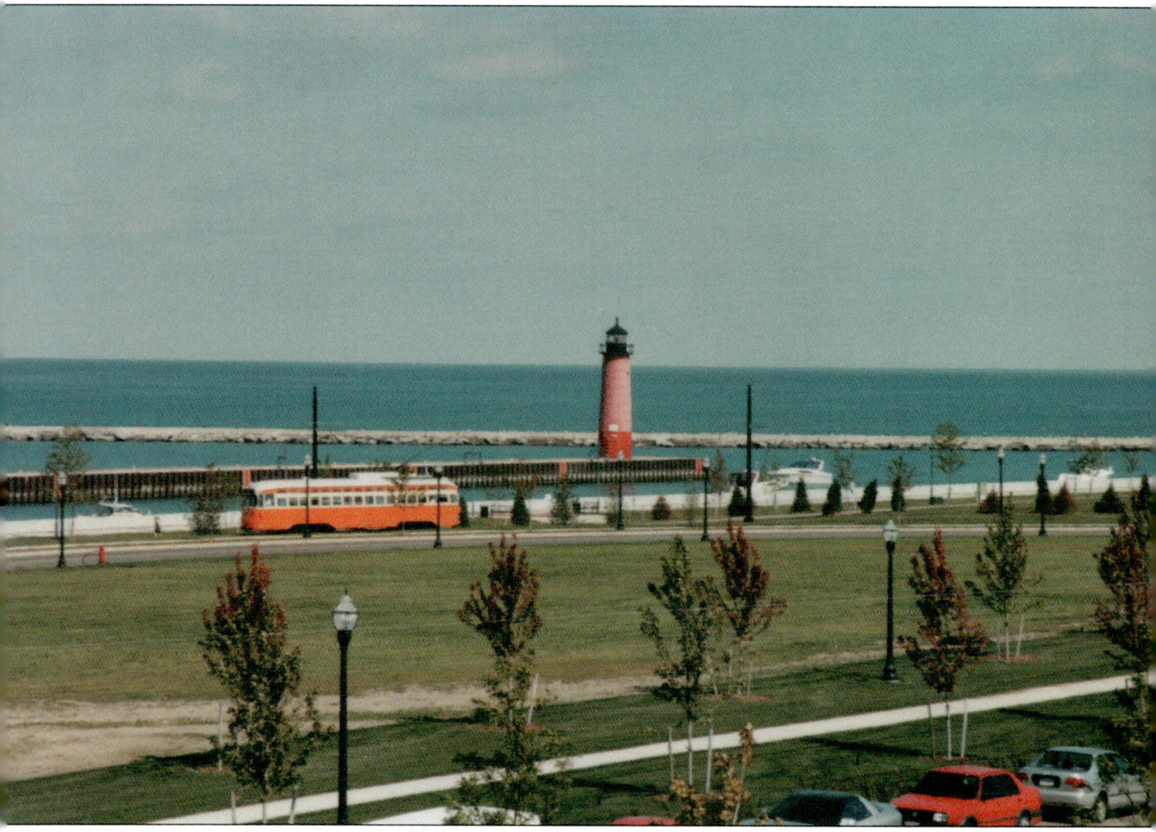

This image shows one of the Kenosha streetcars during its inaugural trip around the tracks. The two-mile loop is a modern-day, scaled-down recreation of Kenosha's original streetcar system, which ran from 1903 to 1932. The five cars are restored 1951 Red Rocket streetcars from Canada and follow a scenic path through Harbor Park, the lakefront, two historic districts, the Metra train station, and the downtown business district. Each car is painted to match a historical color scheme of a North American trolley transit system. Behind the trolley in this photograph is the Kenosha North Pier Lighthouse. It was built in 1906 and matches a lighthouse in Milwaukee. This lighthouse is painted the typical red of many Lake Michigan light towers, although it began its life on the lake painted white. (Courtesy of the Kenosha Public Museum.)

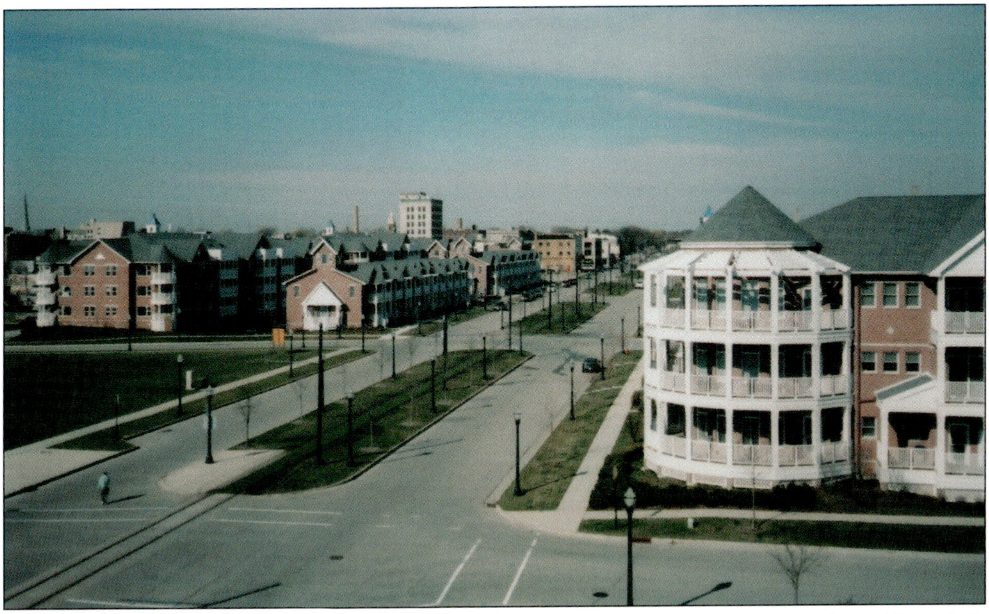

These apartments and townhouses by the harbor are a recent development along Kenosha's lakefront. Back and to the left lies the city's historic downtown, and running through the middle of this image are the trolley tracks that pass through downtown and up around the lakefront. (Courtesy of the Kenosha Public Museum.)

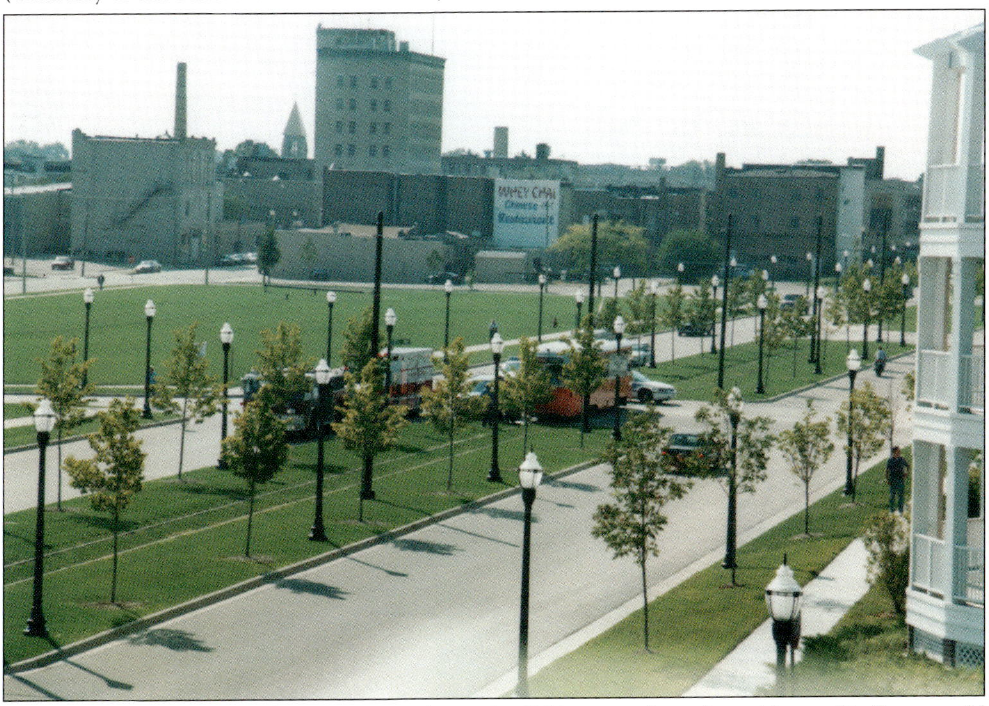

Kenosha's first iteration of streetcars in the early 1900s was rife with accidents. Trolleys would derail, and people would get hit at crosswalks. That is part of the reason why this picture from the trolley's early days might be alarming. It looks like there has been an accident at the streetcar tracks. (Courtesy of the Kenosha Public Museum.)

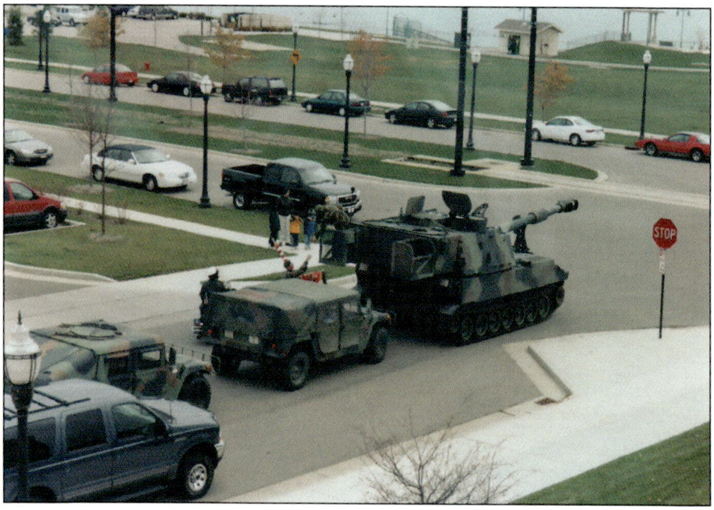

Every year, the Civil War Museum hosts a Veteran's Heritage Day celebration. It honors Kenosha's presence in the Civil War, World War I, World War II, the Korean War, and the Vietnam War. Military memorabilia is displayed, veterans are thanked in a dedication ceremony, and military vehicles go on parade. (Courtesy of the Kenosha Public Museum.)

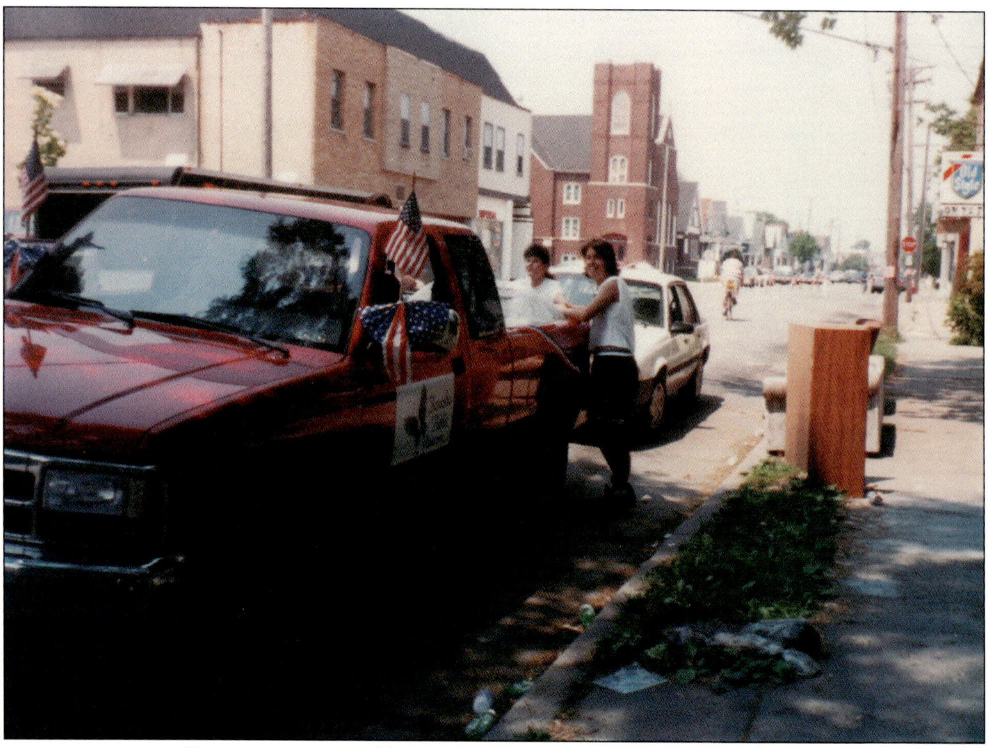

In a continuing effort to support and honor local veterans, Kenosha also hosts a Civic Veterans Day Parade every year. The event starts at 60th Street and 22nd Avenue, parades downtown and through Library Park, then finishes up at 56th Street and 3rd Avenue. This picture shows the Kenosha Public Museum truck getting ready to go. (Courtesy of the Kenosha Public Museum.)

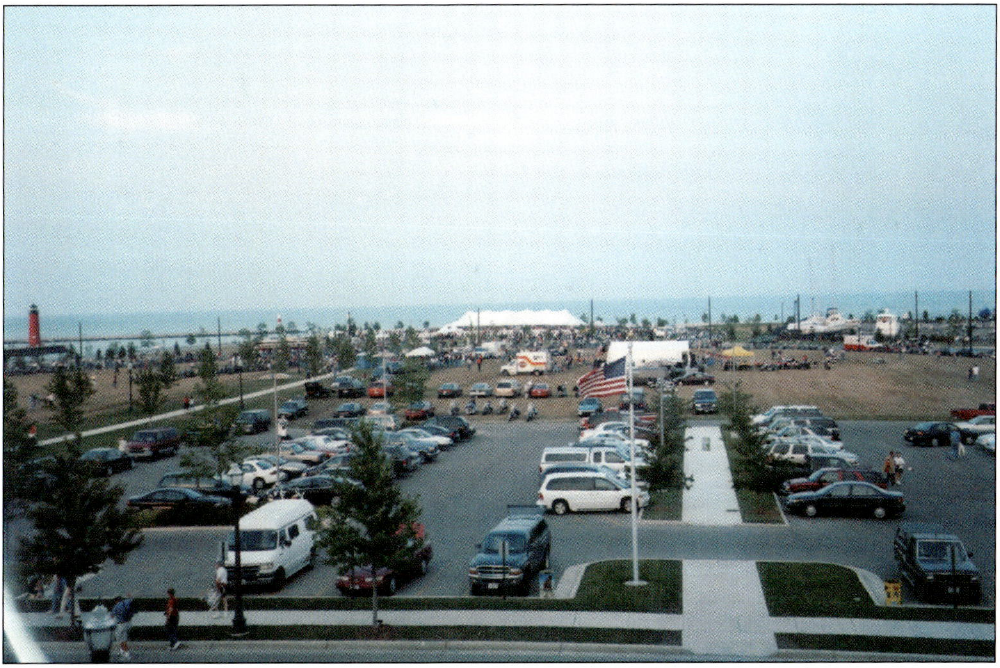

Harbor Thunder is a celebration for Harley Davidson riders held along Kenosha's shoreline. It is a free event and commemorates Harley's anniversary. The event and parade in these pictures was for Harley's 100th. Kenosha has a long history with the Harley Davidson Company. Uke's Harley Davidson has been a fixture in the city since April 1, 1930; it is the oldest Harley dealership in Wisconsin. Frank "Uke" Ulicki was such a motorcycle fan that he never owned a car. Now, the dealership is owned by Uke's son, Keith. When Keith was born, Uke actually brought him home from the hospital on a Harley motorcycle. (Courtesy of the Kenosha Public Museum.)

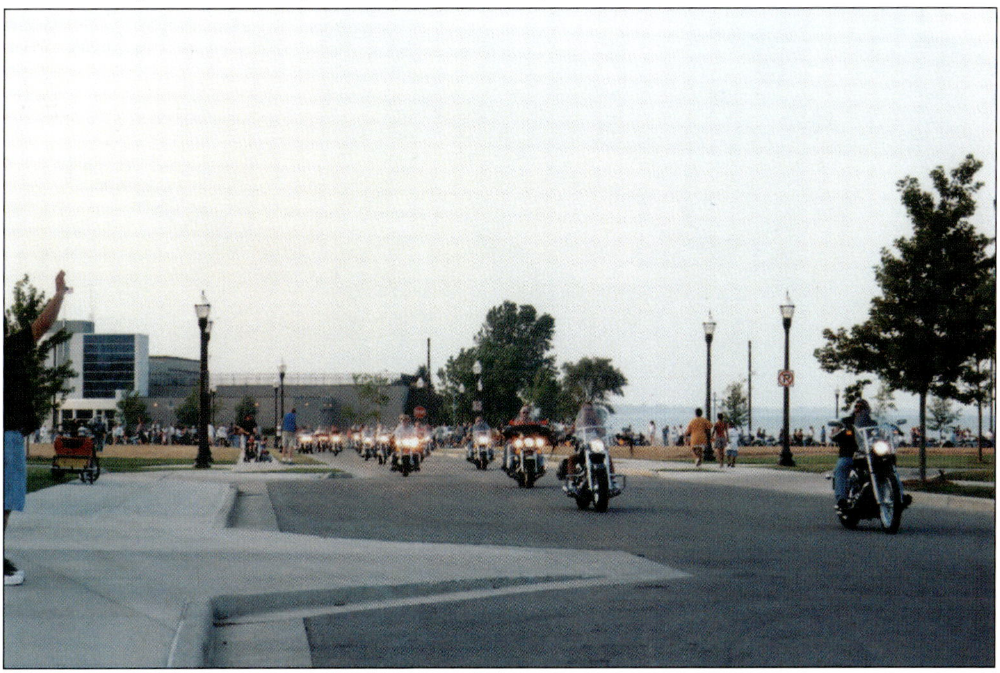

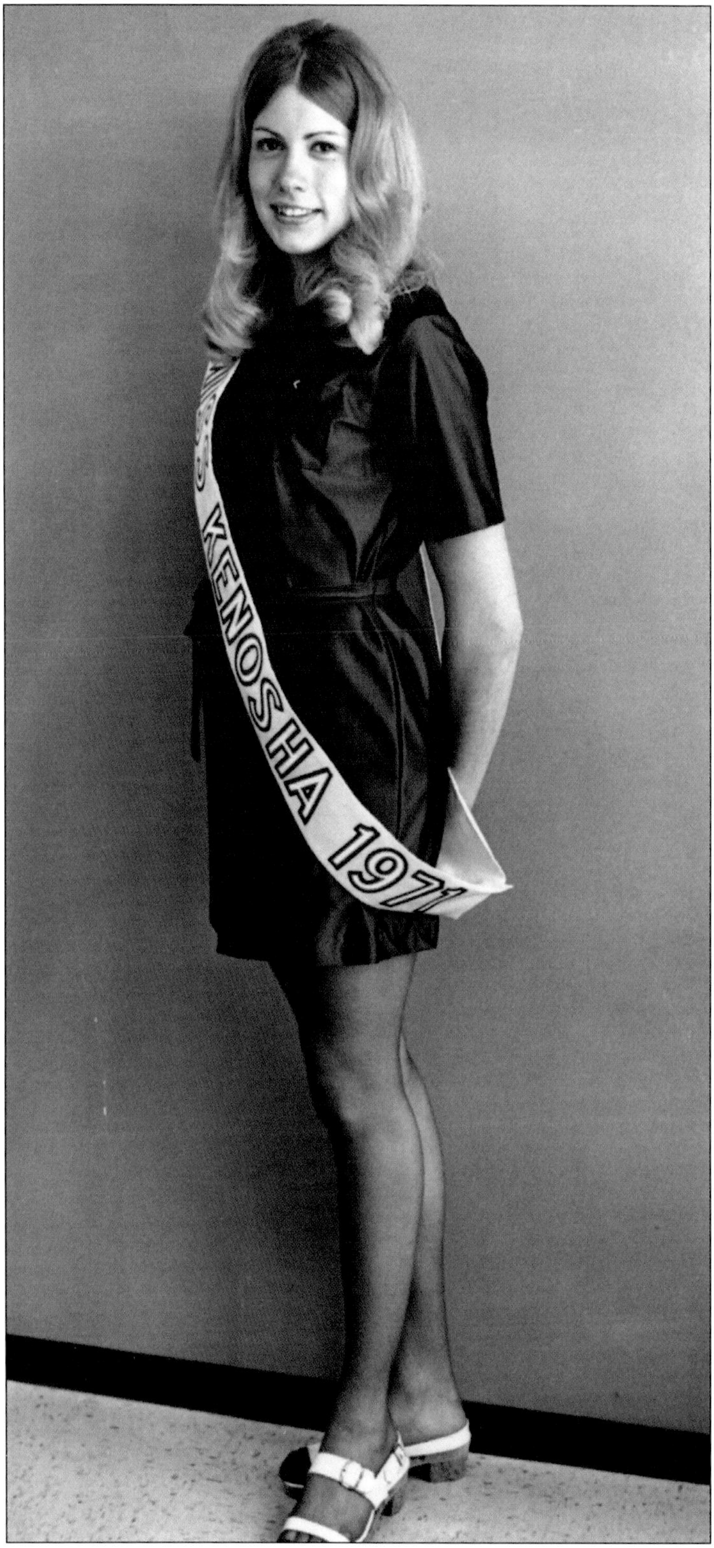

Kenosha's community joins together frequently to celebrate the town. The Miss Kenosha scholarship pageant has been ongoing in the city for more than 80 years. This image shows Dawn Moore, Miss Kenosha 1971. She was a freshman at Carthage College at the time, although she was originally from Lake Geneva. Crowned queens from the Miss Kenosha pageant go on to compete in the Miss Wisconsin pageant, and the winner of that heads to the Miss America pageant. Contestants must all select a charity platform and compete in the following categories: interview, talent, evening wear, and physical fitness/swimsuit. Only two Miss Kenoshas have won the Miss America pageant: one in 1989 and one in 2012. The winner of the Miss America pageant receives a $50,000 scholarship, and monetary prizes are handed out for the category winners as well. (Courtesy of the Carthage College Archives.)

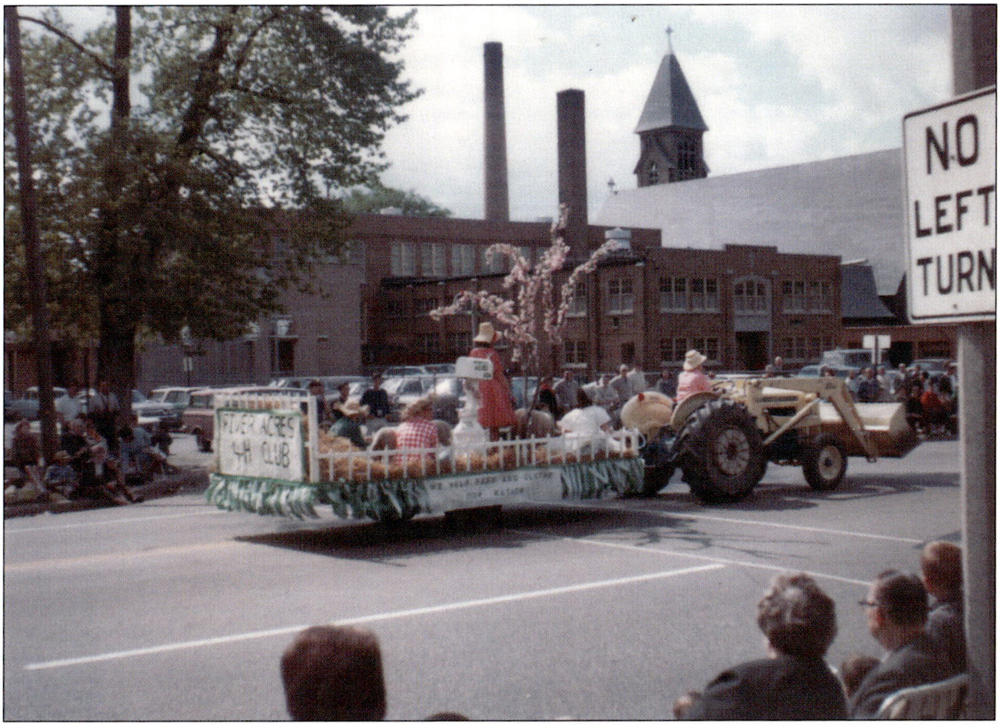

Kenosha loves a parade. The town's community events are a big reason it is such a huge tourist destination. Here, the 4-H Club float heads down the street during the 1970 Memorial Day Parade. About 35,000 people attended the annual parade that year. (Courtesy of the Kenosha County University of Wisconsin-Extension.)

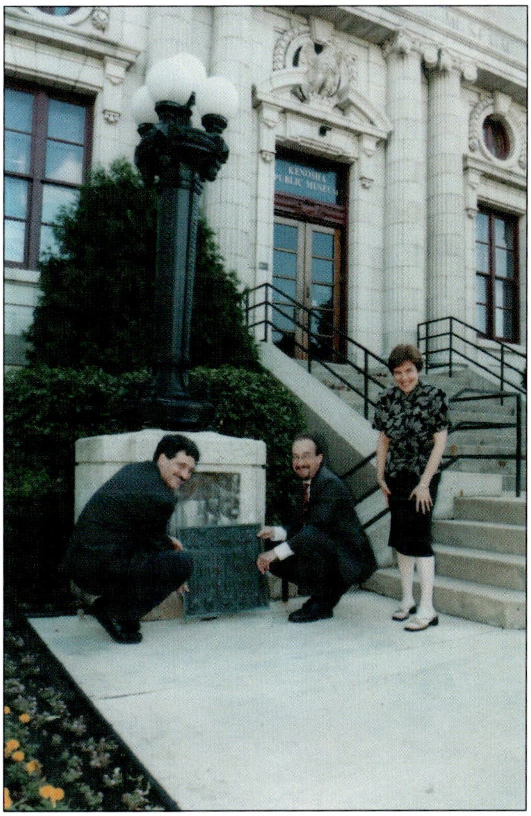

The Kenosha Public Museum opened in 1936 and spent 65 years in the renovated historic post office building outside Civic Center Park. In this photograph, from left to right, Mayor John Antaramian, museum curator Dan Joyce, and museum director Paula Touhey remove the plaque outside the old building to bring to the new location. (Courtesy of the Kenosha Public Museum.)

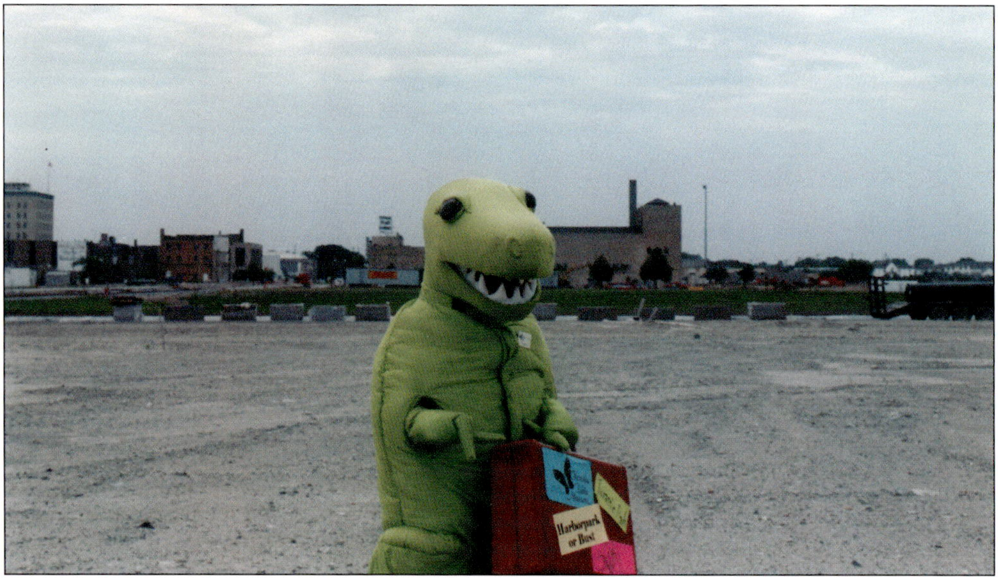

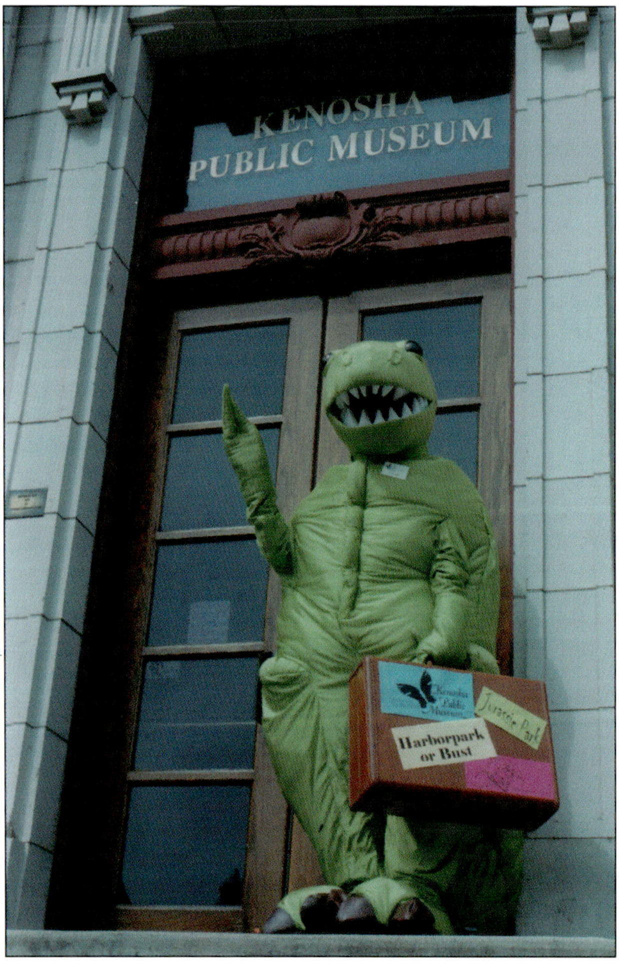

Ty-Rex was the original mascot for the Kenosha Public Museum. In these images, Ty-Rex is getting ready for the museum's move to its new location, waving goodbye from the old doorstep and standing on the grounds of the new location. The woman under the mascot costume was Laura Tyunaitis. Tyunaitis noted that the costume for Ty-Rex is all one piece and warms up inside like a children's snowsuit. Not everyone tasked with wearing the suit can hack it; the opening for the headpiece is very narrow and tends to only fit teenagers. (Courtesy of the Kenosha Public Museum.)

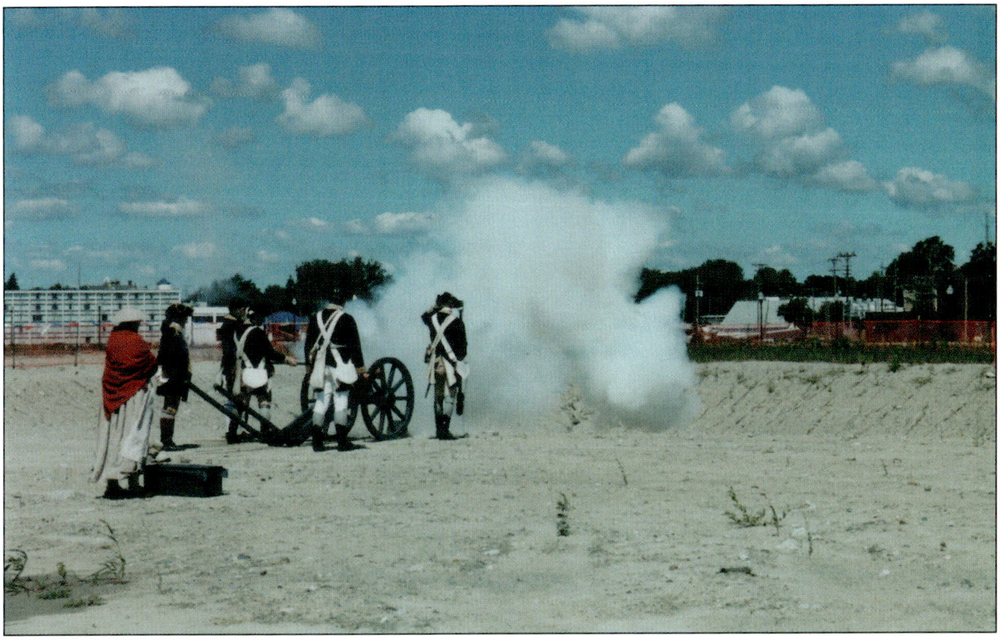

The ground breaking ceremony for the new museum started with a bang—the cannon blast of a troop of Revolutionary War reenactors. The new location is on the east end of Harbor Park, with a commanding view of the lake and quick access to many downtown shops and restaurants. (Courtesy of the Kenosha Public Museum.)

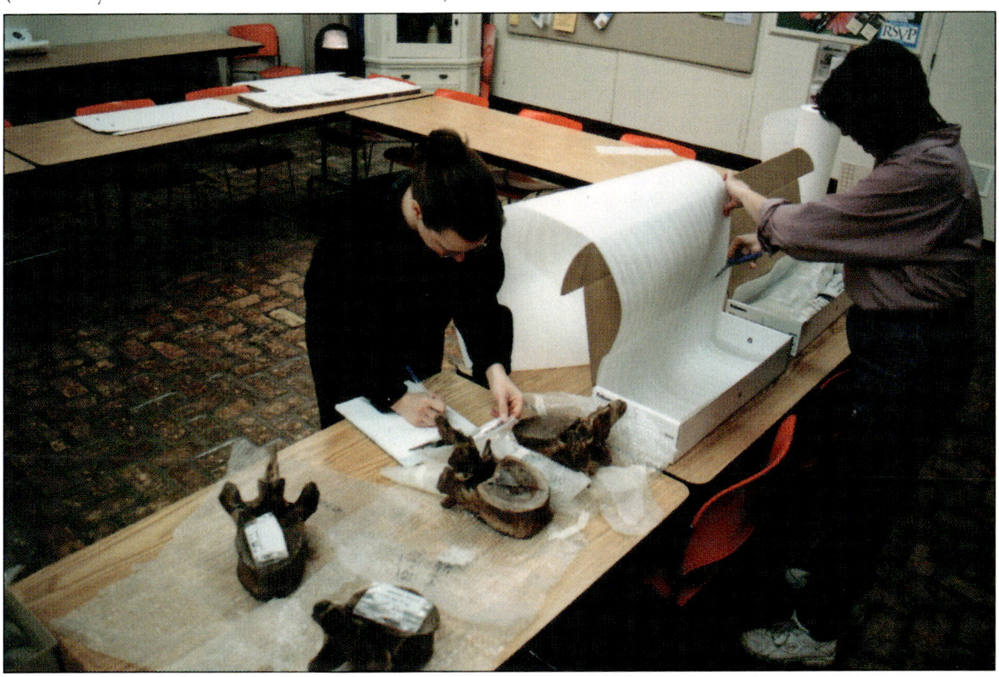

With more than 80,000 items in its collections, sorting, labeling, and packing all of the museum's exhibits was a daunting task. Two museum employees are seen here cataloging and packing a set of bones, to be carefully reconstructed in the proper order once they arrive at the new museum. (Courtesy of the Kenosha Public Museum.)

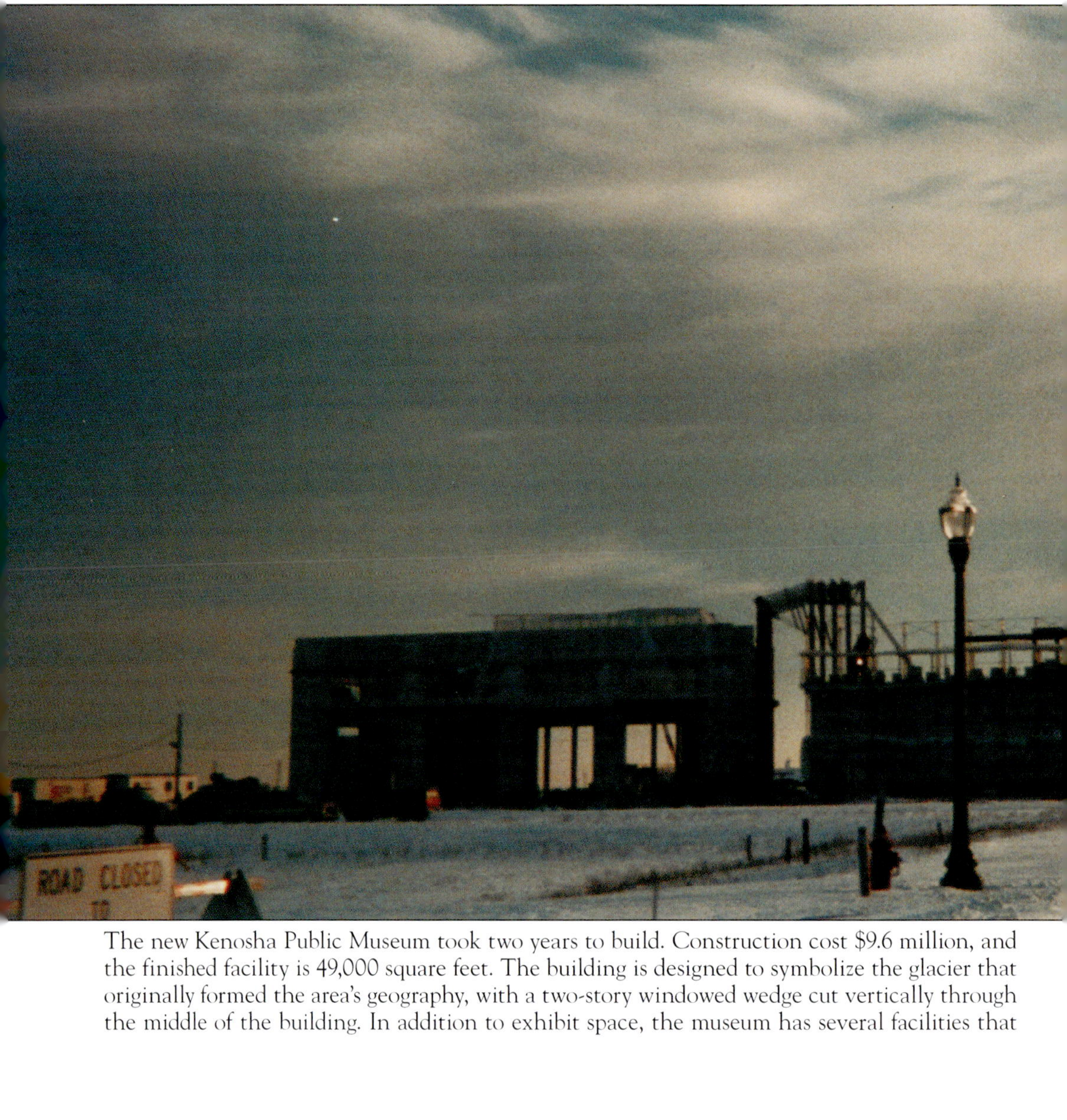

The new Kenosha Public Museum took two years to build. Construction cost $9.6 million, and the finished facility is 49,000 square feet. The building is designed to symbolize the glacier that originally formed the area's geography, with a two-story windowed wedge cut vertically through the middle of the building. In addition to exhibit space, the museum has several facilities that

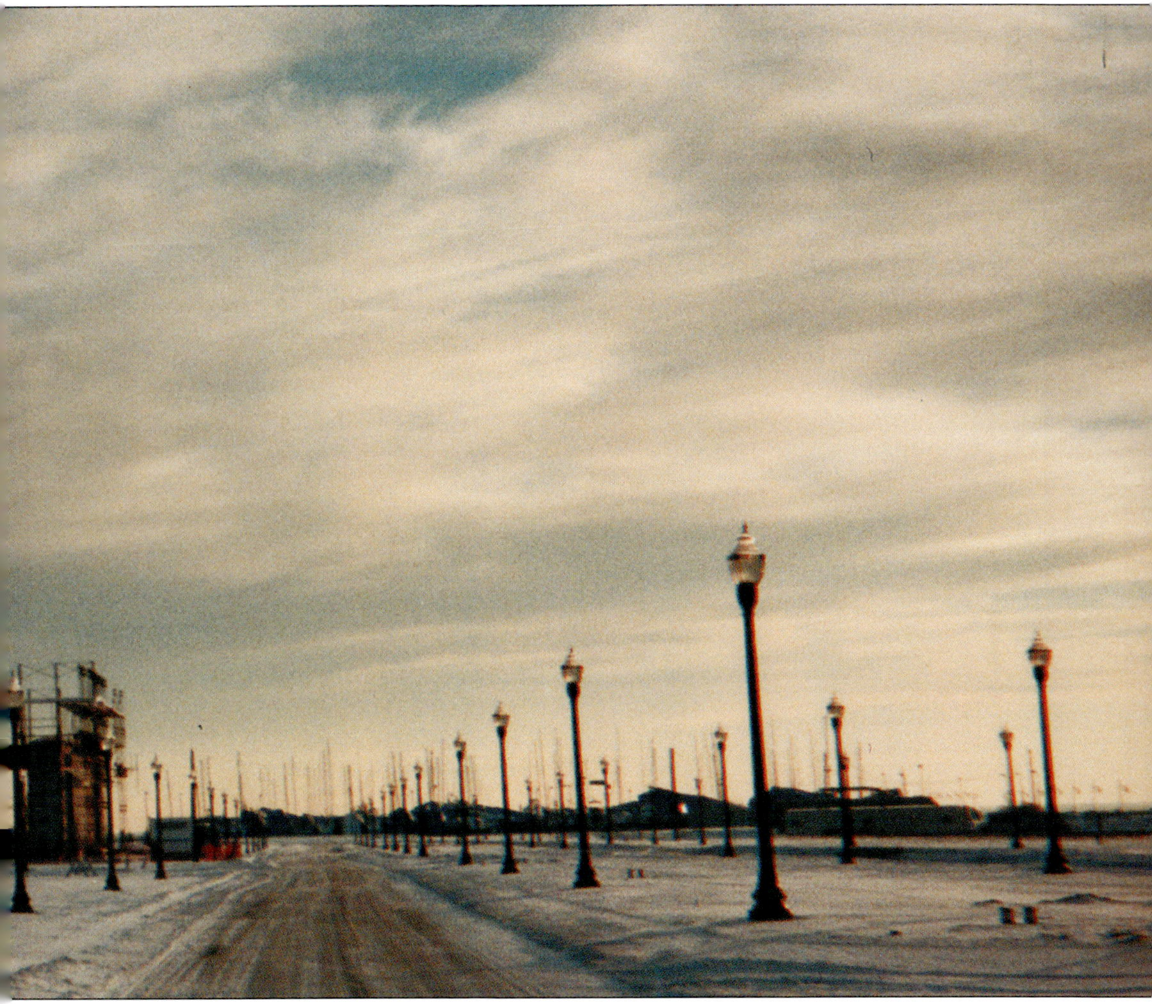

can be rented out for classes, seminars, or events. The architecture company responsible for the design, Engberg Anderson, won two awards for the museum: the International Institute of Masonry Design Award and the WCREW Real Estate Development Showcase Award. (Courtesy of the Kenosha Public Museum.)

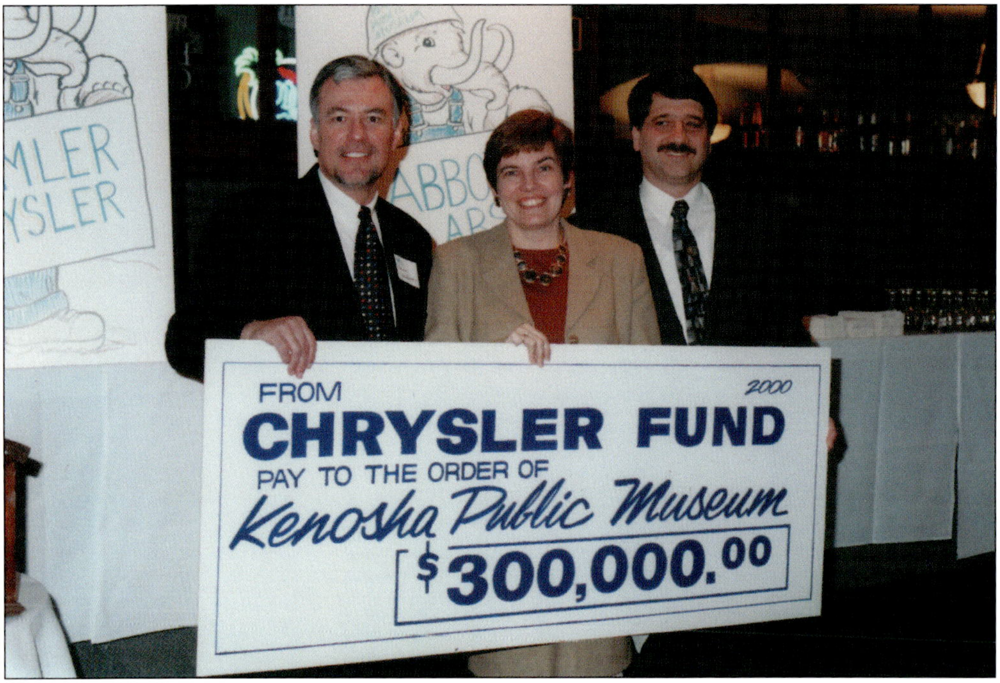

Construction of the new museum required copious funding, and community businesses did what they could to help raise money. Above, Chrysler plant manager Bruce Coventry (left) and Kenosha mayor John Antaramian present a $300,000 check to museum director Paula Touhey at Madrigano Marina Shores, Kenosha's largest banquet hall. Below, representatives from M&I Bank and city officials present the museum board with a $125,000 check. Both of these checks were received a year before the new museum opened and were used to fund remaining construction and install new exhibits in the space. (Both, courtesy of the Kenosha Public Museum.)

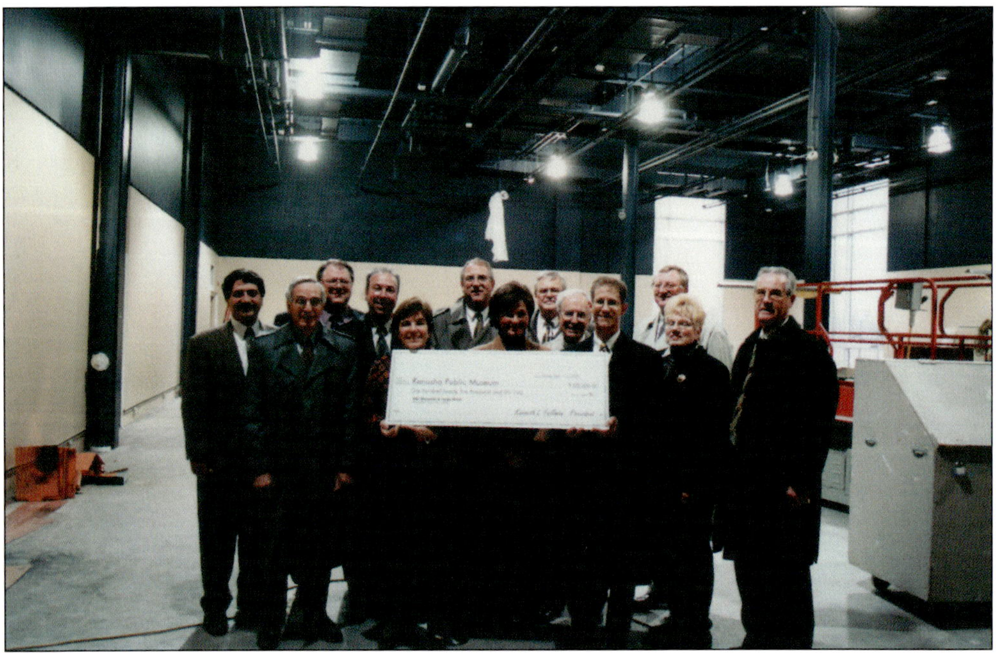

Before the new museum was open to the public, the Rotary Club of Kenosha West was able to attend a hard-hat party for a sneak peek of the building. That same day, the Rotary Club presented a $100,000 check to the museum to help install new exhibits. (Courtesy of the Kenosha Public Museum.)

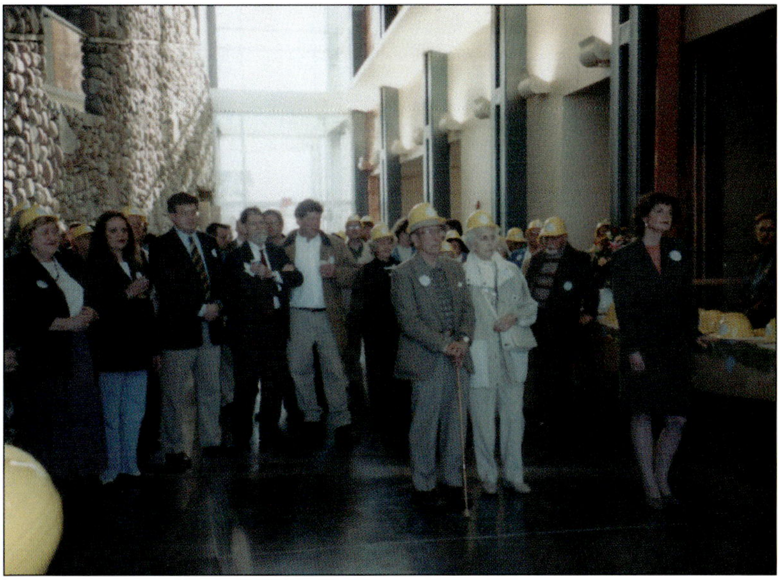

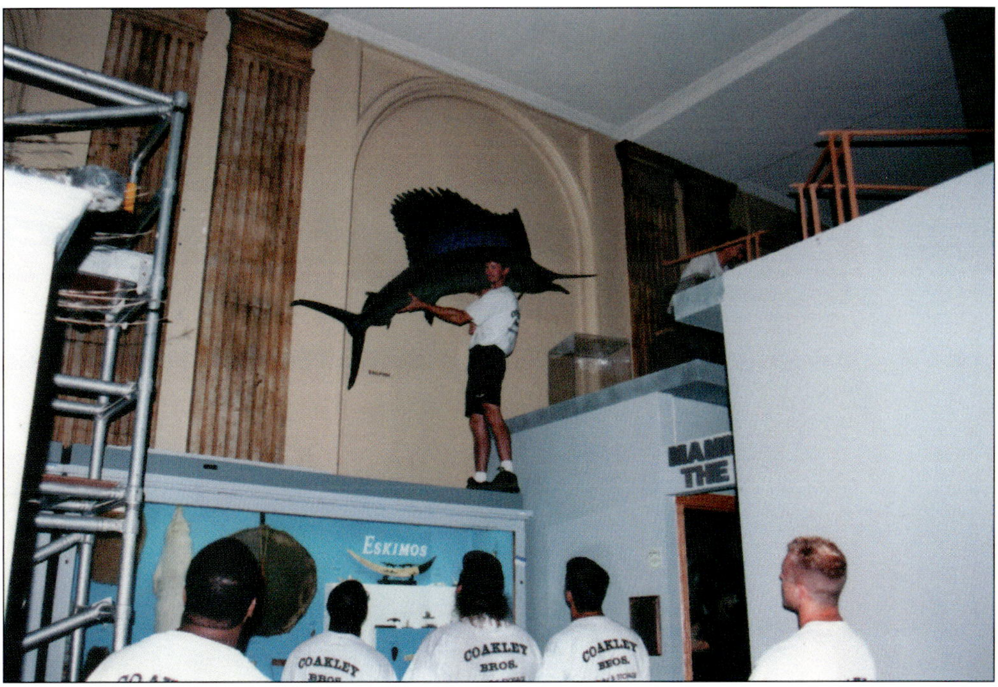

The museum's collections include more than just bones—they also include items like this, a full-size sailfish. These fish live in the warmer parts of the ocean and grow between four and five inches per year, to an average length of 10 feet and an average weight of 200 pounds. (Courtesy of the Kenosha Public Museum.)

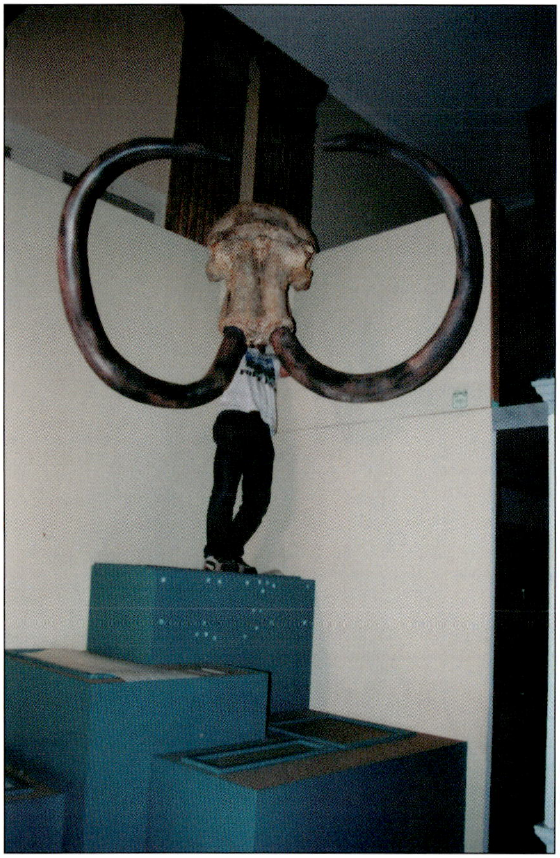

The museum houses two mammoth skeletons, both found within 15 miles of downtown Kenosha. This set of tusks belongs to the Schaefer mammoth found in Paris, Wisconsin. The Schaefer mammoth is believed to be the oldest known mammoth butchered by humans east of the Mississippi. (Courtesy of the Kenosha Public Museum.)

This is the museum's other mammoth, the Hebior mammoth. It is a reproduction of the largest wooly mammoth ever excavated. The Hebior is dated at 14,500 years old and the bones show signs that it was butchered by humans, which means that humans lived in Wisconsin since 1,000 years before the oldest discovered human community in the western hemisphere. (Courtesy of the Kenosha Public Museum.)

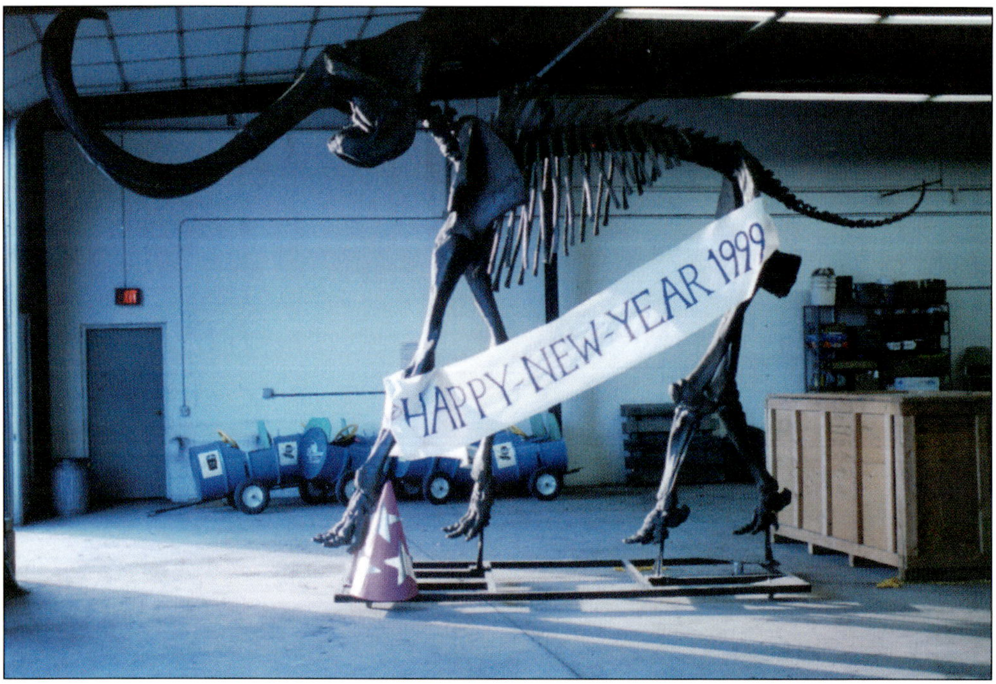

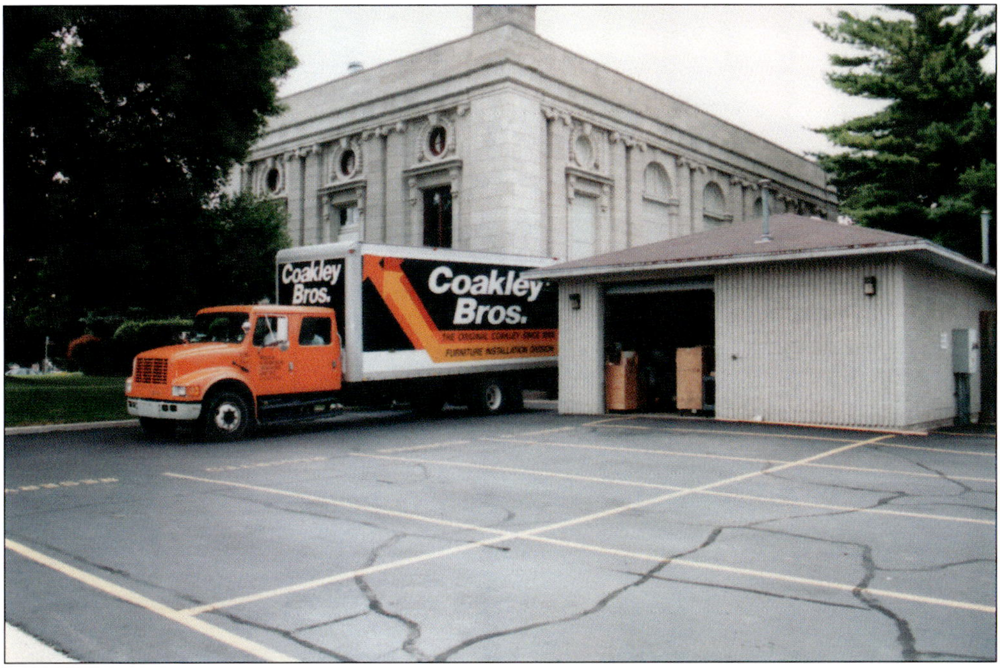

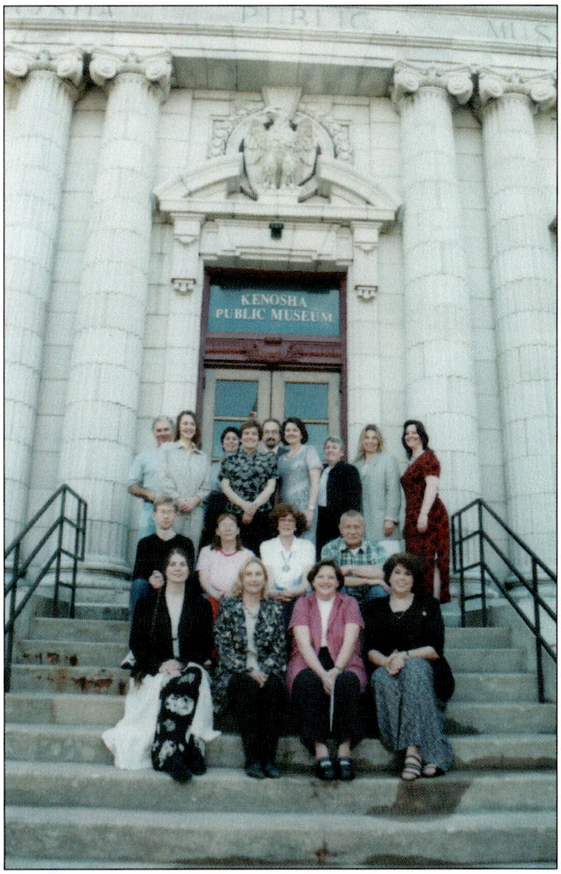

The move to the new museum was not far; the two buildings are only separated by six tenths of a mile. In the picture above, one of the moving trucks is getting ready to take another load to the new building. At right, the staff poses on the steps outside the old museum for a group picture on the last day of work in the old building. Once the museum moved to its new location, the old building became the Dinosaur Discovery Museum, which is owned by the public museum system. It's like the staff never had to leave! (Both, courtesy of the Kenosha Public Museum.)

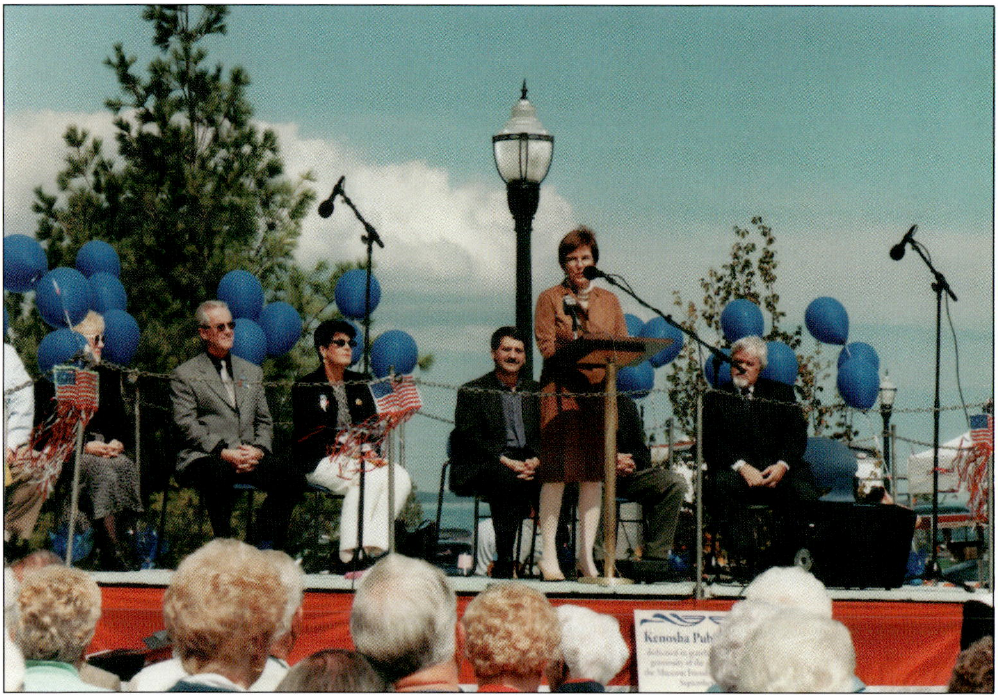

Three months after the museum's move, the staff held a grand opening event. There was a ceremony with speeches by city and museum elite as well as a ribbon cutting. Above, Paula Touhey, the museum director, is speaking to the crowd at a dedication ceremony. Below, Kenosha mayor John Antaramian joins Touhey in front of the museum for the ribbon cutting. The new, uniquely designed building allowed for exhibit expansion (virtual, permanent, and rotating); more space for events, seminars, and classes; new technology; and a better overall experience for guests learning about Kenosha's history. (Both, courtesy of the Kenosha Public Museum.)

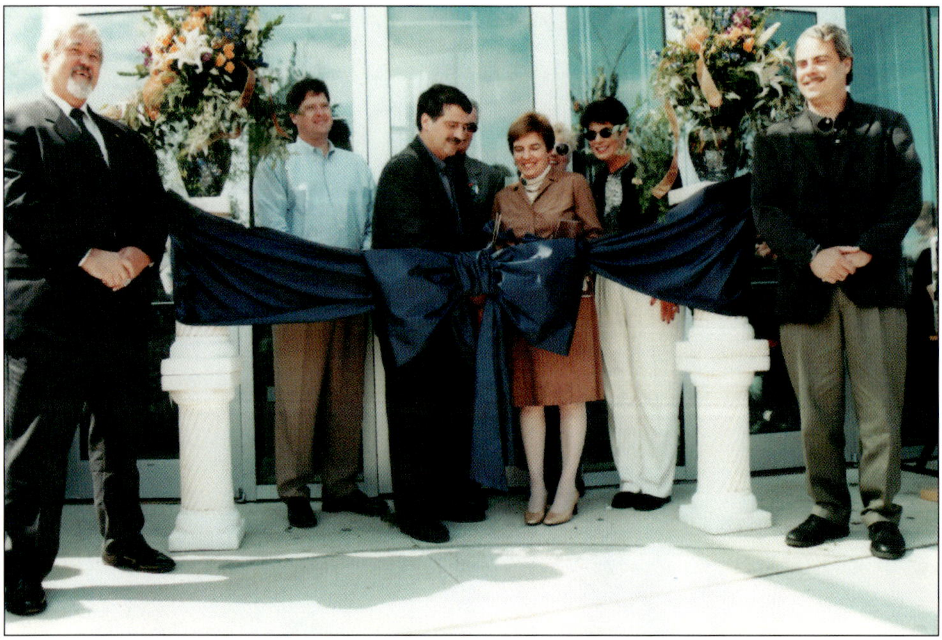

Long ago, all of Kenosha was completely underwater. After the ice age, when the glaciers receded, huge fish like this were brought to the surface. This process is chronicled in the Wisconsin Story exhibit, which is where the movers in this photograph are bringing the reproduction. (Courtesy of the Kenosha Public Museum.)

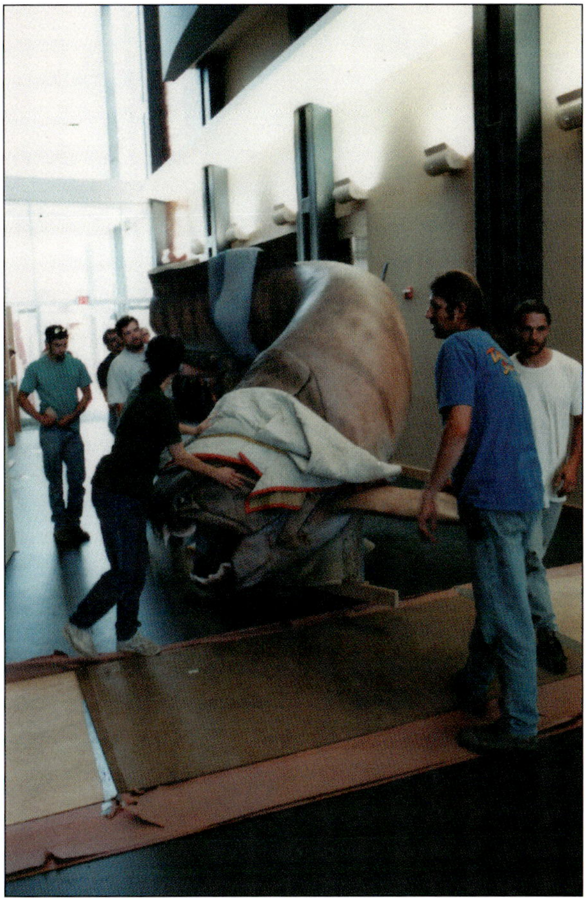

In 2007, the Kenosha Public Museum welcomed a third addition to its group of facilities: the Civil War Museum. This museum was built right next to the Public Museum and has a unique mission to focus solely on the upper Midwest's involvement in the Civil War. (Courtesy of the Kenosha Public Museum.)

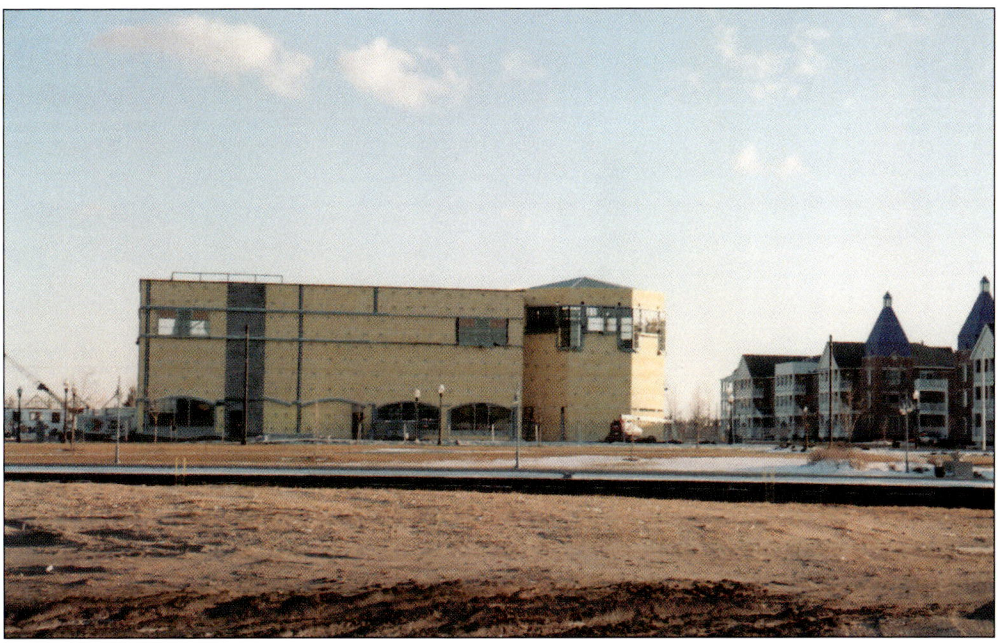

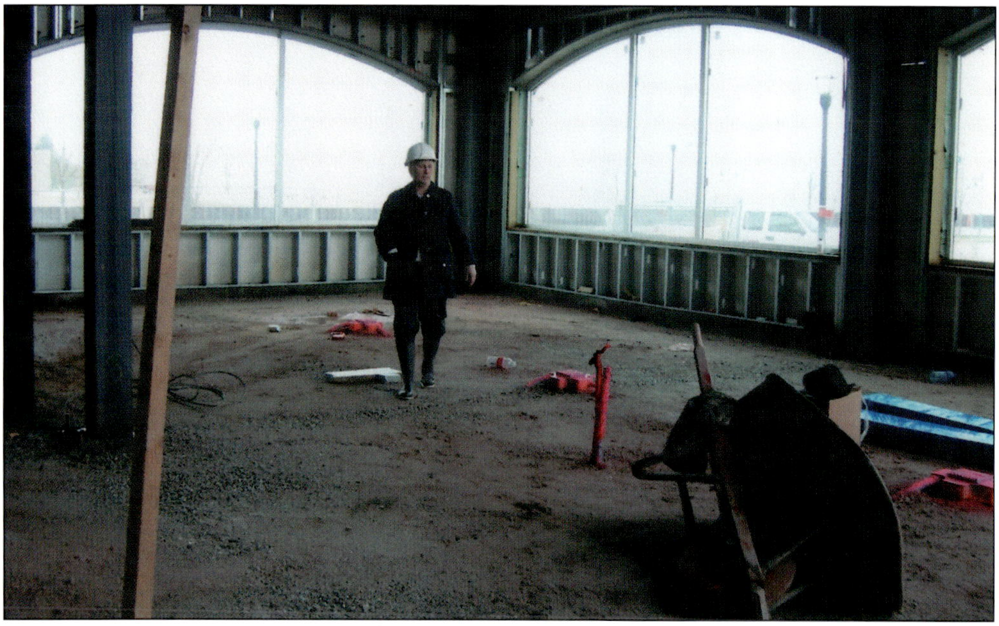

Because the Civil War Museum only focuses on six states (Illinois, Indiana, Iowa, Michigan, Minnesota, and Wisconsin), it has the unique ability to tailor its exhibits to the perspective of the 750,000 area men sent to fight. In this photograph, Civil War Museum manager Rita Myers walks through what will be the gift shop. (Courtesy of the Kenosha Public Museum.)

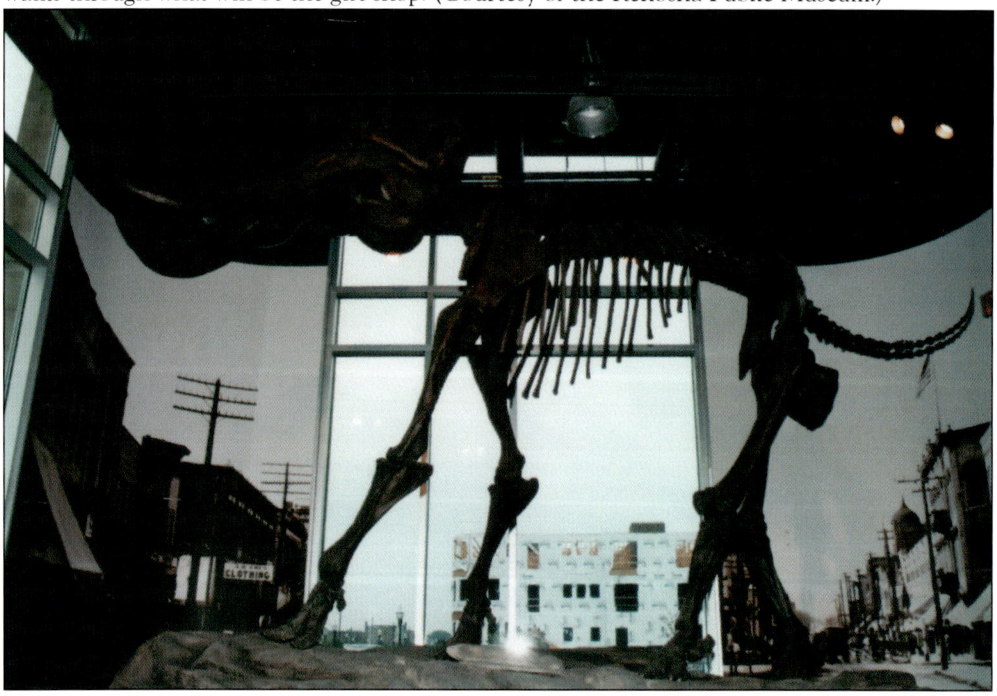

This image shows the Hebior mammoth in its new and complete home inside the Kenosha Public Museum mammoth exhibit. Outside the window is the ongoing construction of new condos that were planned to round out the Harbor Park development and neighborhood. The condos match townhomes across the street. (Courtesy of the Kenosha Public Museum.)

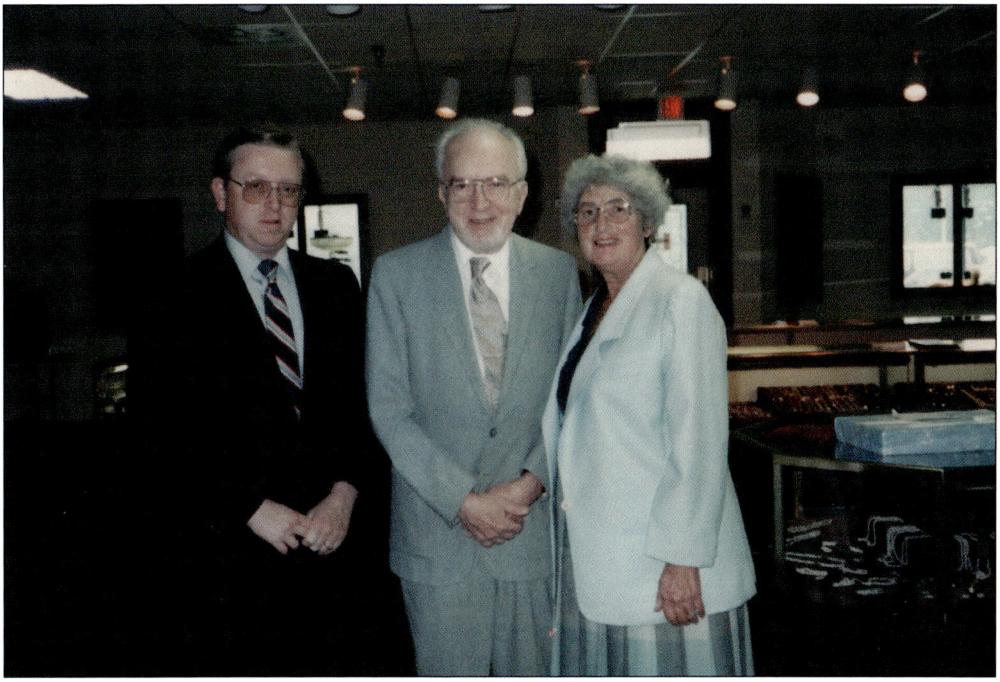

This 1988 photograph shows Herbert Block, his wife Marge, and their son Edward, the family that still owns Herbert's Jewelers today (although Edward's daughter Lisa now runs the store). Herbert's carries a mix of jewelry, but when it first opened, the store stocked everything from engagement rings to dining sets and bowling balls. (Courtesy of Herbert's Jewelers.)

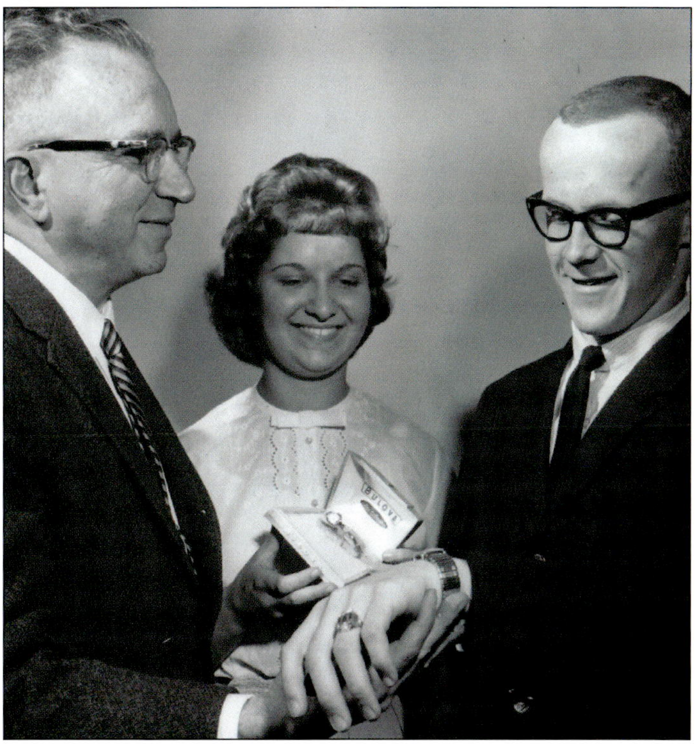

In 1962, Herbert's Jewelers won the civic award in Kenosha. It was well-deserved; since its opening, the business made a lot of strides in the retail jewelry arena, including issuing shoppers passbooks and charging a dollar down payment and a dollar a week as a financing program. (Courtesy of Herbert's Jewelers.)

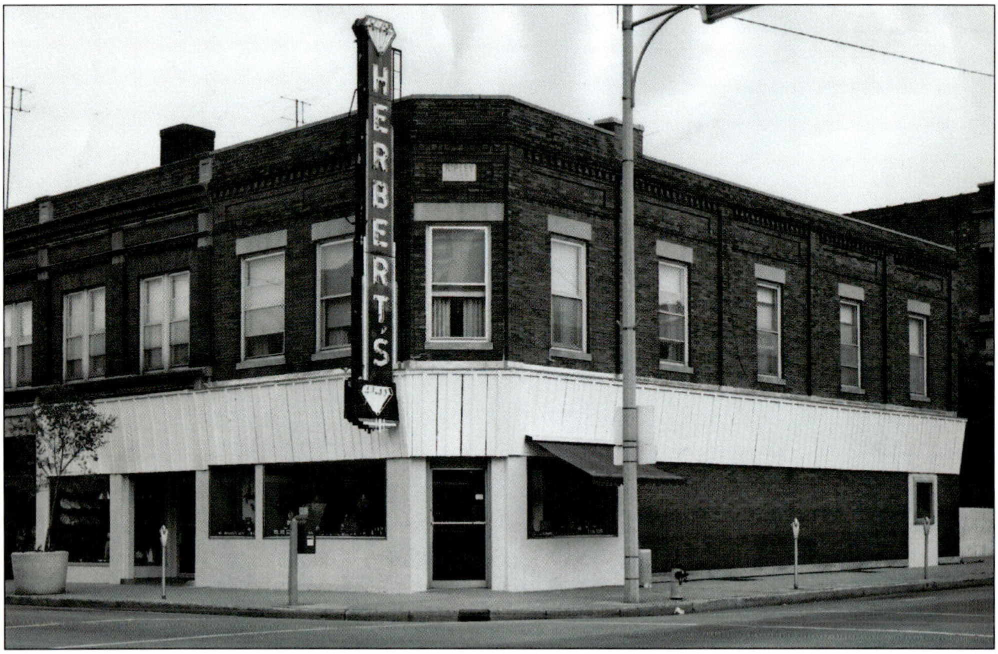

Herbert's originally opened as Herbert's Credit Jewelers, allowing customers to buy pieces on credit. It was groundbreaking; when the store opened in 1938, it was unusual for stores to offer credit to any but their wealthiest customers, yet Herbert offered it to everyone. This is the store after an aesthetic makeover in 1964. (Courtesy of Herbert's Jewelers.)

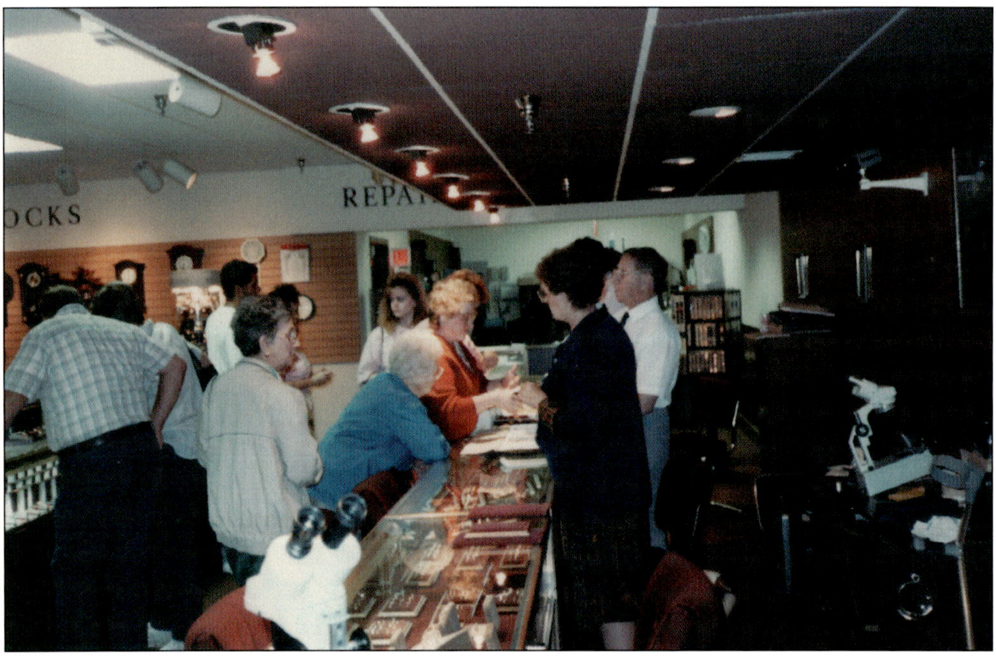

This image shows the interior of Herbert's Pershing Plaza store in 1986. The popularity of the store didn't suffer at all from moving out of downtown. In fact, the store has consistently placed as either a winner or nominee in the *Kenosha News* annual Best of Kenosha competition. (Courtesy of Herbert's Jewelers.)

In 1983, Edward Block moved the store from its original location downtown, where it had been for 45 years, to a location in what would become a new strip mall business district: Pershing Plaza, removed from the historic downtown district but still close enough to reap the city's benefits. In addition to Herbert's, the plaza now contains a Sears, a McDonald's, a nail salon and spa, a Piggly Wiggly, a Little Caesars, and more. These two images show the store's scenery change in progress, with a crane lifting the sign off of the jewelry store's old facade. (Both, courtesy of Herbert's Jewelers.)

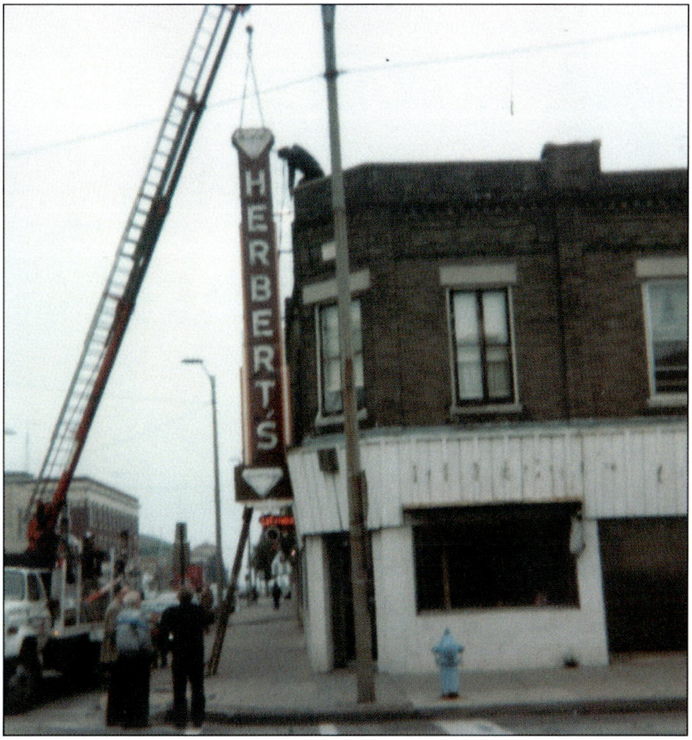

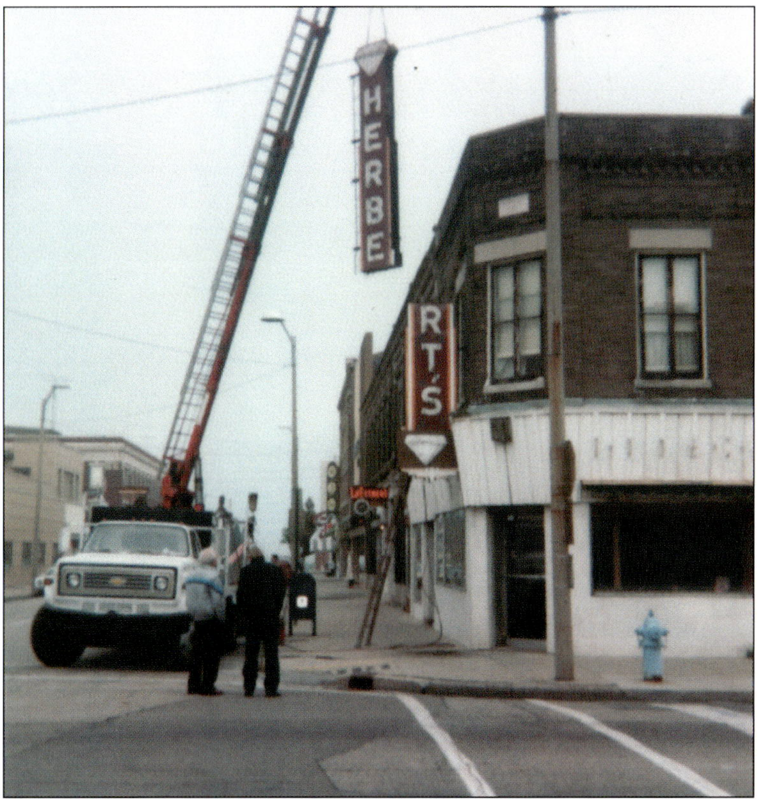

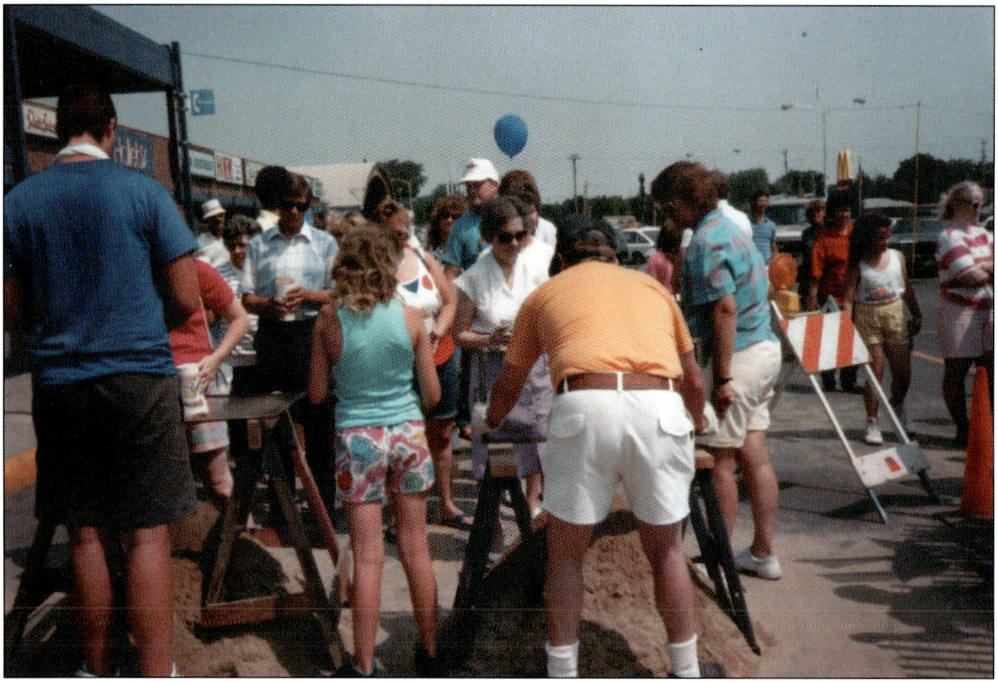

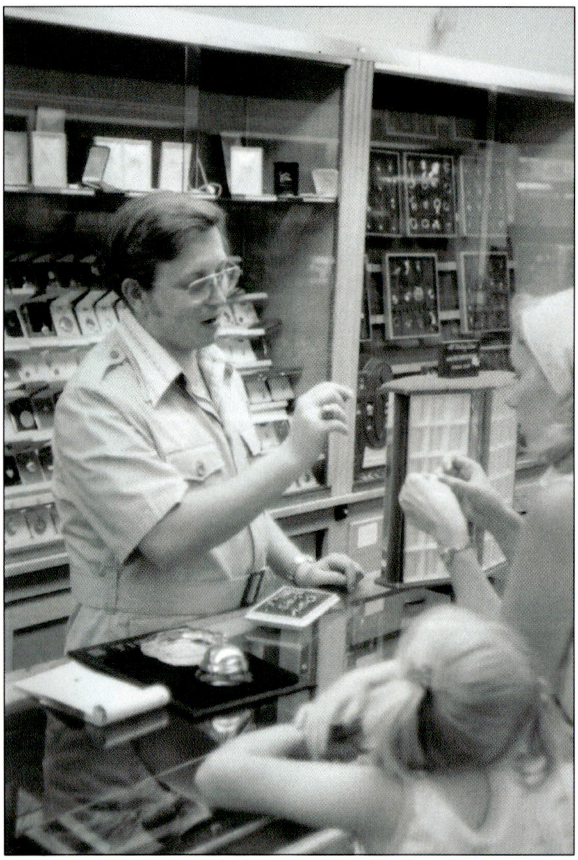

On June 30, 1986, Herbert's Jewelers opened a "gem mine." Shoppers were allowed to come to the store and sift through a giant pile of dirt that Edward Block had sprinkled different gemstones throughout. Customers could keep what they found. The event was a big hit in the community. (Courtesy of Herbert's Jewelers.)

In 1975, Edward Block took over Herbert's Jeweler's from his father, Herbert. Edward enrolled in gemology classes to further his intimate knowledge of the business. Edward played a large part in Kenosha's community by supporting local charities and groups. He ran the store until he passed away in October 2011. (Courtesy of Herbert's Jewelers.)

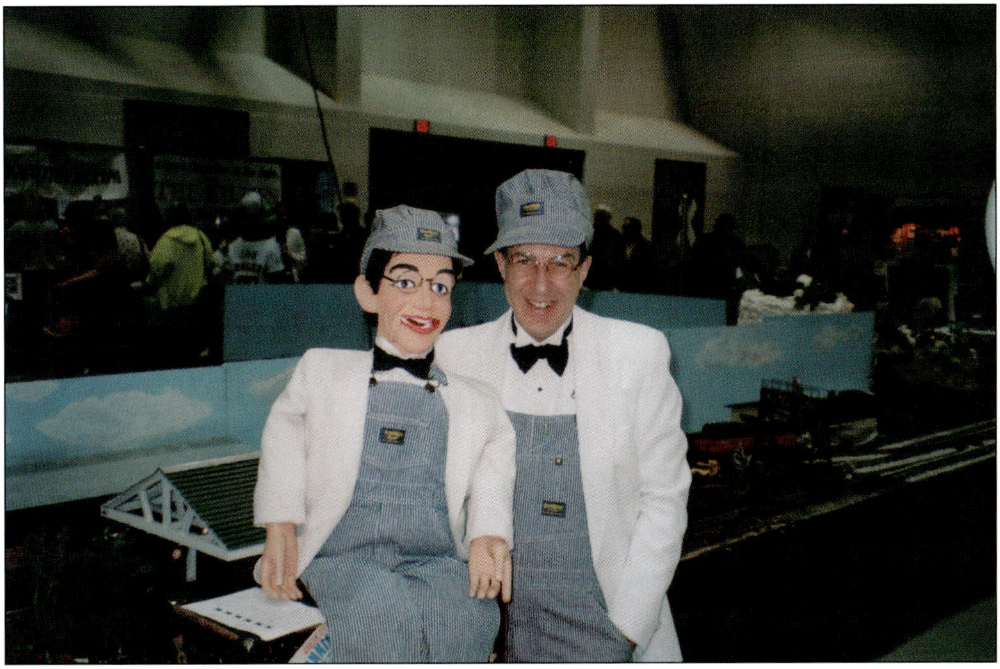

The Kenosha Expo is held every year at the University of Wisconsin-Parkside Frank J. Petretti Fieldhouse. The Chamber of Commerce organizes the event, allowing community members to meet many area business owners. This image shows a member of the G-Scalers Model Train Club with his ventriloquist dummy. (Courtesy of the Kenosha Public Museum.)

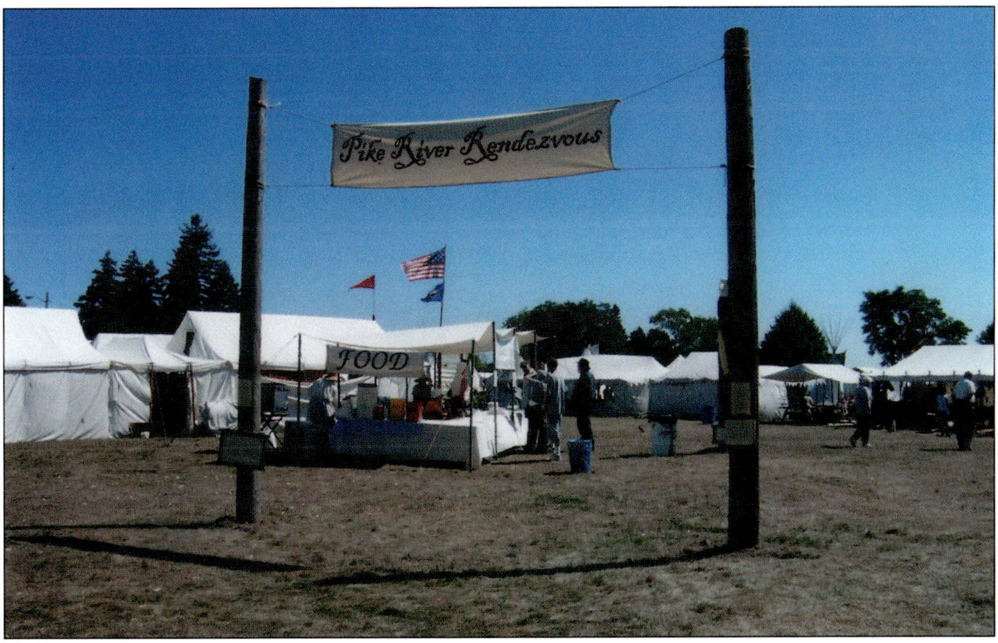

Kenosha did not always go by that name. When the town was settled in 1835, it was called Pike Creek. It was not until incorporation in 1850 that the name *Kenosha* came into being. The Pike River Rendezvous event celebrates the historical Pike Creek settlement. (Courtesy of the Kenosha Public Museum.)

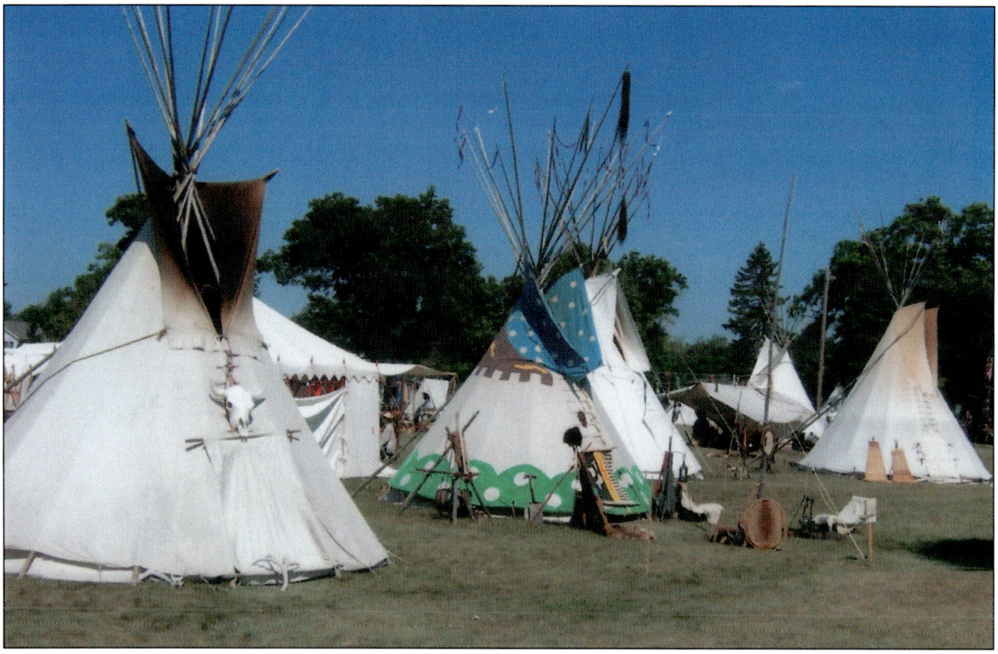

The Pike River Rendezvous is held on Simmons Island. More than 350 reenactors come out and set up 150 camps. Visitors can come talk to them about how life was in Kenosha during the fur-trading days. There are also craft and trade demonstrations. (Courtesy of the Kenosha Public Museum.)

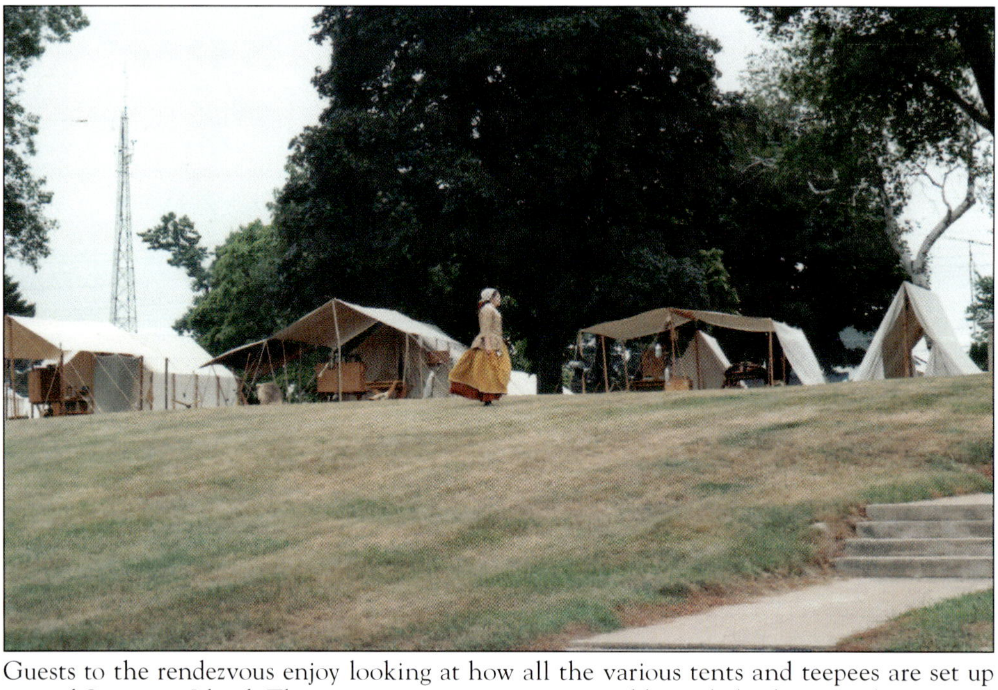

Guests to the rendezvous enjoy looking at how all the various tents and teepees are set up around Simmons Island. The reenactors wear costumes and have daily chores to do—visitors can help with those tasks as well. It truly is a historical experience. (Courtesy of the Kenosha Public Museum.)

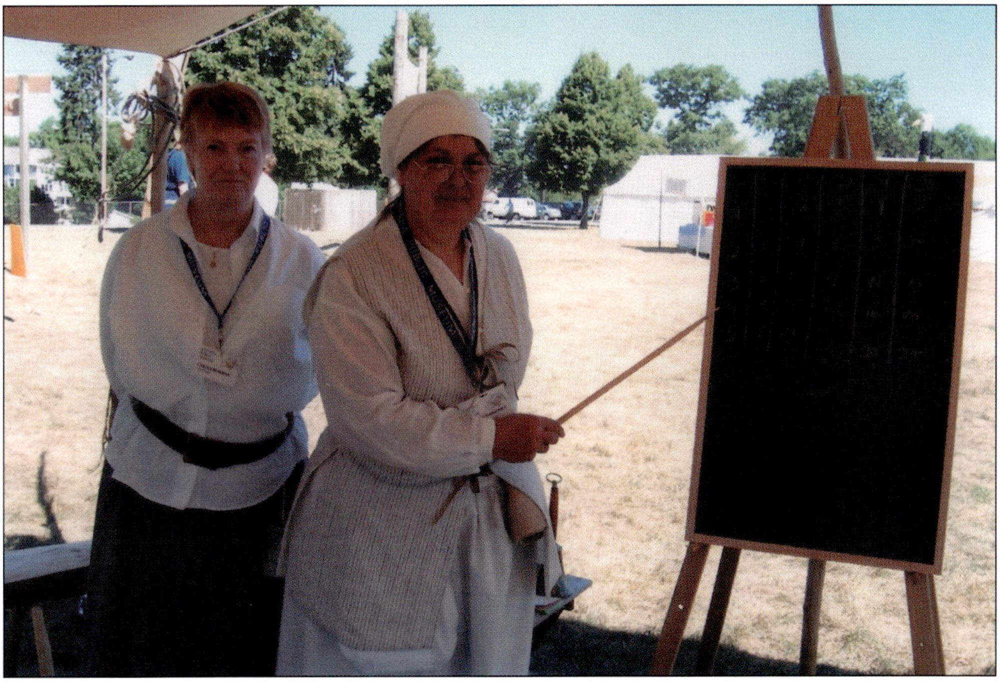

Reenactors at the rendezvous go all out, even teaching everyone how math was done in the old days, such as with these multiplication tables. Guests can sit and attend a class going over these principles, taught as it was back in the early 1800s. (Courtesy of the Kenosha Public Museum.)

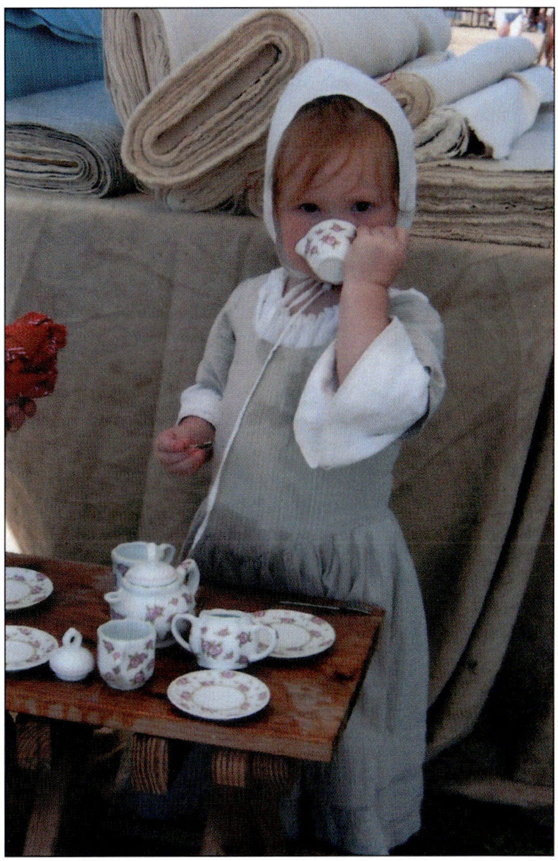

The rendezvous is a great place for kids. They can play period games and make crafts in the family area, and there is an ample supply of fair food available. There are even horse-drawn carriage rides as a shuttle from the parking area to the event. (Courtesy of the Kenosha Public Museum.)

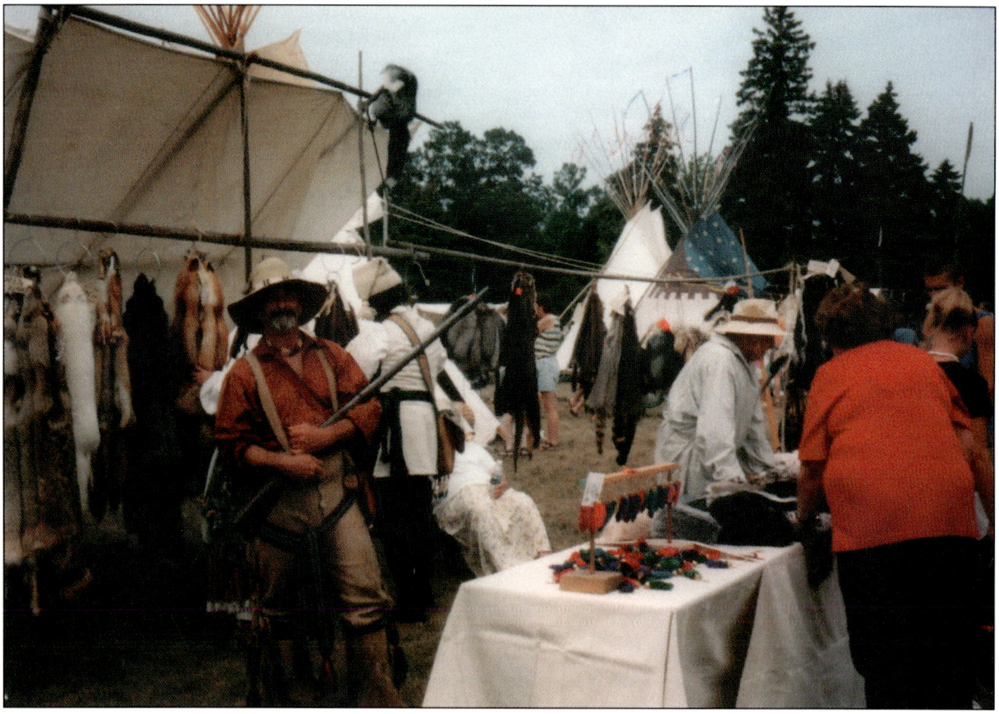

In addition to speaking with fur trappers, like this one at the rendezvous, guests can see a pirate battle, watch jugglers, hear live period music, attend church, and buy souvenirs and gifts. The event is held the first full weekend in August every year. (Courtesy of the Kenosha Public Museum.)

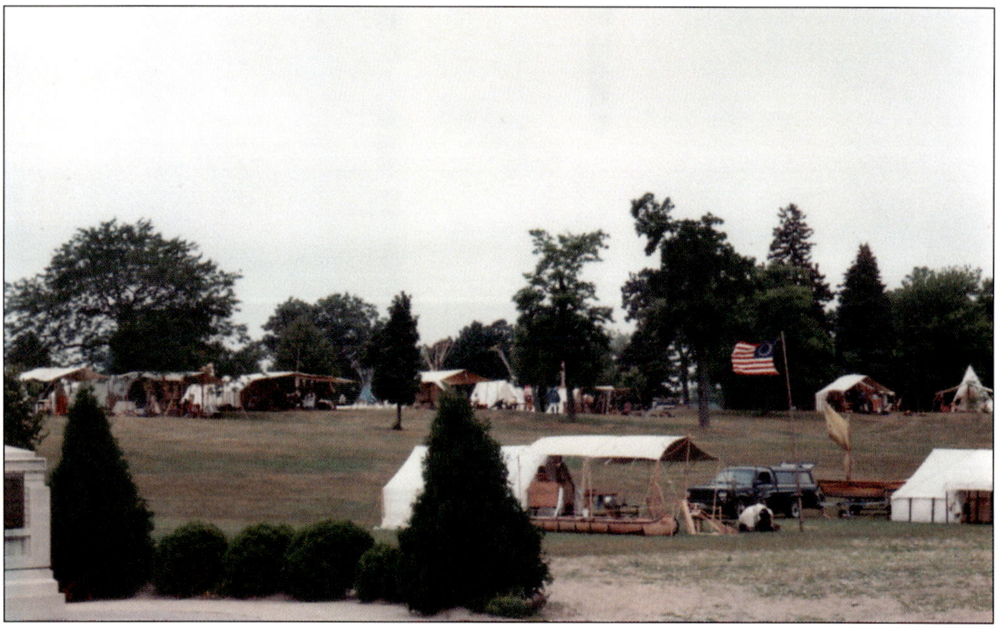

Simmons Island truly is the best place to host the rendezvous. It is centrally located along the waterfront right next to Pike Creek, and has a beach, two lighthouses, and an extensive park. The land there was first settled as the original site of Pike Creek before Kenosha was incorporated. (Courtesy of the Kenosha Public Museum.)

Two

Arts and Edutainment

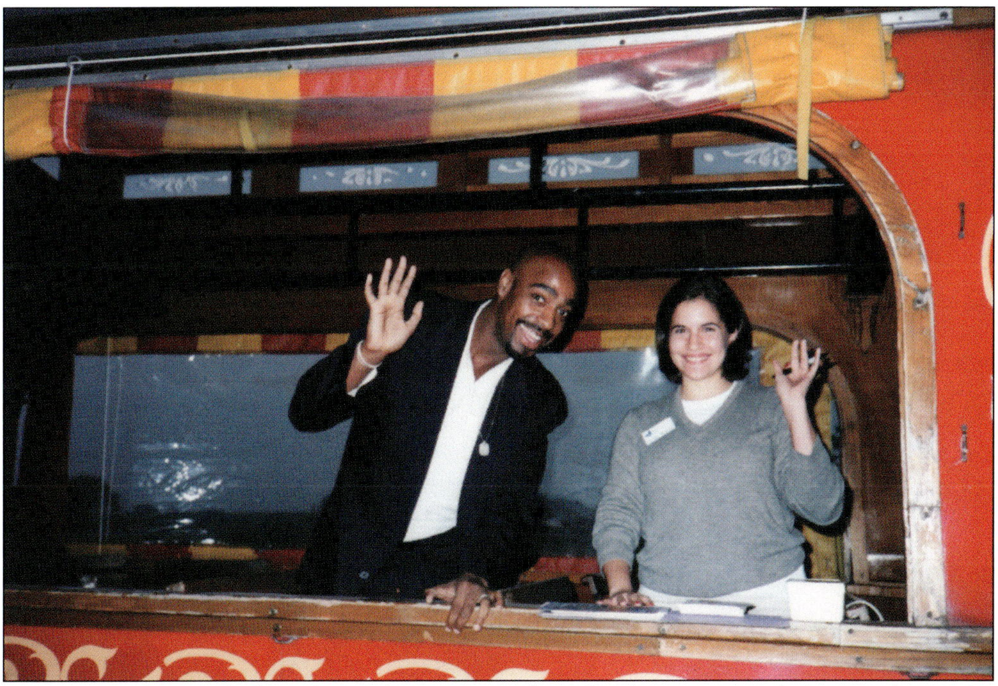

Jeffrey Sams, known for his roles in the movies *Soul Food* and *Waiting to Exhale*, visited Kenosha in the 1990s to celebrate the opening of his latest film, *Just Write*. The movie was financed by five dentists and a hospital administrator, all from the Kenosha area. (Courtesy of the Kenosha Public Museum.)

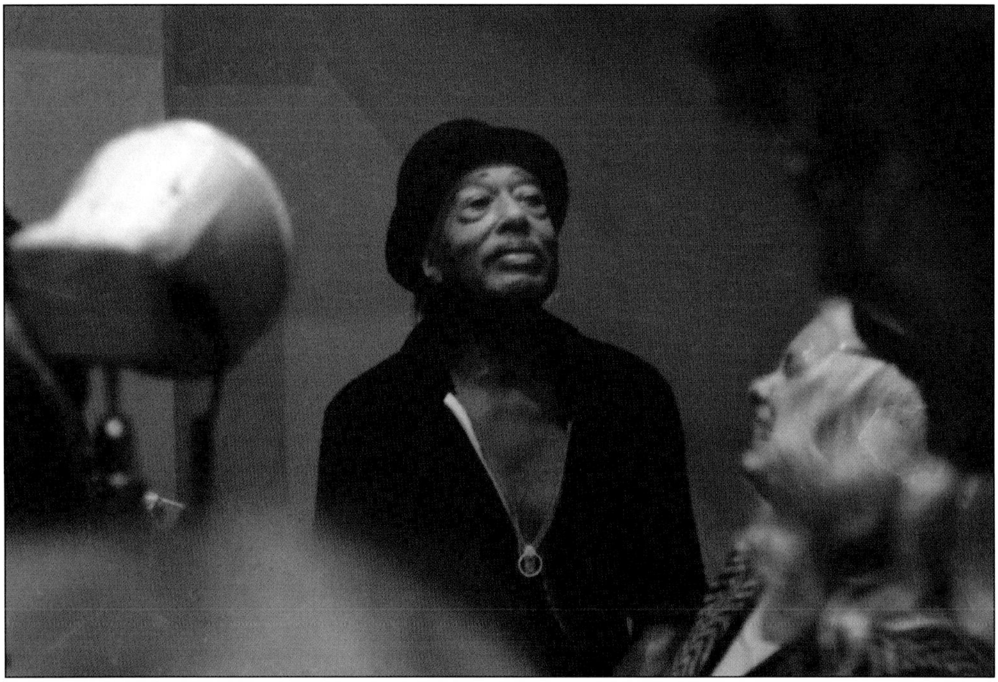

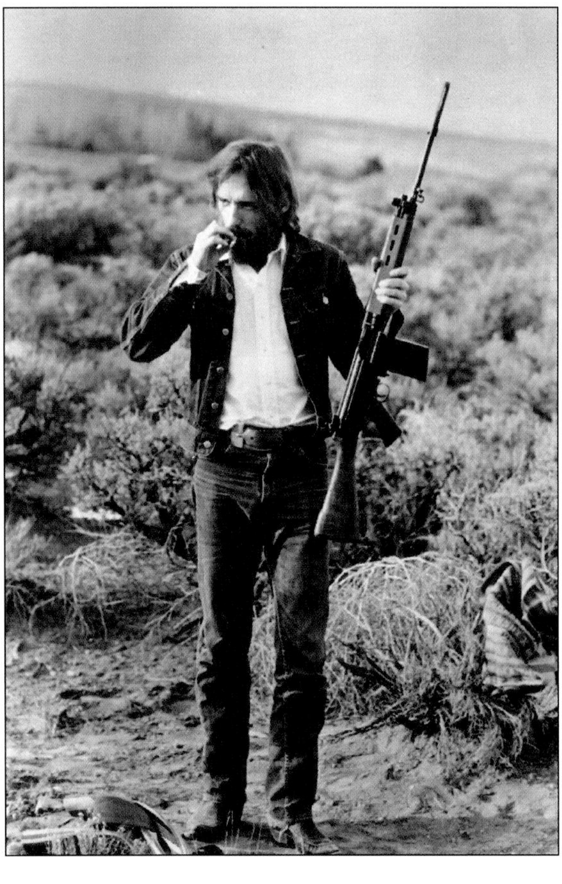

This 1973 photograph shows Duke Ellington, who had come to Kenosha with his orchestra to perform a concert of sacred music with the Carthage College Choir. This was Ellington's second performance at the college, the previous having been the year prior. Ellington died in 1974. (Courtesy of the Carthage College Archives.)

In 1971, Dennis Hopper (shown here) released a documentary about himself called *The American Dreamer.* Hopper deliberately kept the film out of public circulation, but he did take a movie tour to college campuses, including local Kenosha colleges, so he could show the film. (Courtesy of the Carthage College Archives.)

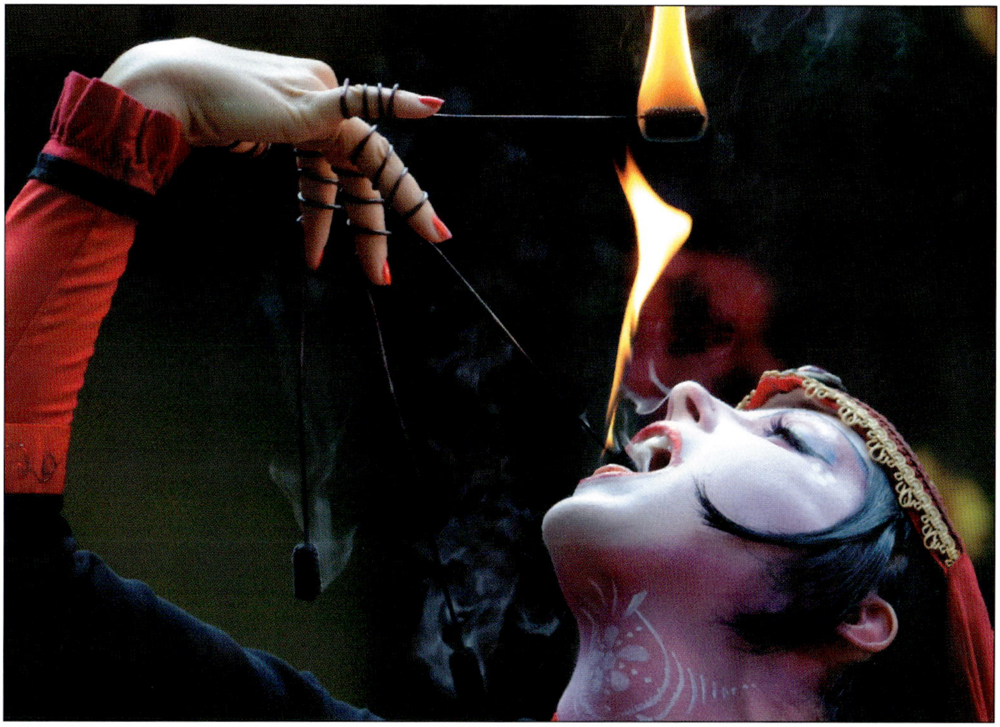

The Bristol Renaissance Faire is one of the largest area attractions in Kenosha. It is known in part for its exciting death-defying acts, like a sword swallower, fire eating, and a fire whip show. The Faire has more than 20 designated areas for shows and events. (Photograph by Robert Streiffer, courtesy of the Bristol Renaissance Faire.)

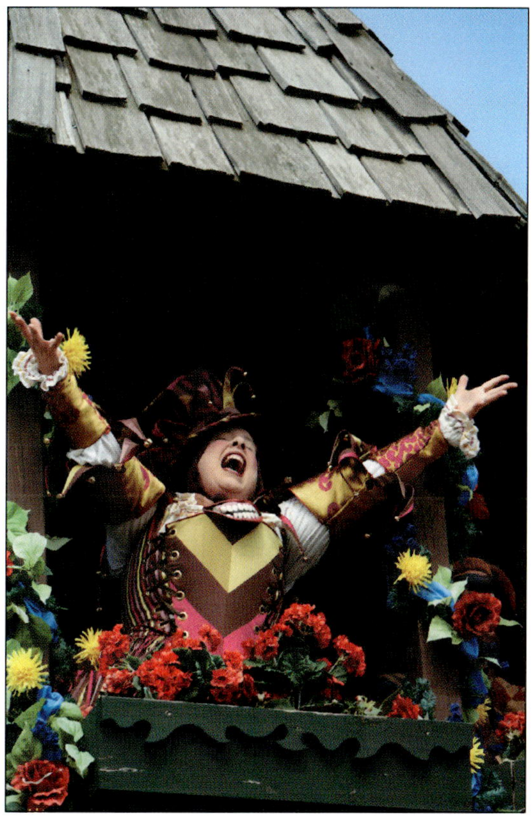

The Faire is a brightly colored and jovial event, with celebrations and parades every day in honor of the Queen. It is nearly impossible to walk even 10 feet without hearing the iconic shout of "Huzzah," as this woman is doing here. (Photograph by Ivan Phillips, courtesy of the Bristol Renaissance Faire.)

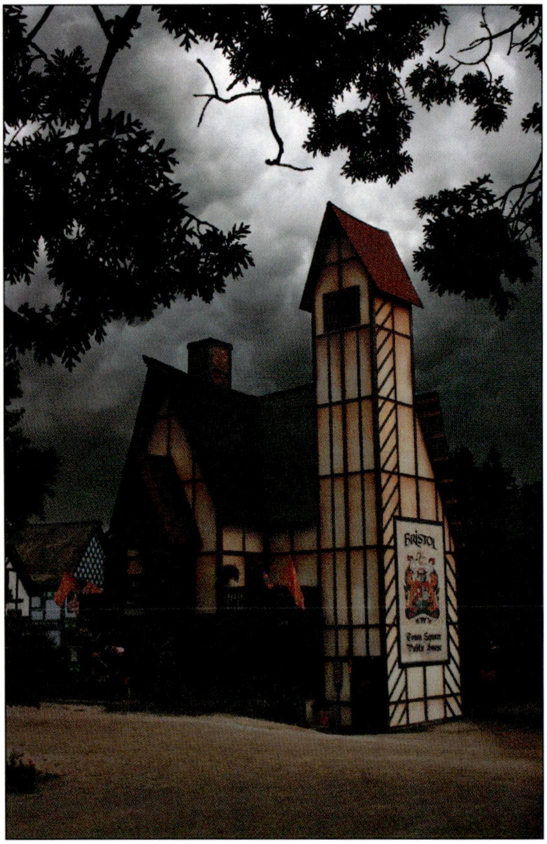

The Faire is a permanent construction that sits on 30 acres. It recreates an English village from 1574, and many visitors come in period costume. Of course, others come in more outlandish costumes not true to the period, such as *Star Wars* stormtroopers and Lord of the Rings characters. (Courtesy of the Bristol Renaissance Faire.)

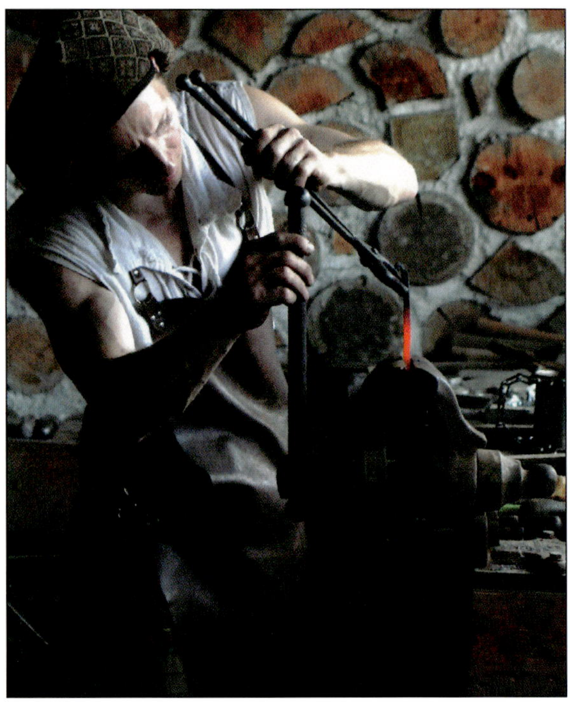

Every year, artisan craftsmen run retail booths at the Faire. Some offer live demonstrations and classes, like this blacksmith, while others simply sell their wares. On any given day, visitors can leave with everything from handmade leather shoes and journals to hand-forged weapons and bars of made-from-scratch soap. (Photograph by Kathy Kucia, courtesy of the Bristol Renaissance Faire.)

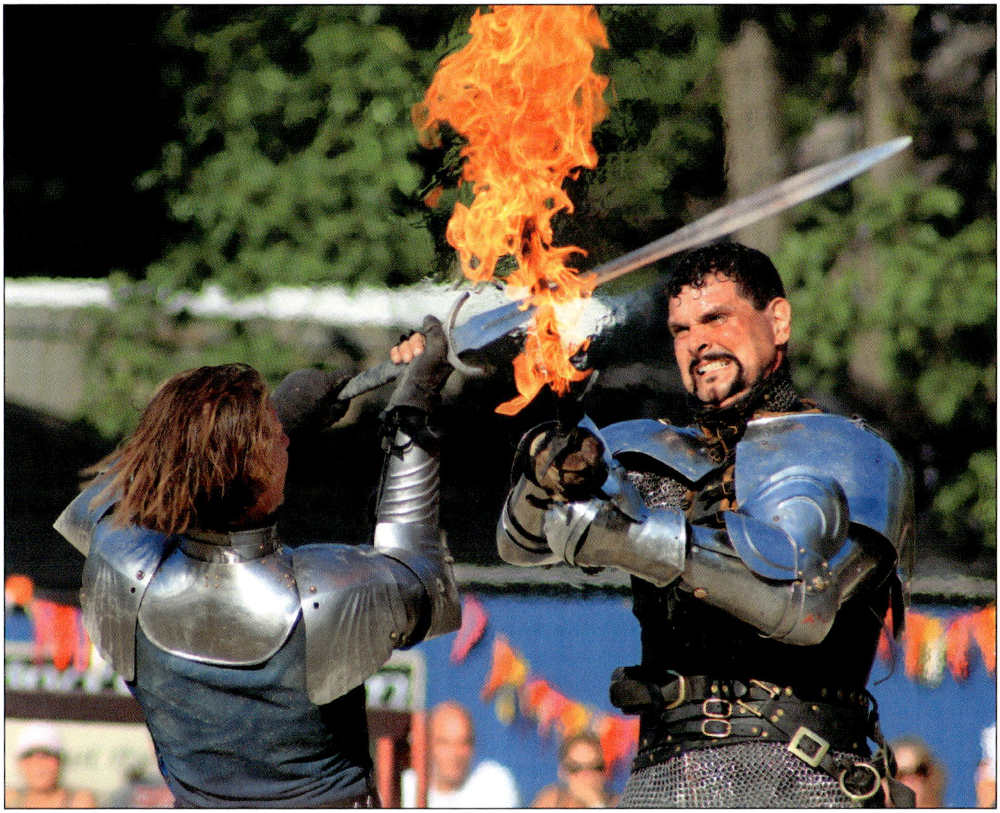

One of the most anticipated events at the Faire is the joust, where armored knights take each other on by horseback in an epic battle to win the favor of the crowd and queen. And sometimes, the jousts end in fiery swordfights like this one, determining the victor without the aid of his noble steed. (Photograph by Cynthia Suits, courtesy of the Bristol Renaissance Faire.)

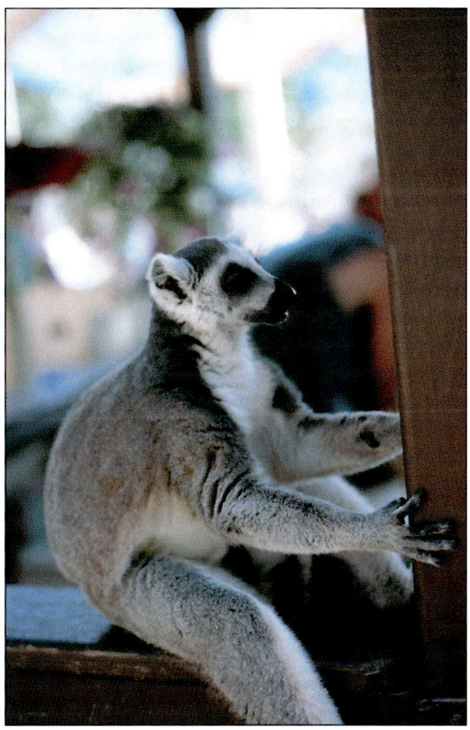

Part of the fun of the Faire is seeing the unique and unusual animals, like the one pictured here. Guests can ride elephants and camels, as well as watch hawks being released. Visitors can also buy puppets and marionettes of different animals to walk around the Faire. (Photograph by Sheila Teruty, courtesy of the Bristol Renaissance Faire.)

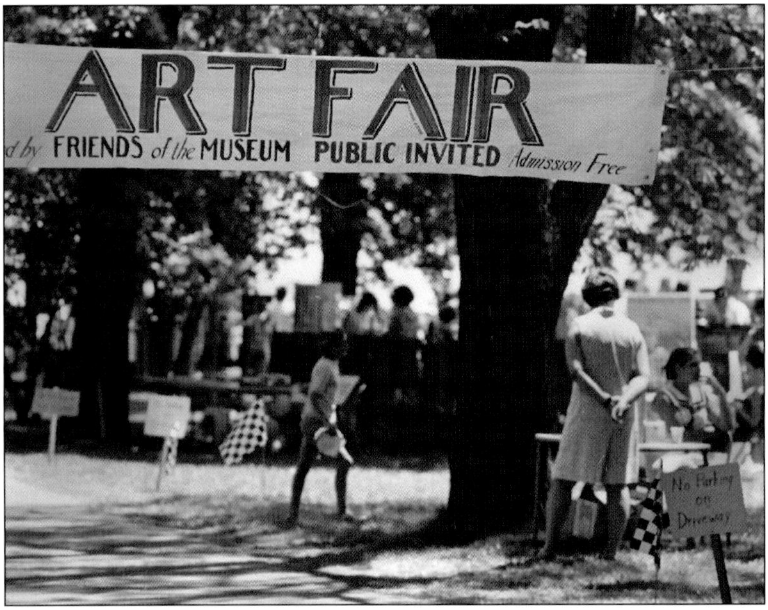

Since 1964, the Library Park Art Fair has been a popular event in downtown Kenosha. The city has a strong artistic flair (as evidenced by the many art galleries within its borders) and celebrates that whenever possible. This 1970 picture shows the entrance to the art fair. (Courtesy of the Kenosha Public Museum.)

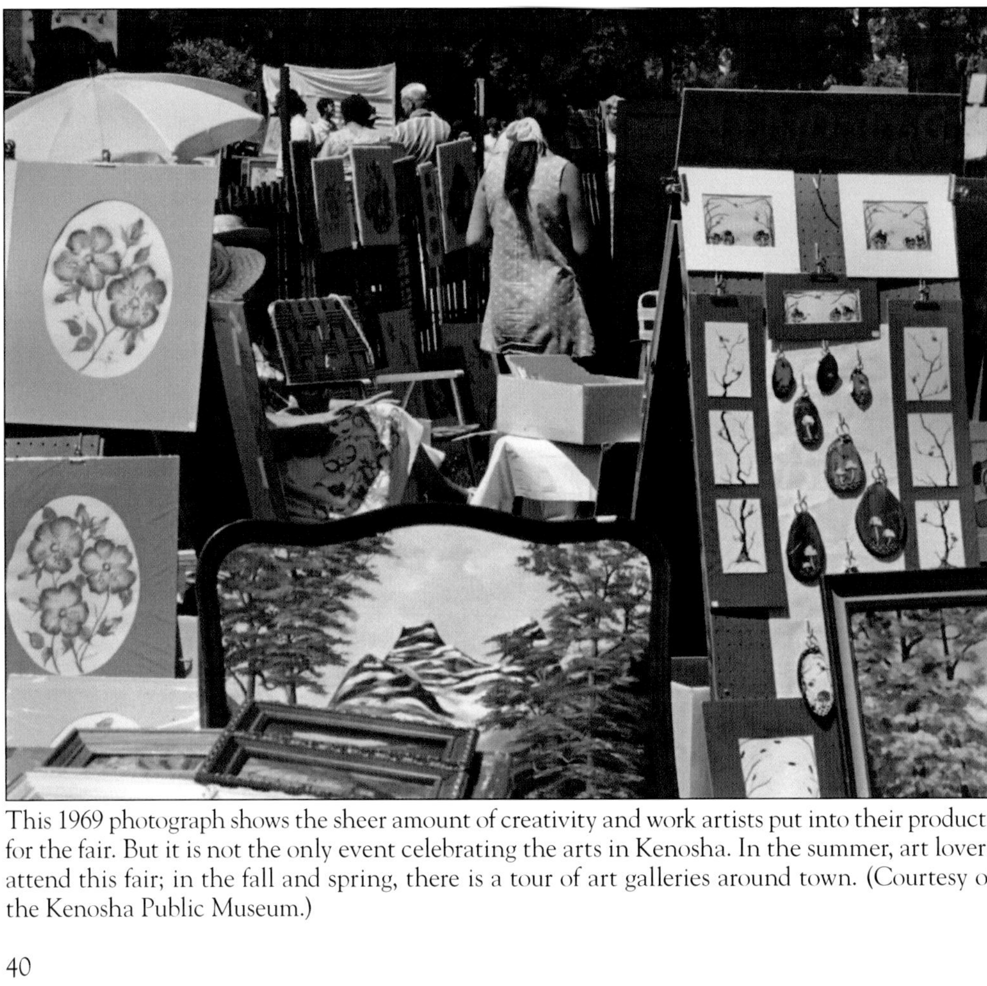

This 1969 photograph shows the sheer amount of creativity and work artists put into their products for the fair. But it is not the only event celebrating the arts in Kenosha. In the summer, art lovers attend this fair; in the fall and spring, there is a tour of art galleries around town. (Courtesy of the Kenosha Public Museum.)

The pottery and paintings shown in this 1969 art fair photograph are indicative of the myriad types of art that can be found at the fair. Creators of all types would come and set up chairs, tents, shelves, and racks on the grass at the park, hoping to make a sale. (Courtesy of the Kenosha Public Museum.)

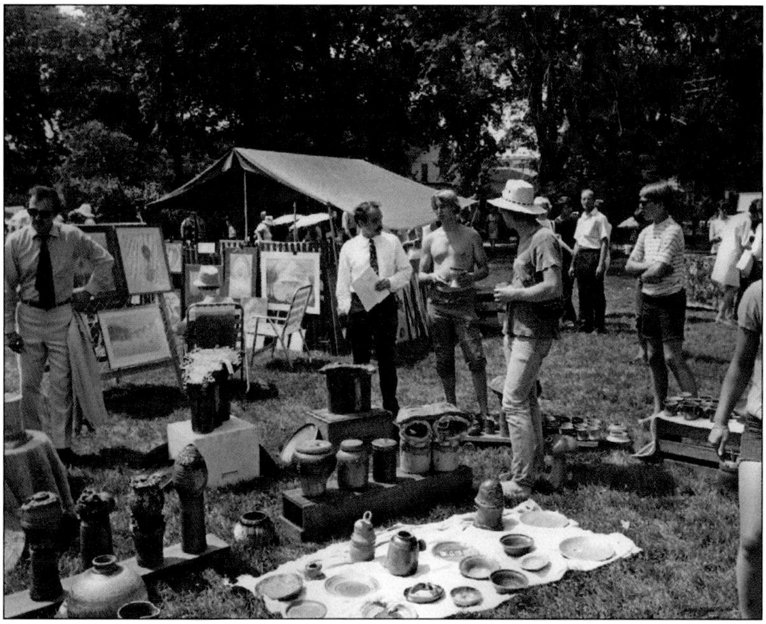

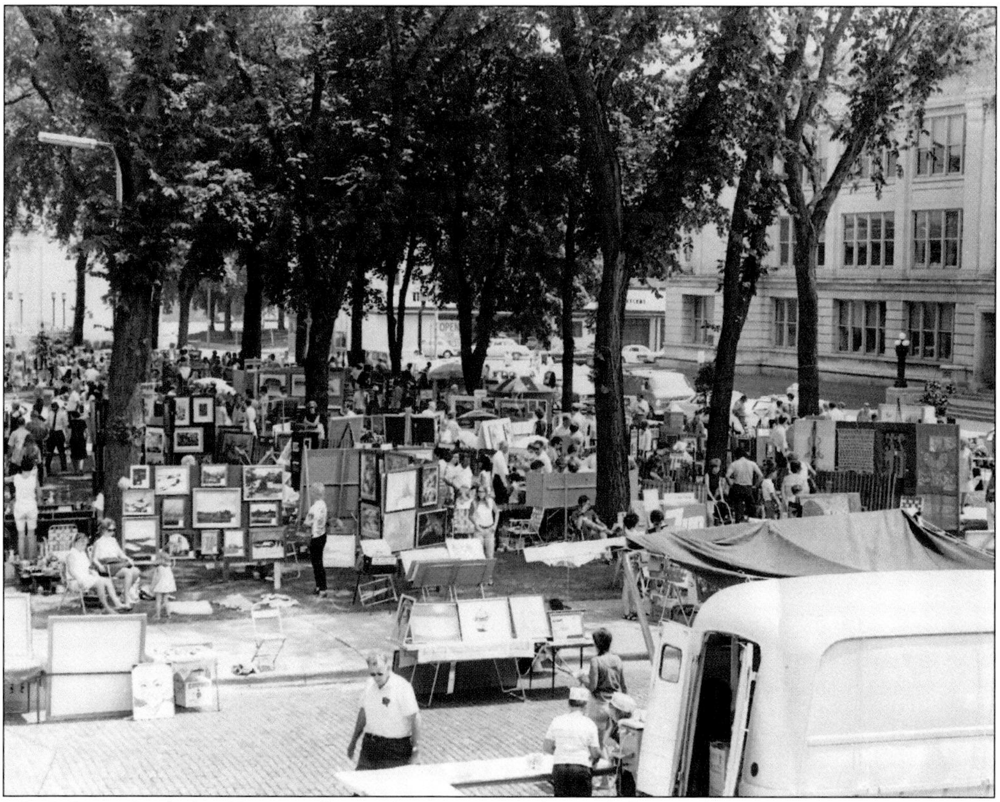

The Library Park Art Fair was located in its namesake park for nearly 50 years. This 1970 image provides an idea of how crowded the park could get with artwork. When the fair moved to its new location, the name changed from Library Park Art Fair to Friends of the Museums Art Fair. (Courtesy of the Kenosha Public Museum.)

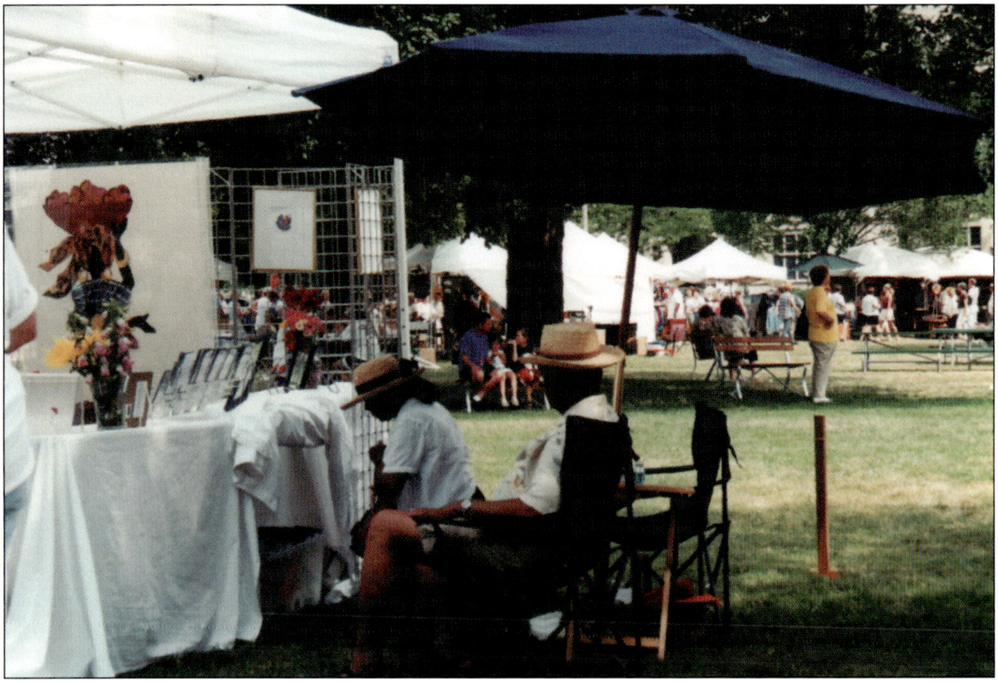

Once the new Kenosha Public Museum was built, the Friends of the Museums Art Fair moved from Library Park over to the Harbor Park. The reason for the move was to make the fair more convenient, and also to show off the new museum buildings. (Courtesy of the Kenosha Public Museum.)

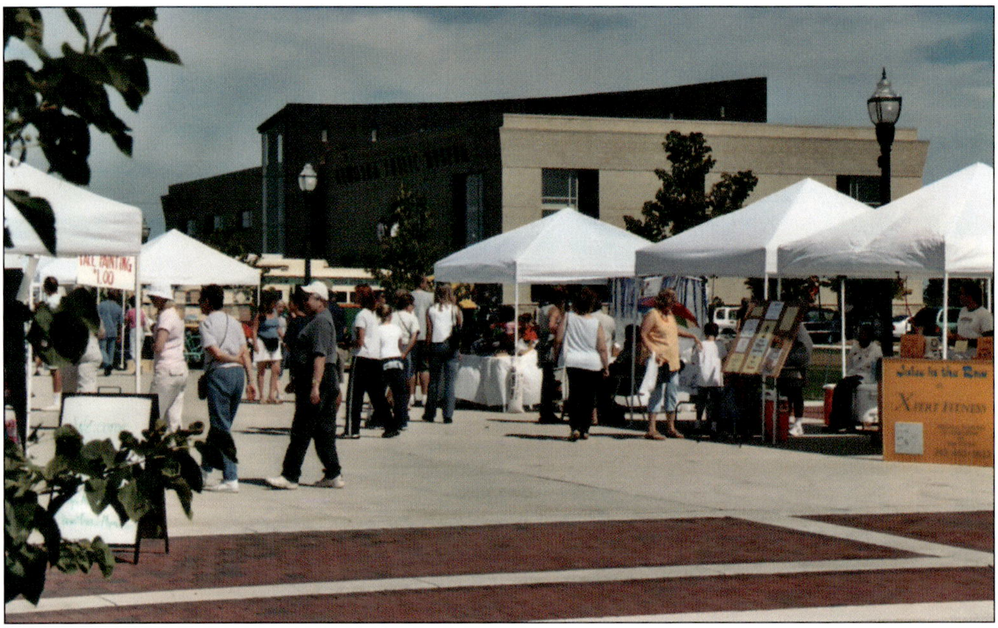

Kenosha has farmers' markets year-round throughout the city. In the winter, the downtown market is held inside an old theater. But in the summer, Harbor Park outside becomes a bustling hub of activity, with farm stands, vendor tents, live music, food samples, and crafts. (Courtesy of the Kenosha Public Museum.)

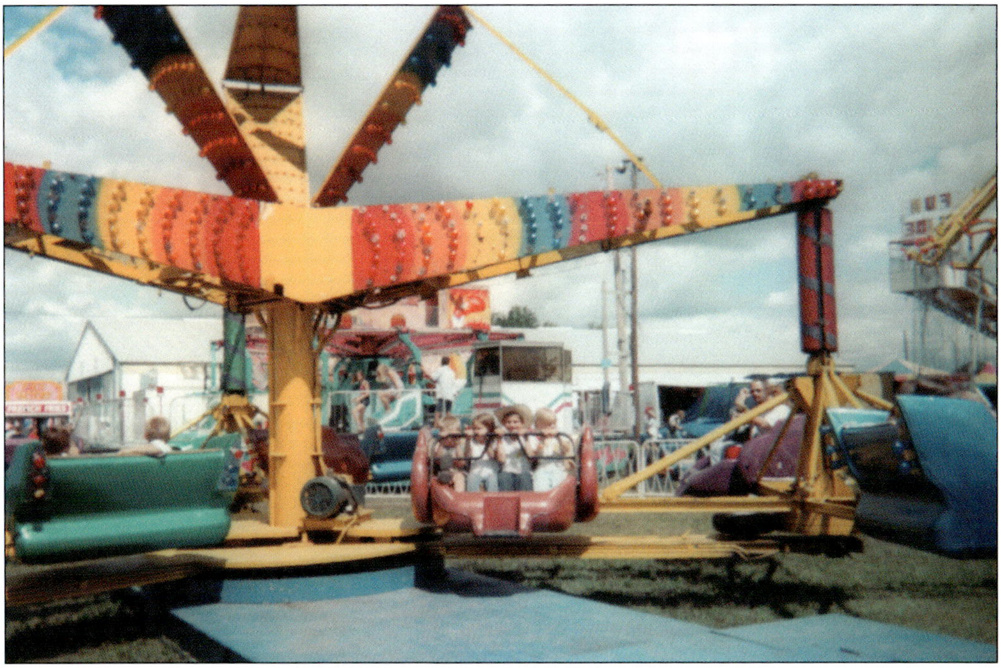

The Kenosha County Fair has been a huge part of the community for 95 years. Not only does it showcase the agricultural and livestock achievements of the area and 4-H Club competitions, it also includes fun rides, entertainment, exhibitions, and food vendors. (Courtesy of the Kenosha County University of Wisconsin-Extension.)

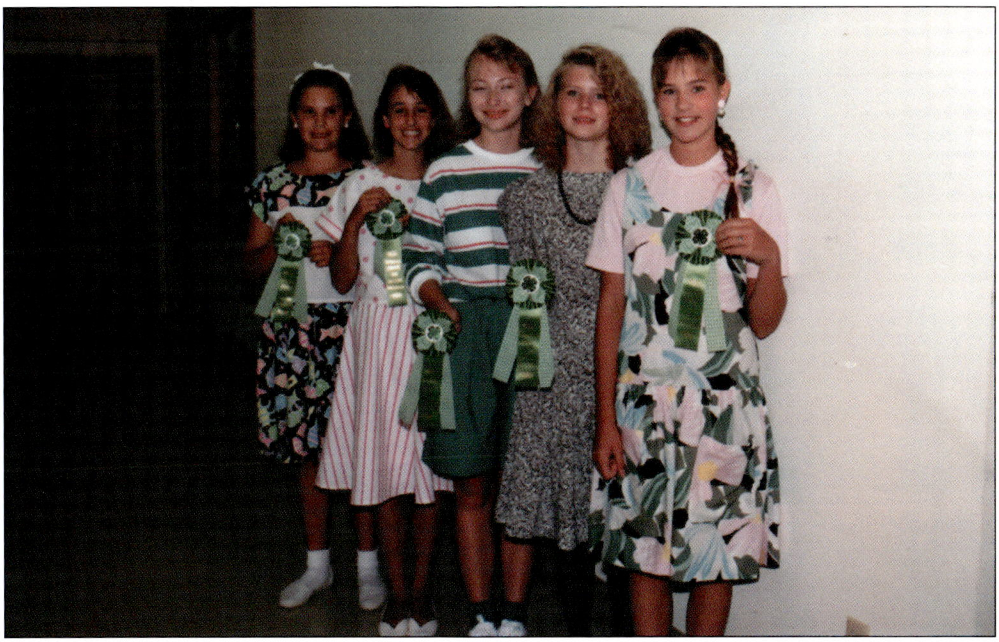

Every year, the Kenosha Extension hosts an event called Fashion Explosion for 4-H members. Designers of all skill levels are able to construct clothing, model it, and win awards for their work. The event comes complete with a class about how to model clothing. (Courtesy of the Kenosha County University of Wisconsin-Extension.)

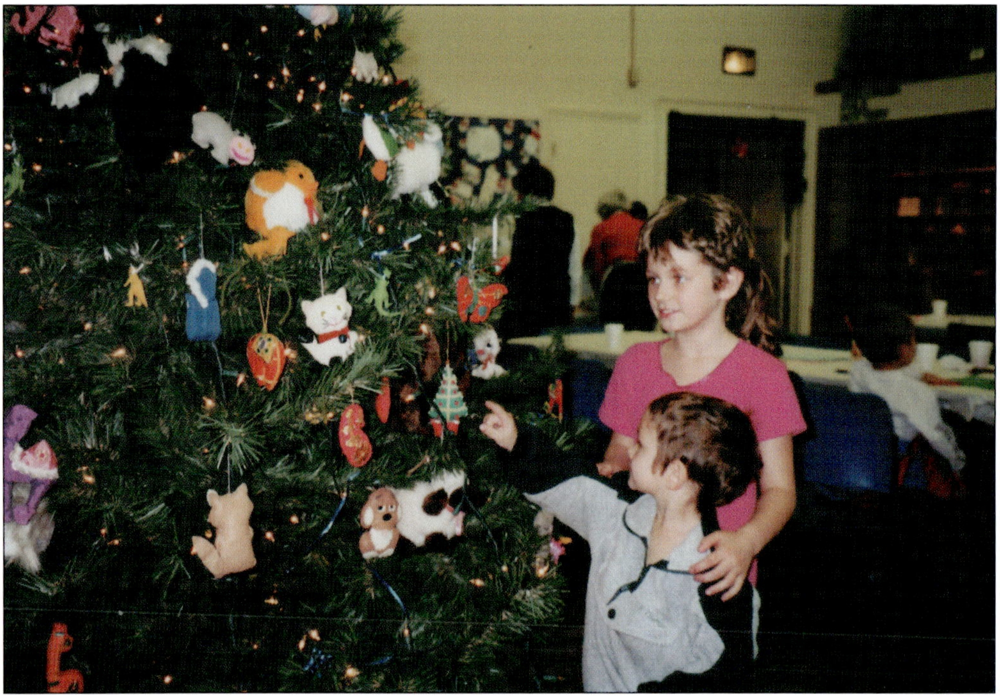

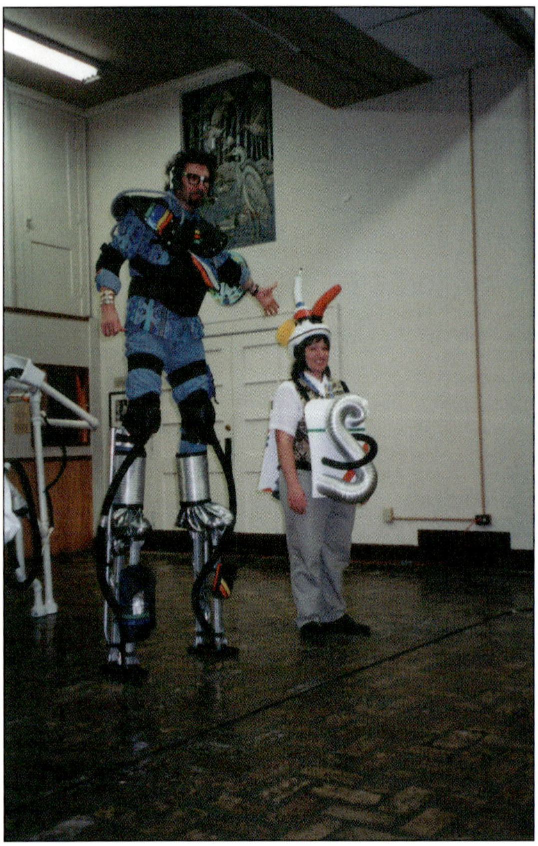

At the Kenosha Public Museum, the holidays become a full-on festival. A scale holiday train is set up in the lobby, there are celebrations for Christmas and New Year's, and there is even a Christmas tree kids can decorate, like these two children are doing in this 1980s photograph. (Courtesy of the Kenosha Public Museum.)

With a historic movie palace and several community- and school-based theater troupes, kids in Kenosha are introduced to the world of acting early. In this photograph, Ron Fry's Theater Company is entertaining children at the public museum. Ron Fry is a local writer, director, actor, and prop maker. (Courtesy of the Kenosha Public Museum.)

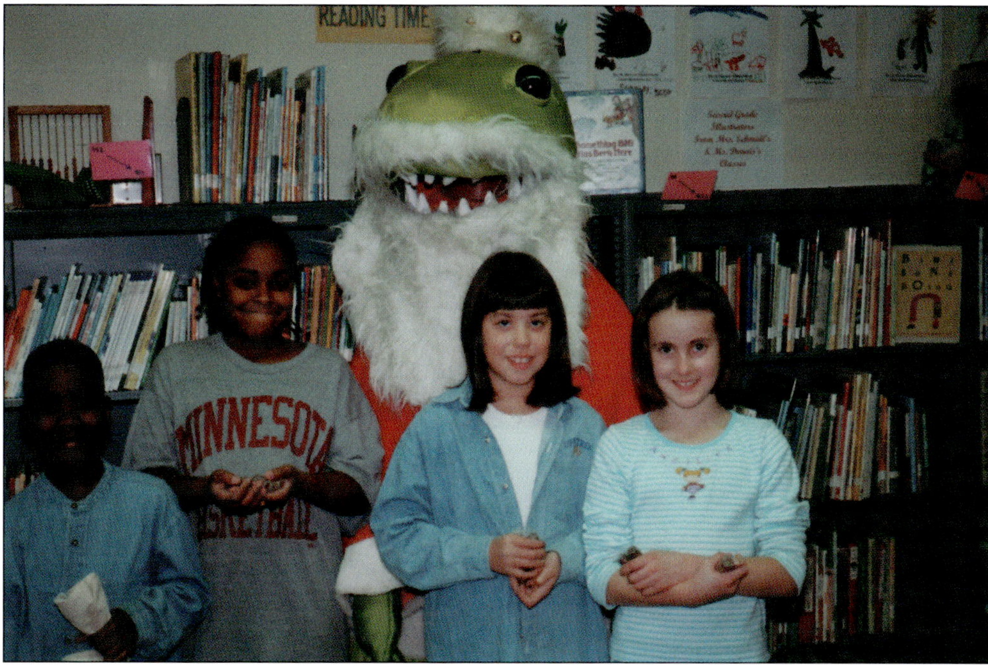

In the 1980s, the public museum's mascot, Ty-Rex the Tyrannosaurus, did his part to spread holiday cheer. In this image, he is playing the part of dino-Santa while visiting a local school. The neon green dinosaur was a constant presence at community events and parades. (Courtesy of the Kenosha Public Museum.)

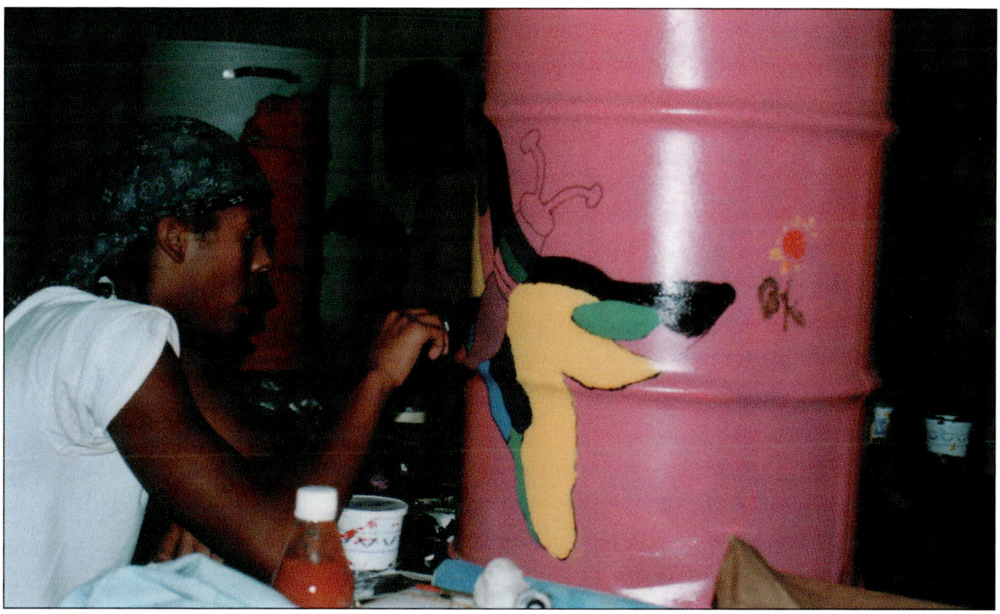

In the early 1990s, Kenosha mayor John Antaramian instituted a summer arts program for kids aged 14 to 17. The Mayor's Youth Employment in the Arts program paired students with local artists for eight weeks. Kids would attend school in the morning and be an artist's apprentice afterwards. This student is painting a trash can for a local park. (Courtesy of the Kenosha Public Museum.)

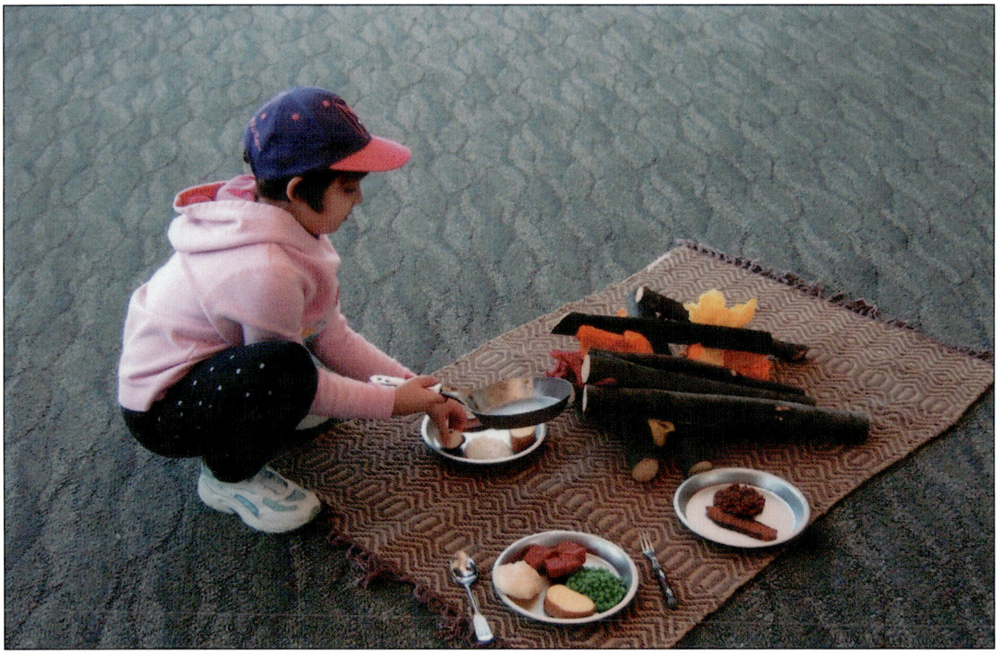

Two of the favorite exhibits for kids in the Kenosha Public Museum's past have been geared towards entertainment while educating. Above, a child is learning to build a fire and cook over it as part of a Sunday Funday exhibit. Below, two kids are searching for dinosaur bones in an exhibit called Hatching the Past. Not only do they get to play around in sand, but they also are learning about the archaeological process—something that might come in handy later, since Kenosha County has been on the front lines of some major archaeological discoveries. (Both, courtesy of the Kenosha Public Museum.)

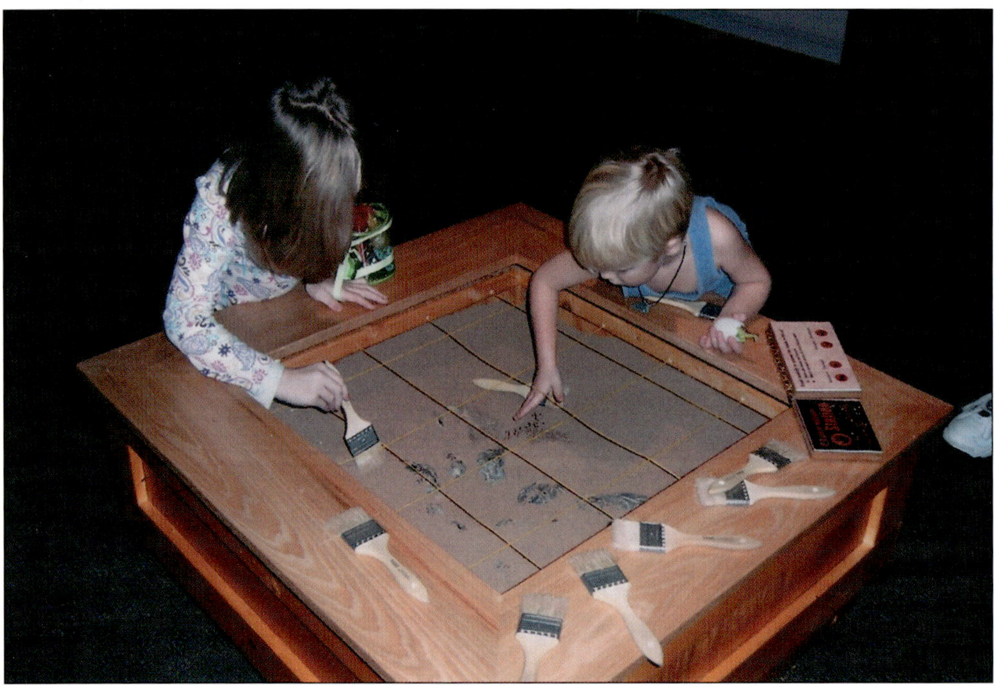

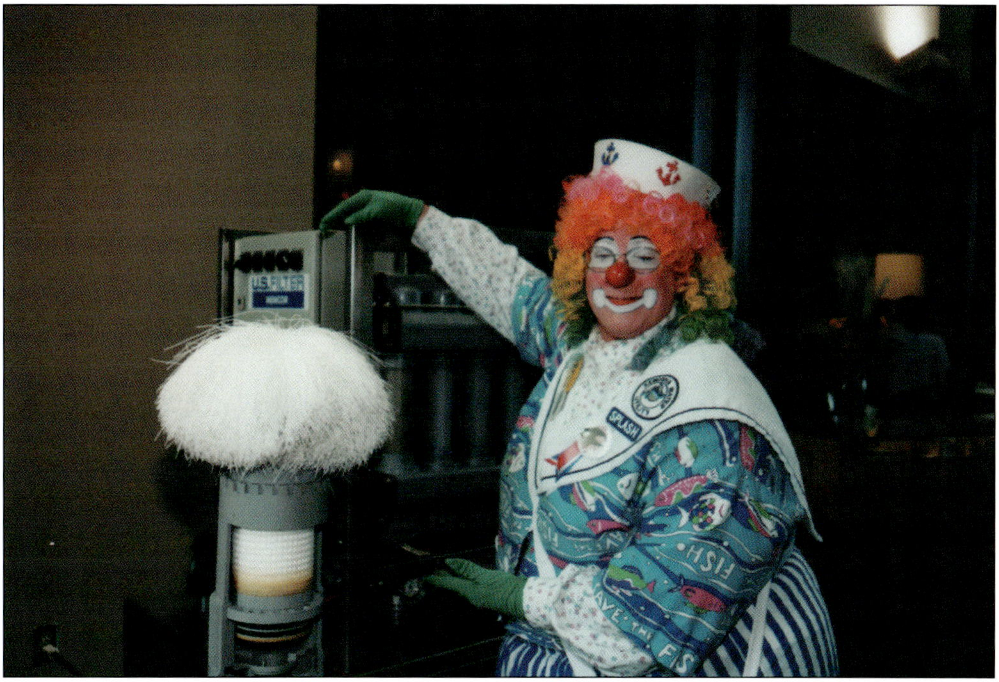

Even the Kenosha Water Utility gets in on the community fun happening around the city. In this picture, a Water Utility employee dressed as a clown presents a demonstration at the public museum's grand opening. The clown's name, aptly, is Splash. (Courtesy of the Kenosha Public Museum.)

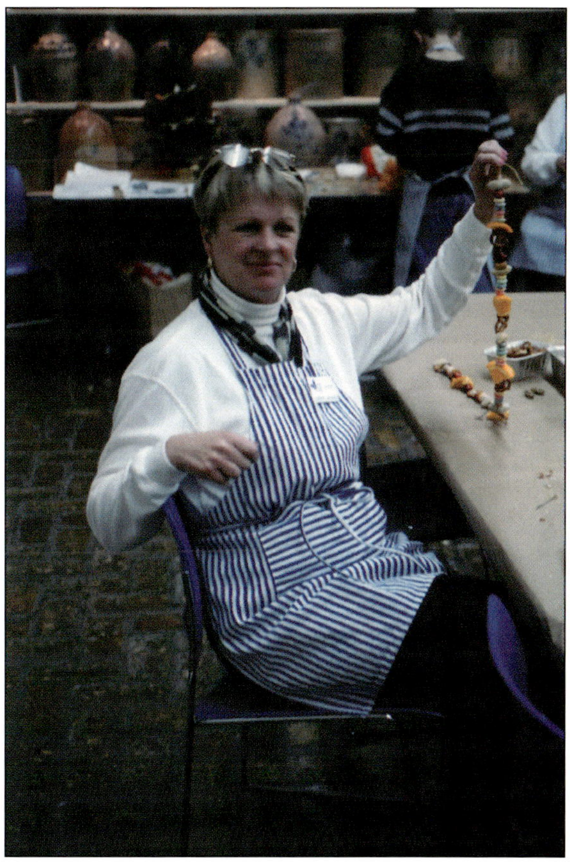

Every winter, the Kenosha Public Museum hosts Frost Fest, a family festival featuring fun things for kids to do during winter break. Every day has a different theme, like how to survive in the Arctic, or creating miniature igloos. Here, museum volunteer Cheryl Bowen is helping to string garland for the festival. (Courtesy of the Kenosha Public Museum.)

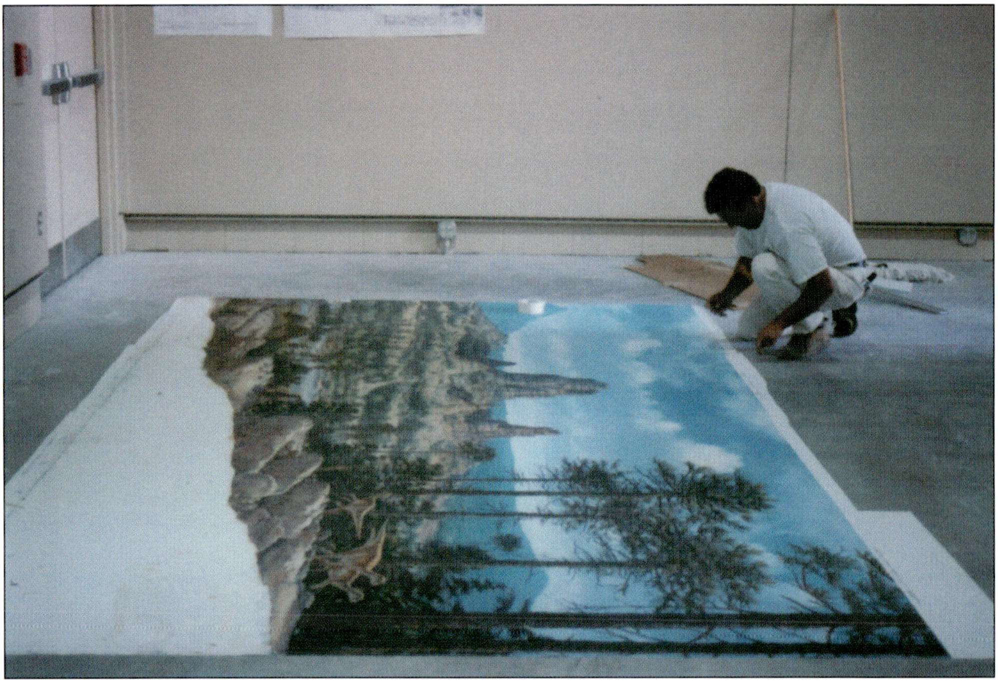

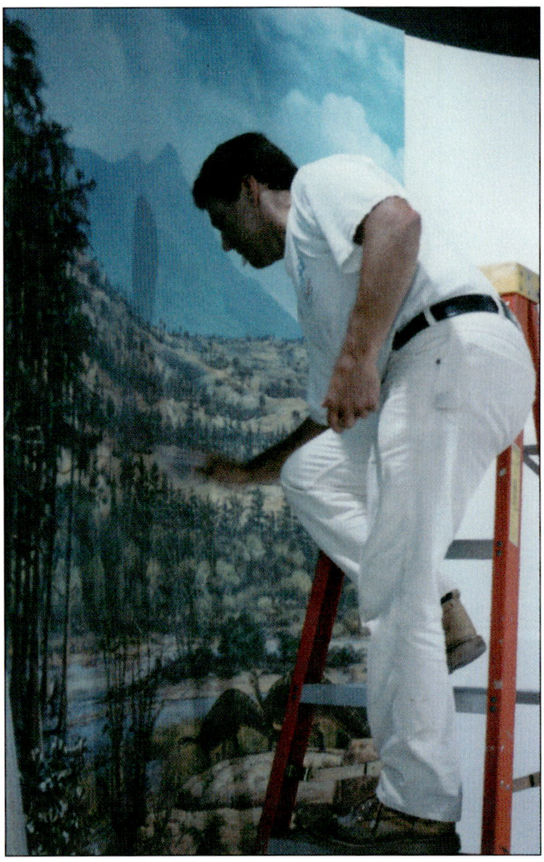

These two images show the installation of the murals in the Wisconsin Story exhibit at the public museum. The exhibit takes museum visitors through the entire history of Wisconsin, starting with the underwater world it once was, then moving to climate change during the ice age (when glaciers covered the area), climate change again that melted the glaciers, ecosystem development, plant and animal evolution, and the lives of the Native Americans who used to occupy this land. This is also the exhibit that contains the museum's two mammoths, as well as coral reefs and ancient underwater monsters. (Courtesy of the Kenosha Public Museum.)

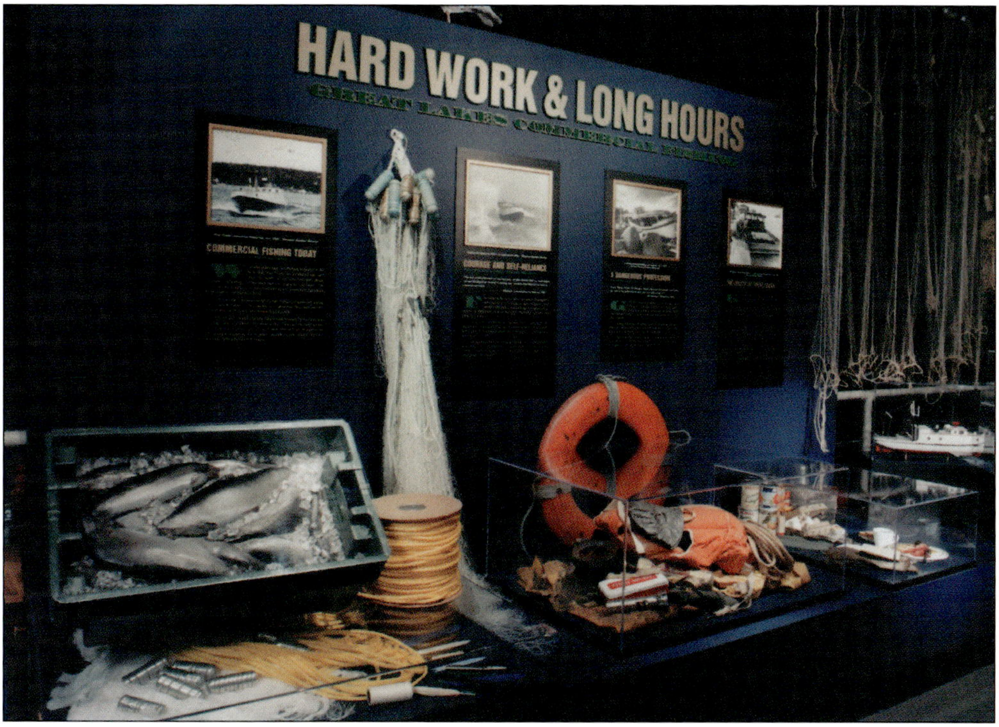

The Great Lakes Commercial Fishing exhibit was the first temporary exhibit to be housed at the new Kenosha Public Museum. Through a display of fish, rope, lifesaving equipment, and more, the exhibit celebrated Kenosha's early history as a commercial fishing port, as well as the fishing business throughout all the Great Lakes. (Courtesy of the Kenosha Public Museum.)

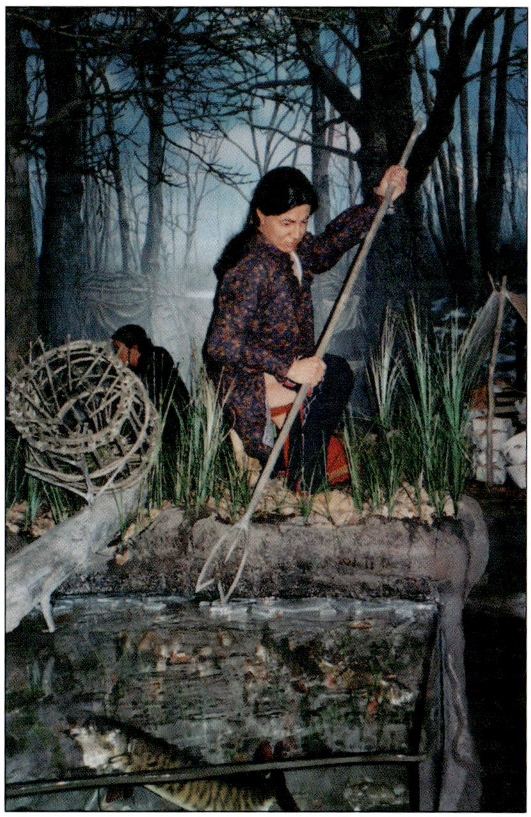

A major focus of the Kenosha Public Museum's collections is the Native American history throughout Kenosha. This scene shows typical spearfishing practices of the native populations: the Potawatomi and Ojibwa. Kenosha actually draws its name from the Ojibwa language moniker for the city: Masu-kinoja, or "a place where fish spawn." (Courtesy of the Kenosha Public Museum.)

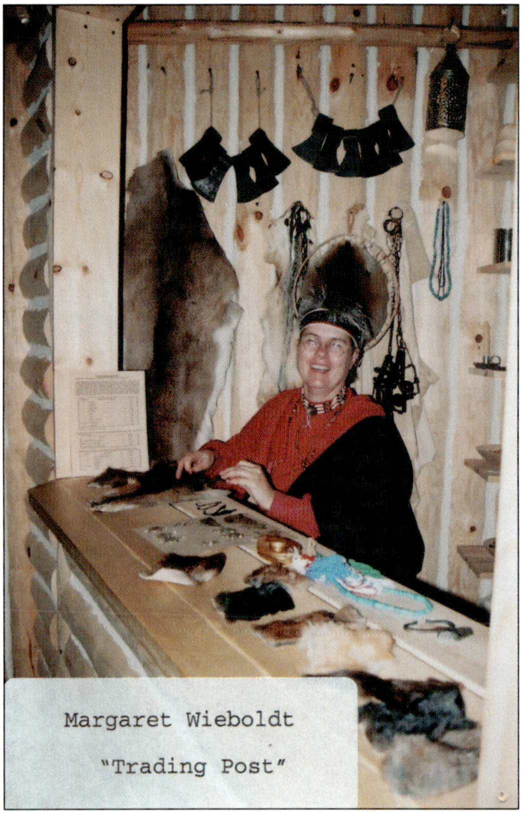

The Trading Post at the public museum is a volunteer-staffed exhibit. The worker dresses up in traditional Native American costume of the early 1800s and runs the trading post just how it would have been run when Kenosha was settled. In this picture, Margaret Wieboldt is staffing the post. (Courtesy of the Kenosha Public Museum.)

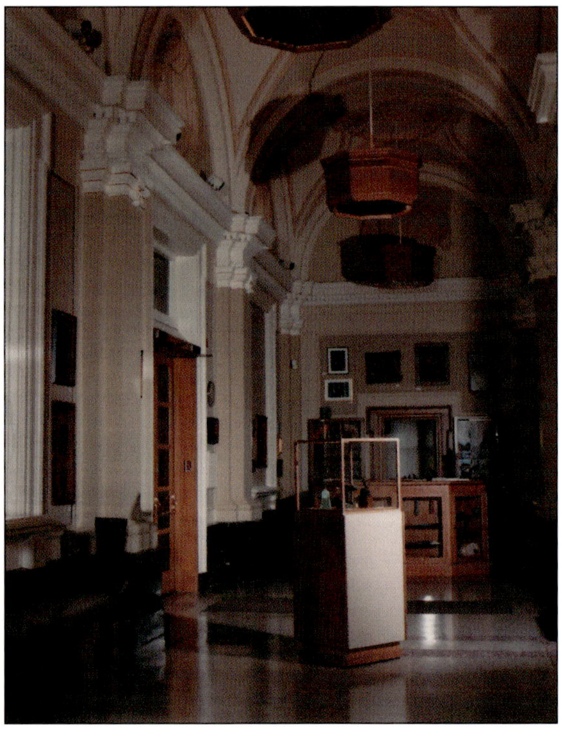

The Friends of the Kenosha Public Museums is a nonprofit organization that supports and promotes the museum through special events, fundraising, and community activities. The group's efforts have often allowed the museum to reap big benefits, such as this renovation of the Friends Gallery in the old Kenosha Public Museum building. (Courtesy of the Kenosha Public Museum.)

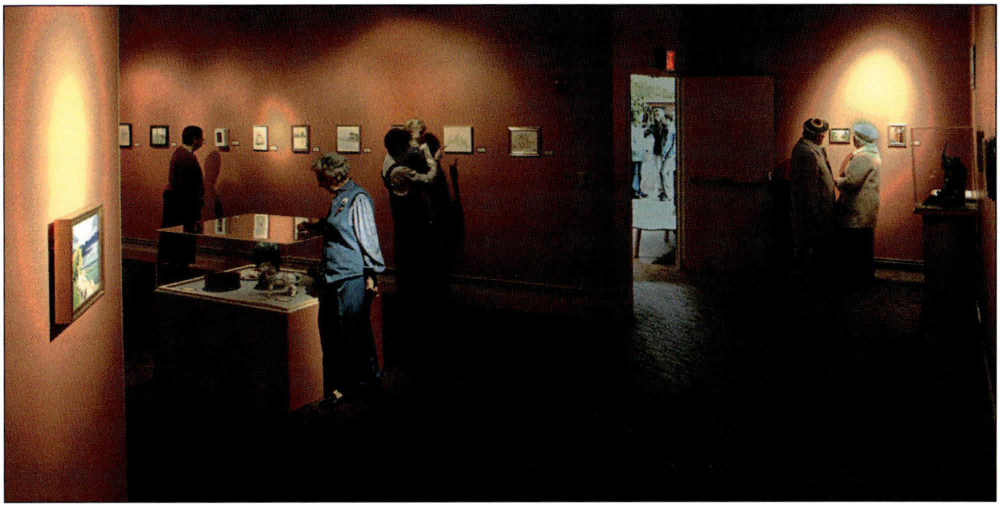

In keeping with the city's continuing mission to combine art, education, and entertainment, the Kenosha Art Association held a Miniature Masterpieces art exhibit at the Kenosha Public Museum. The annual art show limits the paintings to a size of 12 inches by 12 inches, including the frame. (Courtesy of the Kenosha Public Museum.)

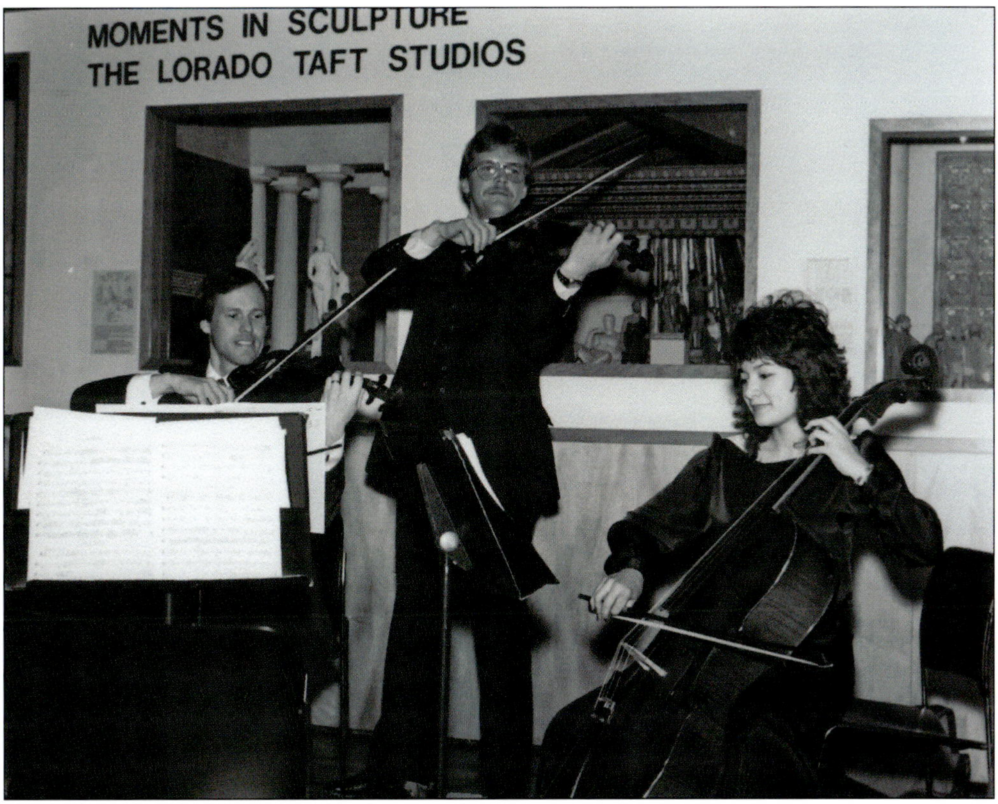

In 1984, the Kenosha Public Museum was celebrating its 50th anniversary. To honor this milestone, the museum threw a swanky gala, complete with a string ensemble. Playing at the gala were David Scripsema (left) and Robert Wells (center). The woman on the right is unidentified. (Courtesy of the Kenosha Public Museum.)

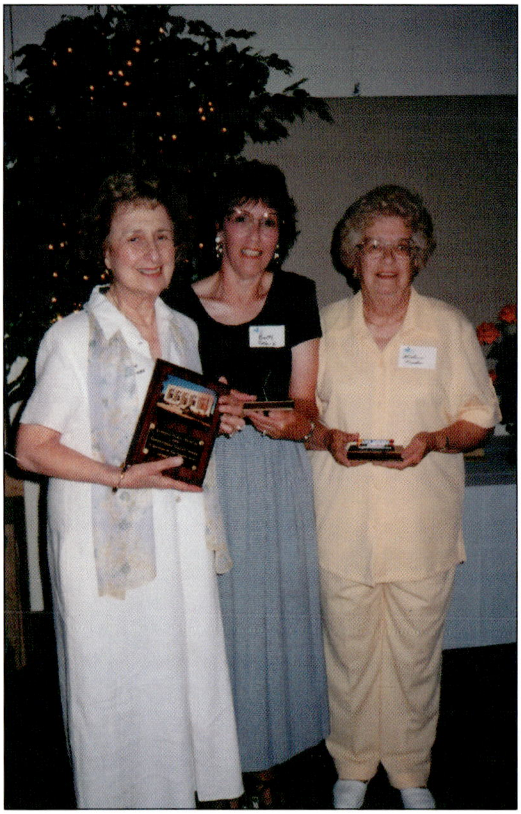

Many of the people working at the public museum on a daily basis are volunteers. The museum holds its volunteers in very high esteem, and every year, it hosts an awards ceremony and party for the group. These pictures show an example of the types of fun awards volunteers can win. At left, from left to right, are Debbie Dorfman, with a distinguished service award; Betty Selin, with a "bent nail" award; and Lillian Tredo, with a lifesaver award. Below, from left to right, are Bill Kazmer with the lifesaver award, and Karen Bessey with the "new kid on the block" award. (Both, courtesy of the Kenosha Public Museum.)

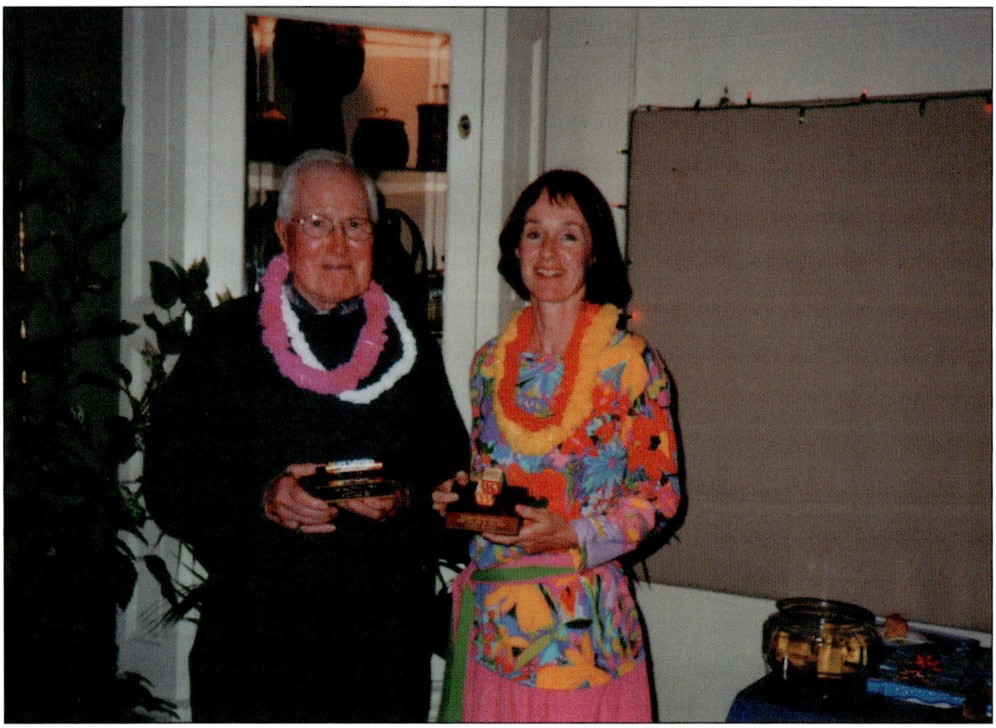

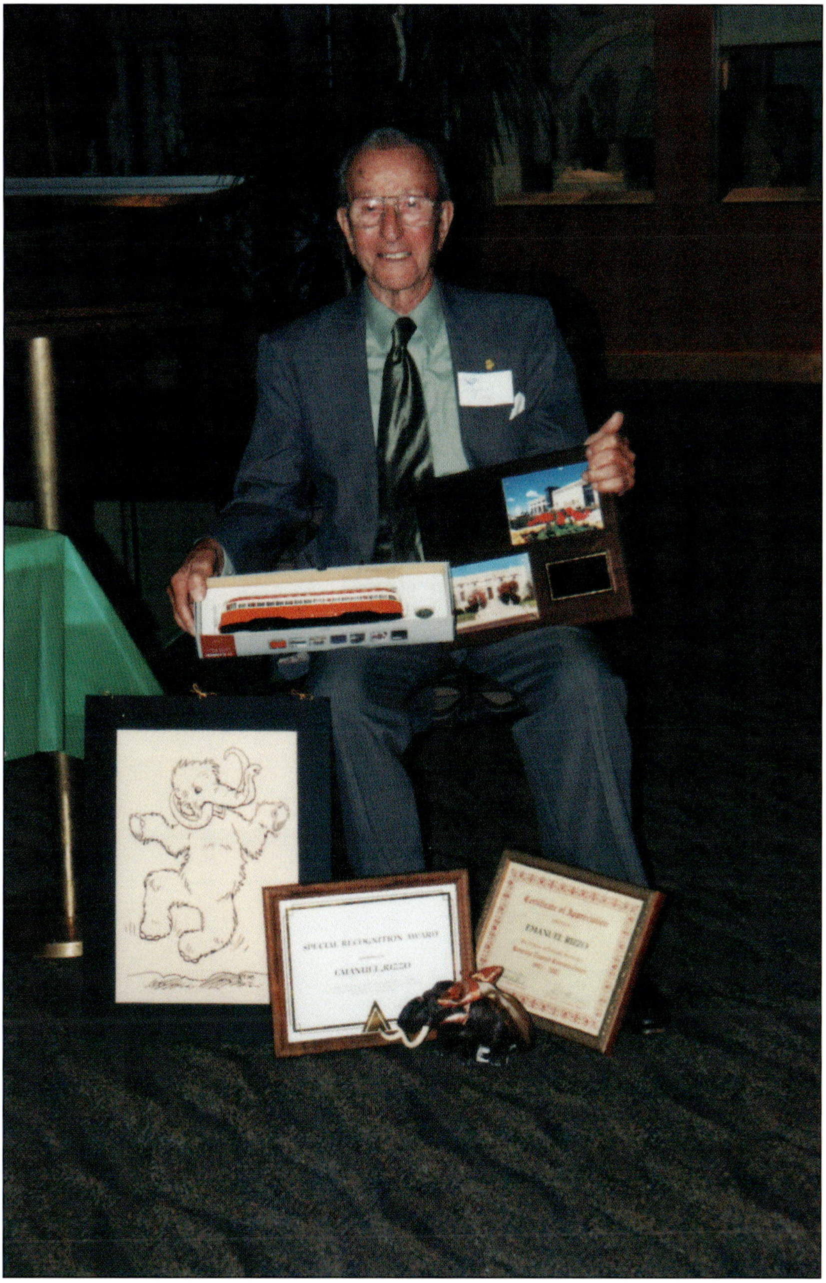

Emanuel Rizzo—or Manny, as he was known to his friends—was a long-standing member of the museum board and a city council alderman. The Public Museum threw him a lavish party when he retired, showering him with gifts. Manny passed away in 2007. He had been a lifelong resident of Kenosha, born in the city in 1912. He served nine consecutive terms as an alderman, longer than any other city council member. Manny was voted unanimously to be city council president, and was also the oldest member on the council at age 73. He was a pioneer in city improvement projects, leading charges to spruce up the parks and community pool. He also helped initiate the water treatment plant expansion. He had a nickname in the city as well: the "Working Alderman." (Courtesy of the Kenosha Public Museum.)

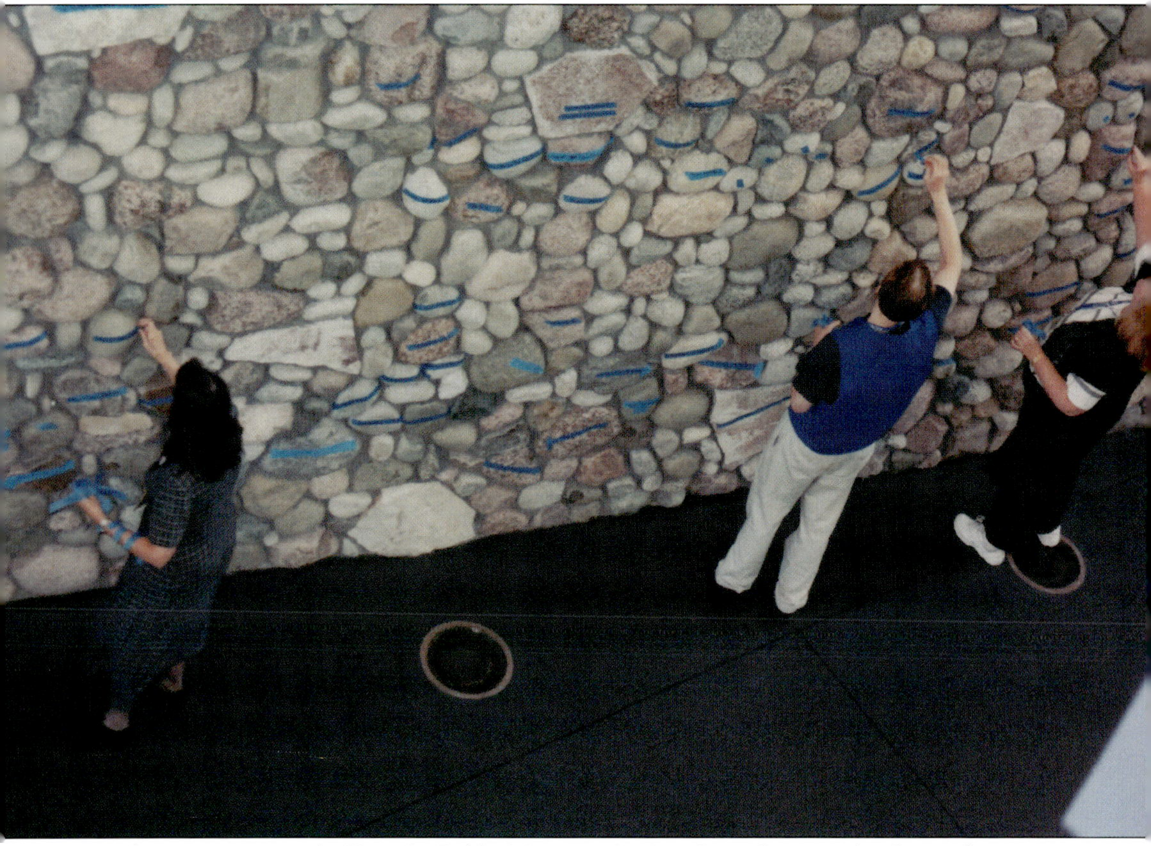

When visitors enter the Kenosha Public Museum, the first thing their eyes land on is the enormous glacial till wall. The wall is created out of fieldstone and towers over the lobby. A unique donation system accompanies the wall. Donors can virtually adopt a boulder in the wall through a kiosk system in the lobby. The would-be donor selects a donation amount on the kiosk, then the screen displays all of the remaining rocks available for purchase. The donor picks the rock, dedicates it to whomever they wish, and then gets a record of virtual ownership. Their information is recorded in the kiosk for other visitors to see. Here, prior to the installation of the program, museum employees are using blue tape to mark which boulders have already been purchased so the names can be entered into the new system. (Courtesy of the Kenosha Public Museum.)

Three

Parks, Recreation, and Agriculture

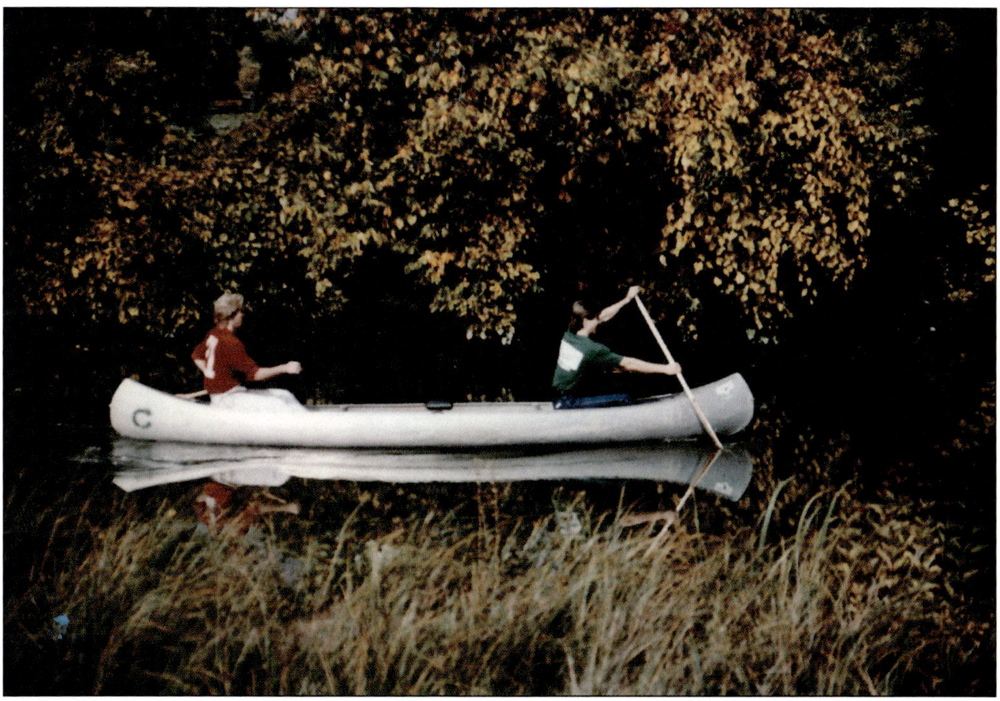

The Pike River was a major player in the original settlement of Kenosha. Its bisection of land with Lake Michigan forms Simmons Island, and it framed the location for the founding of the town. In this picture, two students from Carthage College are doing as the natives once did and canoeing along the Pike. (Courtesy of the Carthage College Archives.)

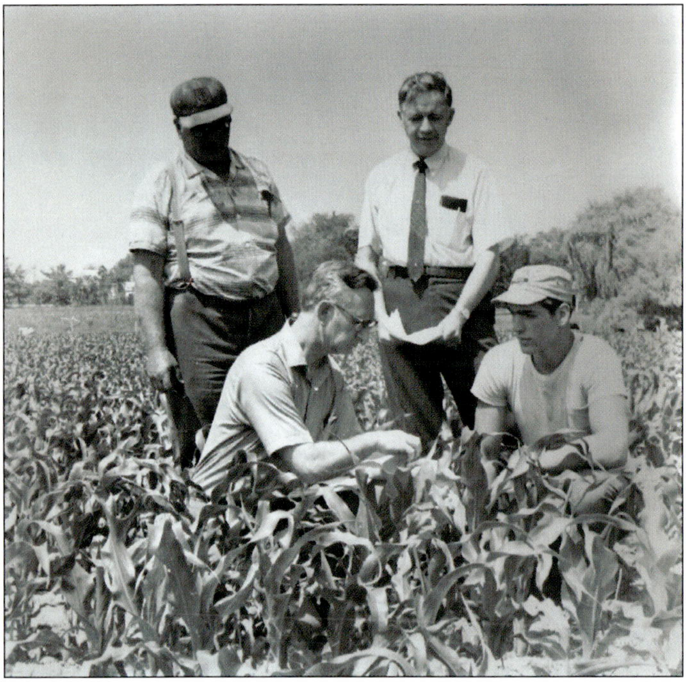

Kenosha may be a metropolitan area, but do not be fooled; it is surrounded on all sides by expansive cornfields. This image from 1971 shows a group of farmers and a member of the 4-H Club investigating a typical type of corn in the area. (Courtesy of the Kenosha County University of Wisconsin-Extension.)

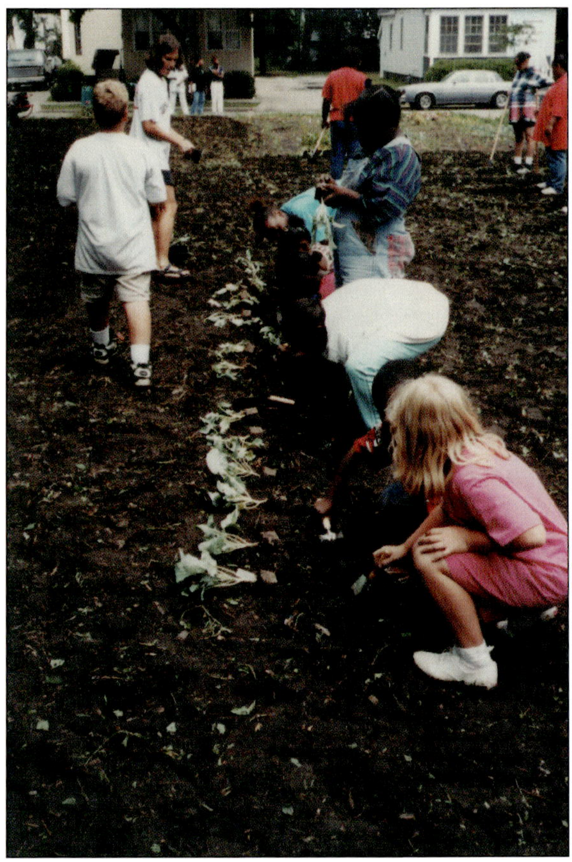

Every year, the Kenosha Extension partnered with the Boys and Girls Club to plant a kids' garden. This garden was the home site for the summer youth nutrition and education program. This image shows a line of children getting ready to plant what looks to be the first crops in the garden. (Courtesy of the Kenosha County University of Wisconsin-Extension.)

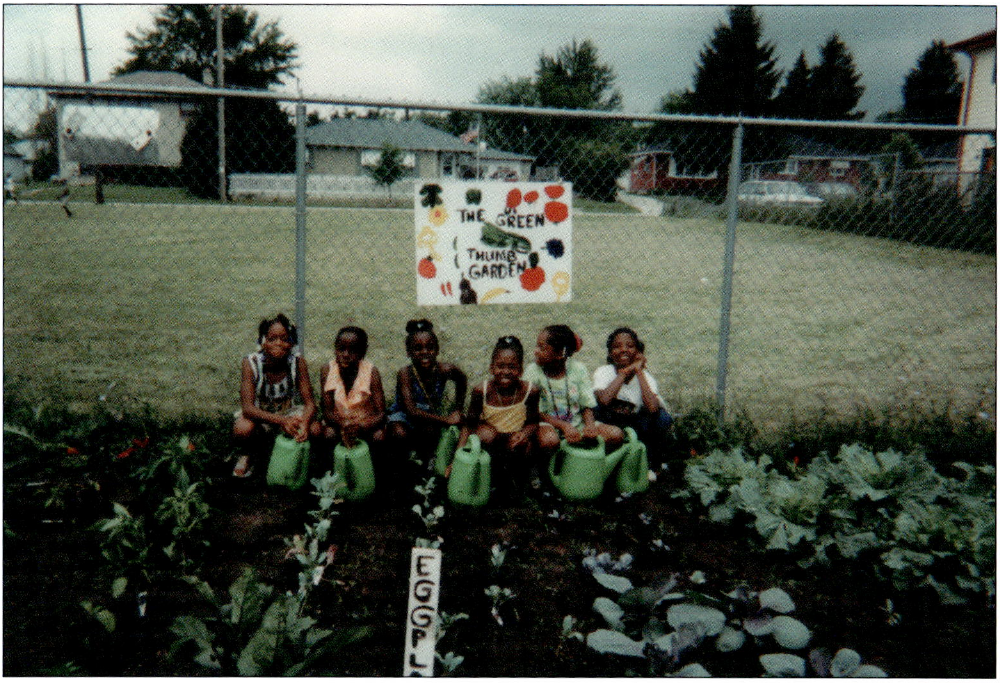

In 1998, the kids' garden was named the Green Thumb Garden. This image shows the land fully planted with crops. The summer youth nutrition and education program was discontinued in 2005, replaced with a Junior Master Gardeners Program in conjunction with Racine County. (Courtesy of the Kenosha County University of Wisconsin-Extension.)

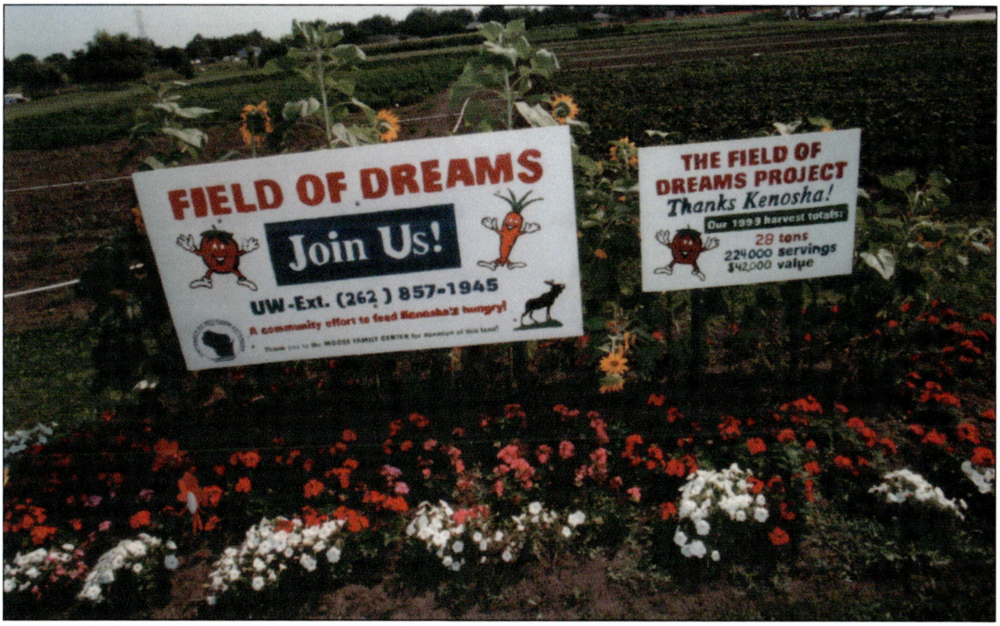

The Field of Dreams is an annual project sponsored by the Kenosha Extension. The garden is on land donated by the Moose Family Center and is used as a goodwill project. Every bit of food harvested from the garden goes right to the community's needy. (Courtesy of the Kenosha County University of Wisconsin-Extension.)

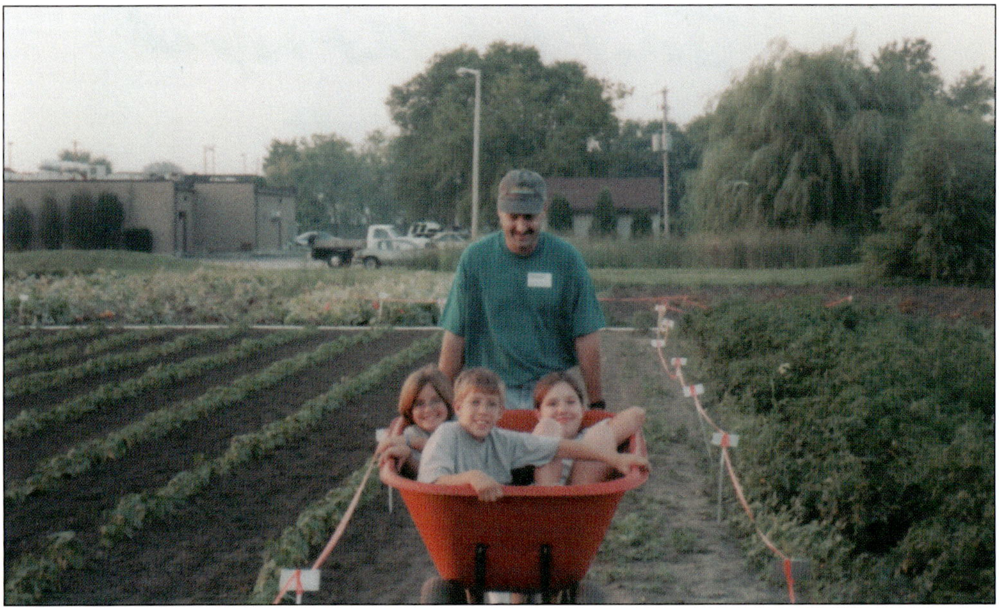

The Field of Dreams produces a massive amount of food every year. In 1999 alone, 28 tons of food were harvested from the field. That equates to 224,000 servings worth $42,000. As such, the garden needs a small army of people to tend the field. More than 300 people to date have worked as volunteers for the project, including the man and three children in the photograph above and the two girls sorting carrots in the picture below. It is not uncommon to find scenes like this throughout the growing season at the farm; it is a healthy combination of work and play. (Both, courtesy of the Kenosha County University of Wisconsin-Extension.)

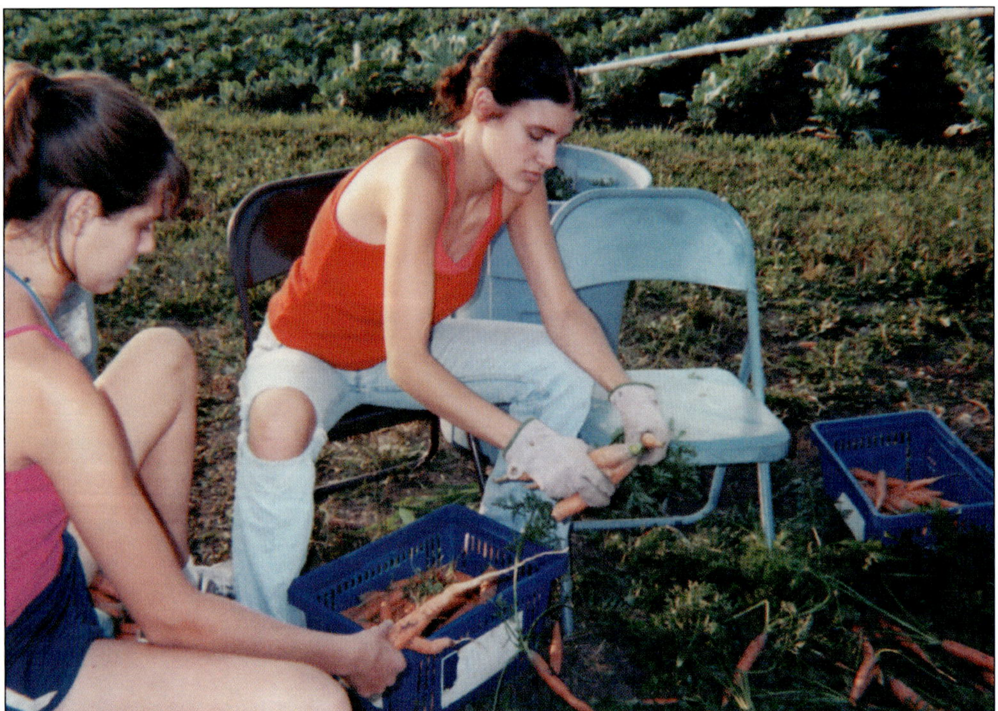

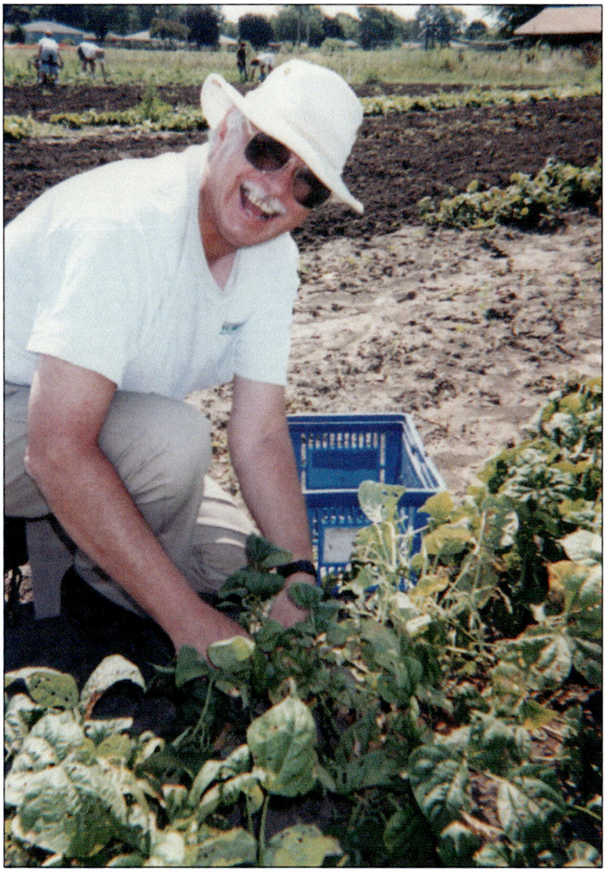

Volunteers for the Field of Dreams are not just youth in the Kenosha Extension program. Adult farmers and helpful community members frequently come out to join in the work, and give everyone pointers along the way, like these two men. Local businesses, churches, and schools often donate supplies and money to help with the annual program as well. The ethnic diversity of the needy in Kenosha is always taken into consideration when deciding which crops to plant, and usually includes some combination of tomatoes, onions, squash, hot peppers, cabbage, sweet corn, beans, and carrots. (Both, courtesy of the Kenosha County University of Wisconsin-Extension.)

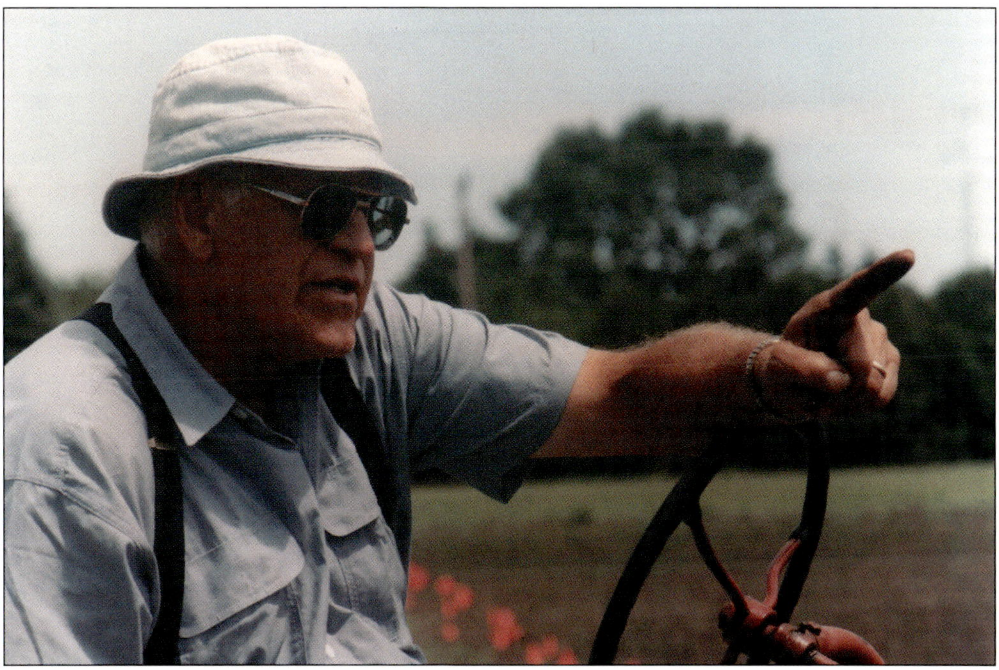

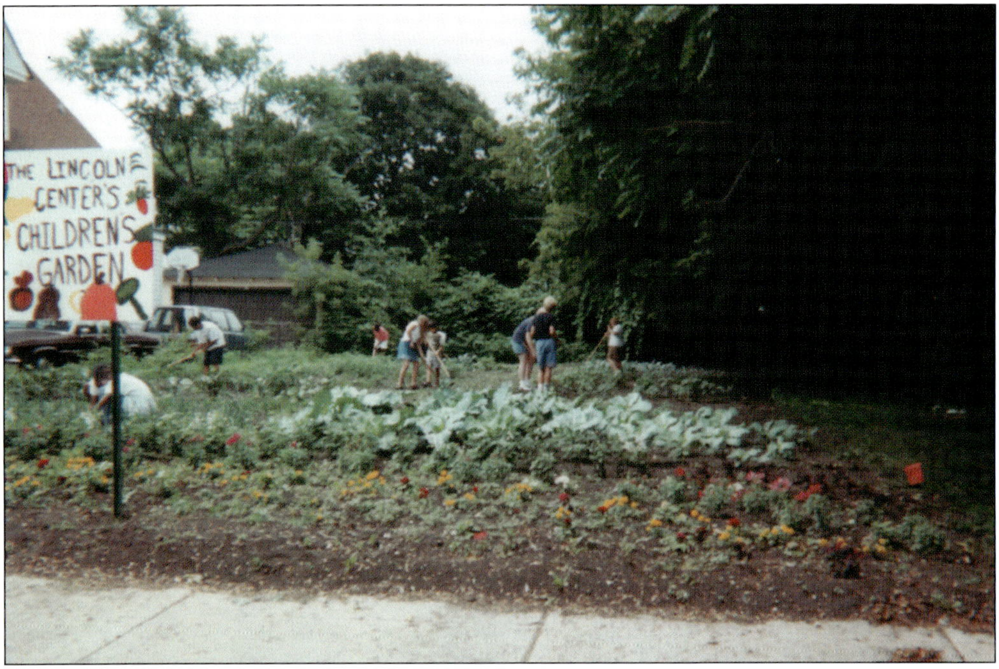

The Lincoln Center Children's Garden is another product of the joint effort between the Kenosha Extension and the Boys and Girls Club. This garden appears to not only have vegetables, but also a few rows of flowers to spruce up the plot. (Courtesy of the Kenosha County University of Wisconsin-Extension.)

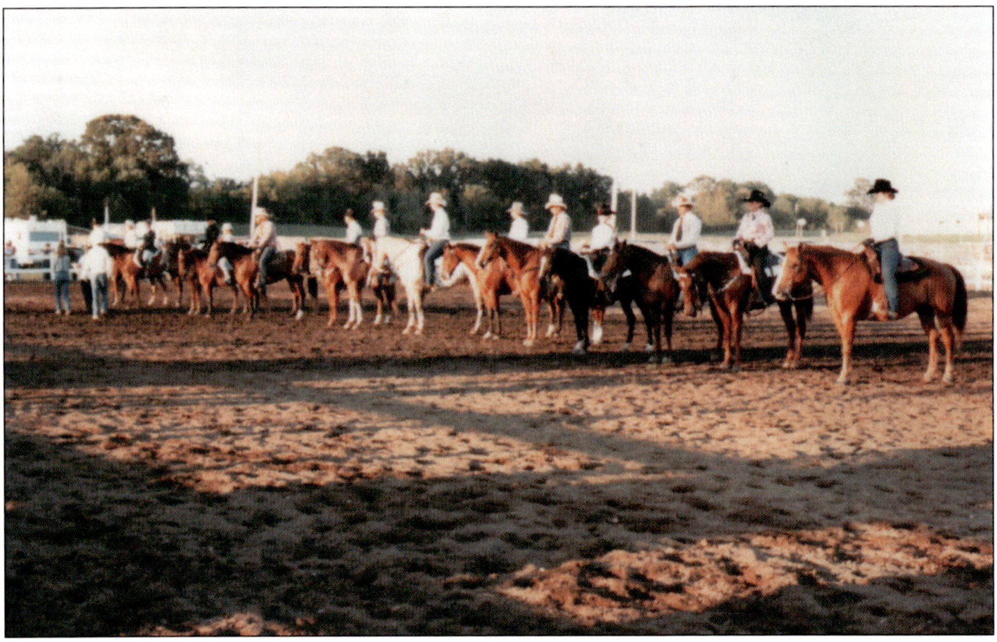

Once kids leave the 4-H Club, they often return for extension events. This 1985 image shows the alumni class of the 4-H Trailblazers competing at the county fair. Alumni class participants age out of regular 4-H once they hit the age of 18. (Courtesy of the Kenosha County University of Wisconsin-Extension.)

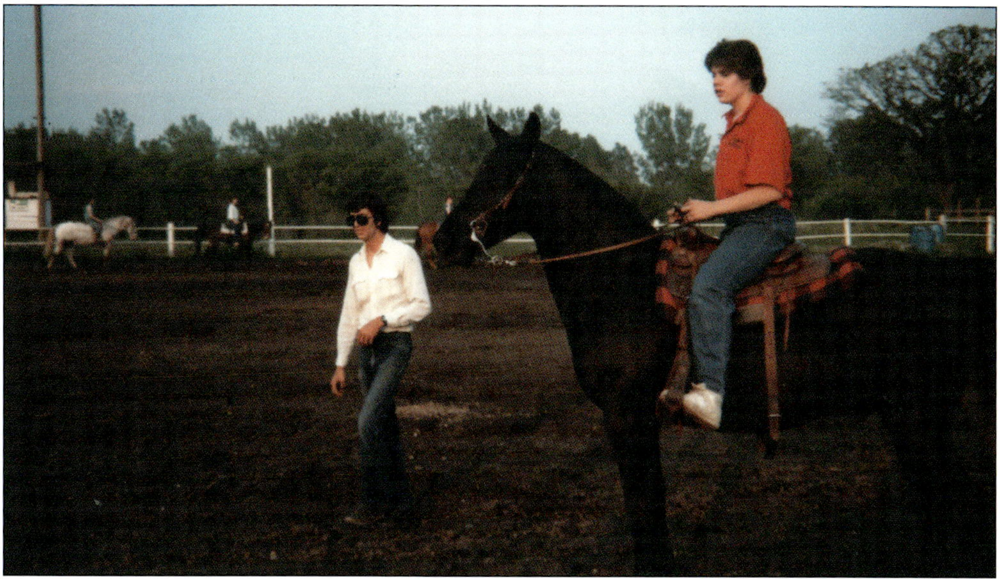

The Trailblazers are the part of the 4-H Club that teaches kids about owning and taking care of horses. Members are encouraged to participate in shows, competitions, and rides, and the group often has its own club rides. This 1988 photograph shows a group class. (Courtesy of the Kenosha County University of Wisconsin-Extension.)

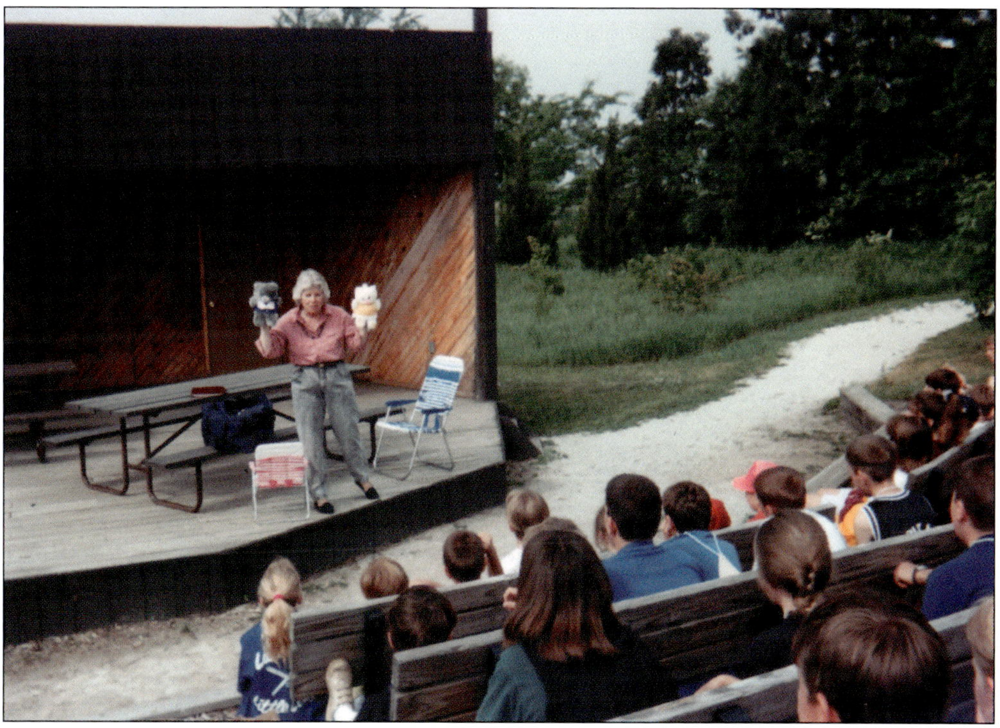

The Pre-4-H Club is a group of children from first grade up to eight years old. Members of this club get to attend a Share the Fun day at 4-H camp, where they learn about 4-H and partake in fun activities, like these kids watching a puppet show. (Courtesy of the Kenosha County University of Wisconsin-Extension.)

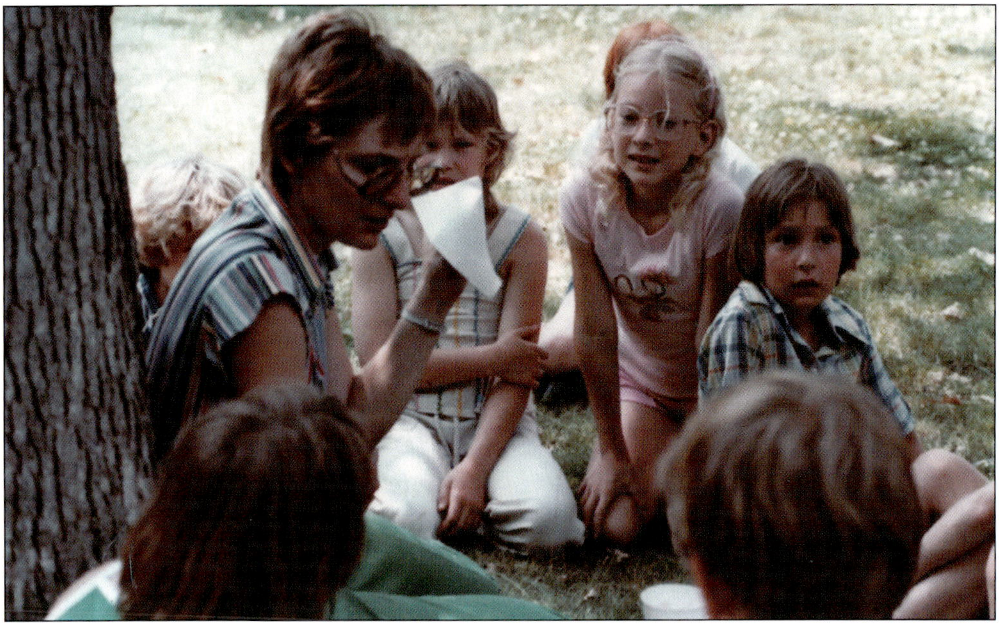

In this photograph, another group of Pre-4-H kids are gathered around a camp counselor at 4-H camp. At camp, the Pre-4-H members learn more about 4-H project areas by participating in hands-on, interactive activities, which often focus on decision making, self-confidence, communication, and relationship building. (Courtesy of the Kenosha County University of Wisconsin-Extension.)

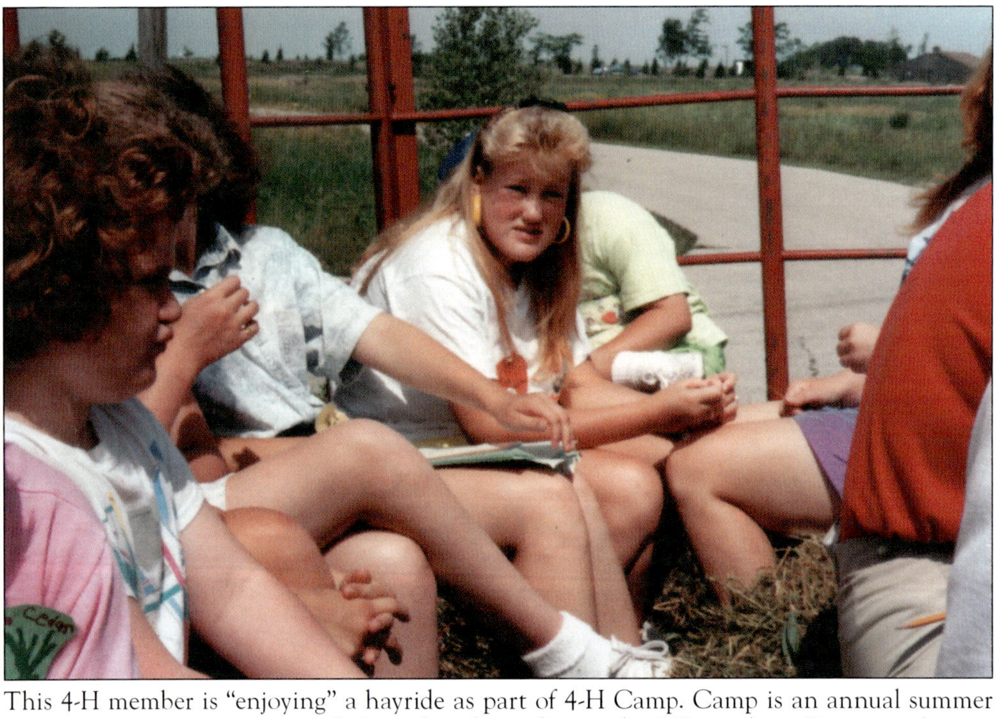

This 4-H member is "enjoying" a hayride as part of 4-H Camp. Camp is an annual summer excursion to an area campground. Attendees do not have to be 4-H members. Campers take part in outdoor activities that teach about swimming, boating, campfires, and more. (Courtesy of the Kenosha County University of Wisconsin-Extension.)

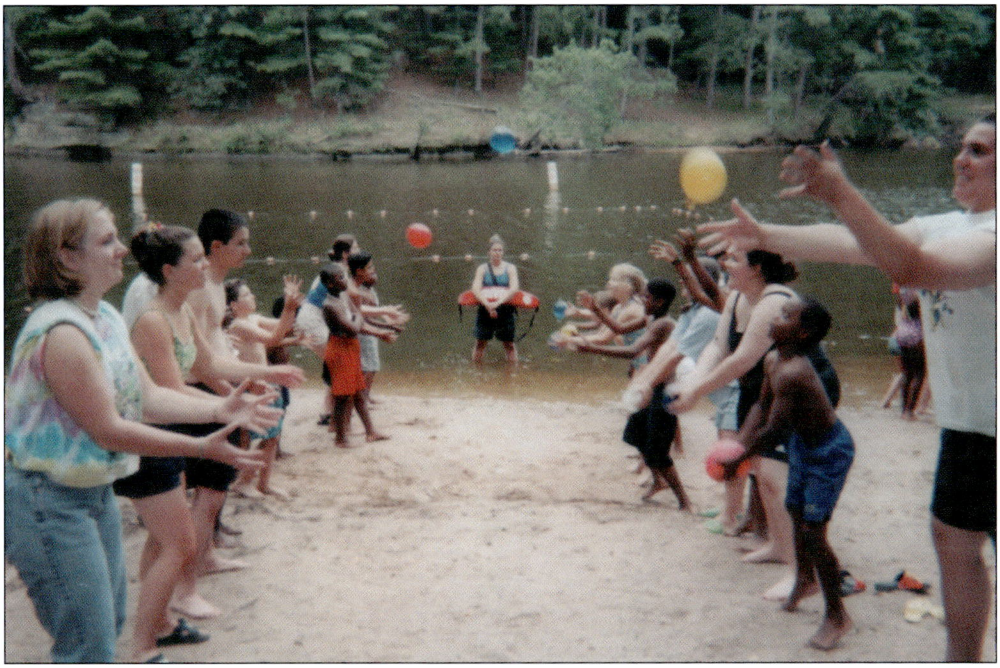

Here, 4-H Club members enjoy a day at the beach during summer camp, with the added bonus of possibly getting pelted with a water balloon. Luckily, a lifeguard is standing by in case the water proves to be too much. 4-H Summer Camp usually takes place over one weekend in June. (Courtesy of the Kenosha County University of Wisconsin-Extension.)

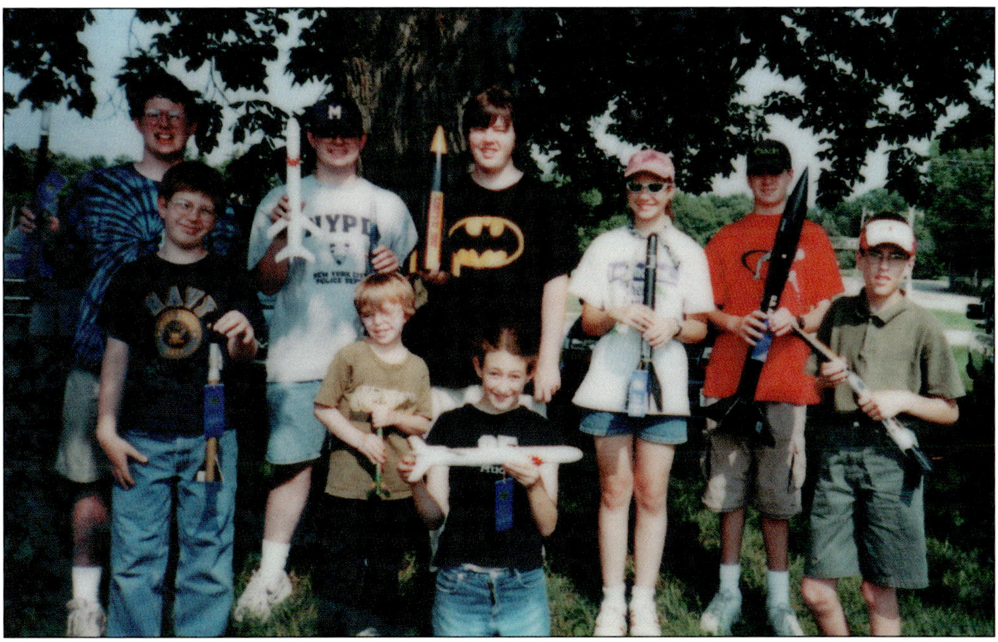

The Kenosha Extension 4-H Club offers area kids an array of opportunities for learning and fun. This group of kids learned about model rocketry and pose before the group's rocket-shooting contest. The rocketry project teaches students how to make a simple single-stage rocket. (Courtesy of the Kenosha County University of Wisconsin-Extension.)

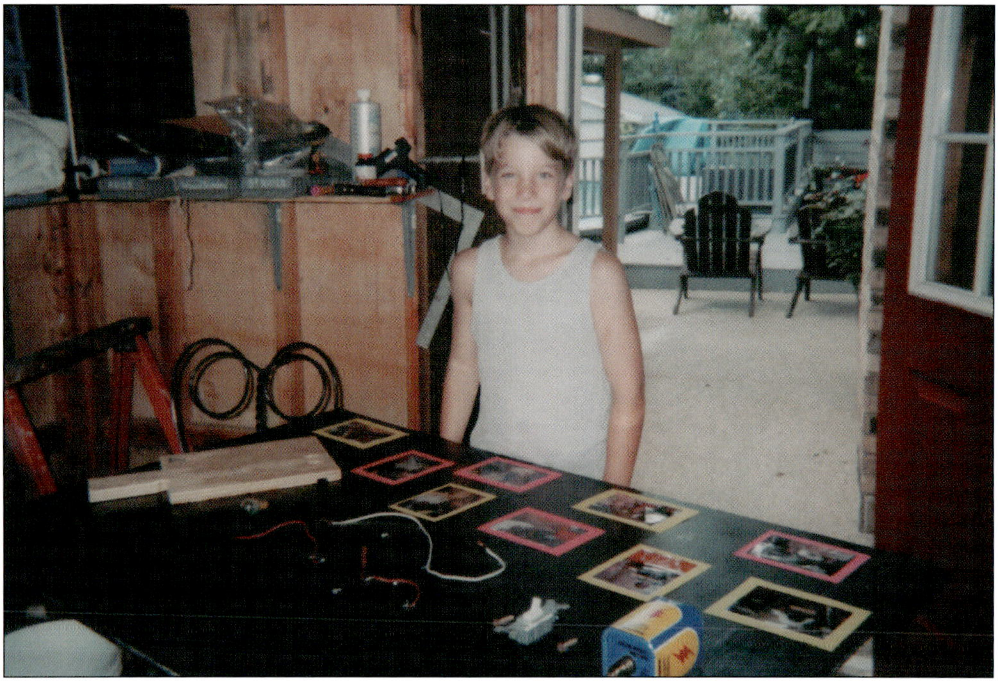

Along with rocketry, Kenosha 4-H members can work on projects involving archery, fishing, scrapbooking, goats, pigs, cows, and more. This boy, Broderick, decided to tackle an electricity project to wire a battery to a light switch. Photographs on the table in front of him show the process step-by-step. (Courtesy of the Kenosha County University of Wisconsin-Extension.)

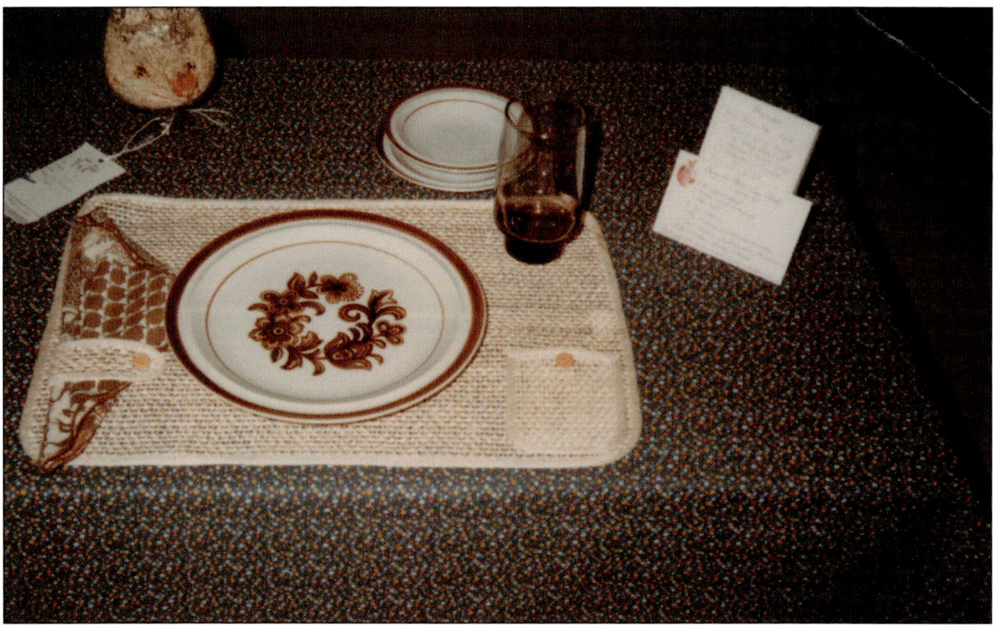

The 4-H Club has always placed an emphasis on home economics, and that includes the art of decorating and setting the table. The Kenosha County Fair usually has several themes that tables can be designed around. This picture shows a 1980 entry in the table-setting competition. (Courtesy of the Kenosha County University of Wisconsin-Extension.)

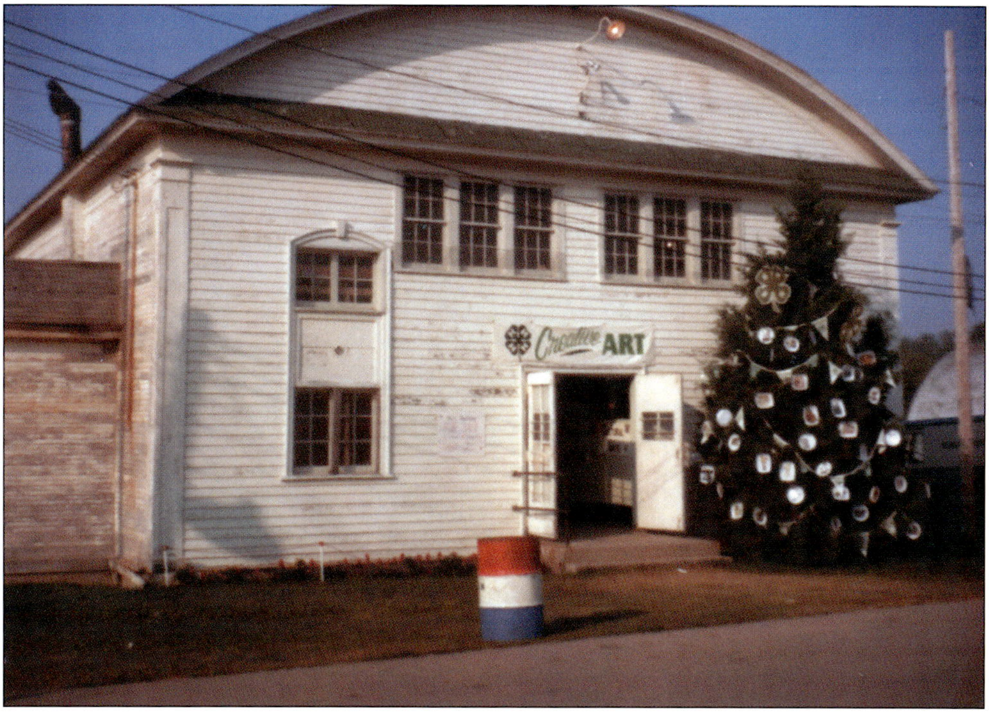

4-H has always had a presence at the Kenosha County Fair, in various buildings throughout the years. Both of these images are from 1978. Above is 4-H's old gym, which functioned as both the home economics building and the creative arts building. Below is one of the club's newer facilities, the overall club building. 4-H in Wisconsin is more than a century old. Throughout its history, Kenosha County has been home to 39 local clubs. The program is still strong, but with less clubs—there are only 13 active ones now. (Both, courtesy of the Kenosha County University of Wisconsin-Extension.)

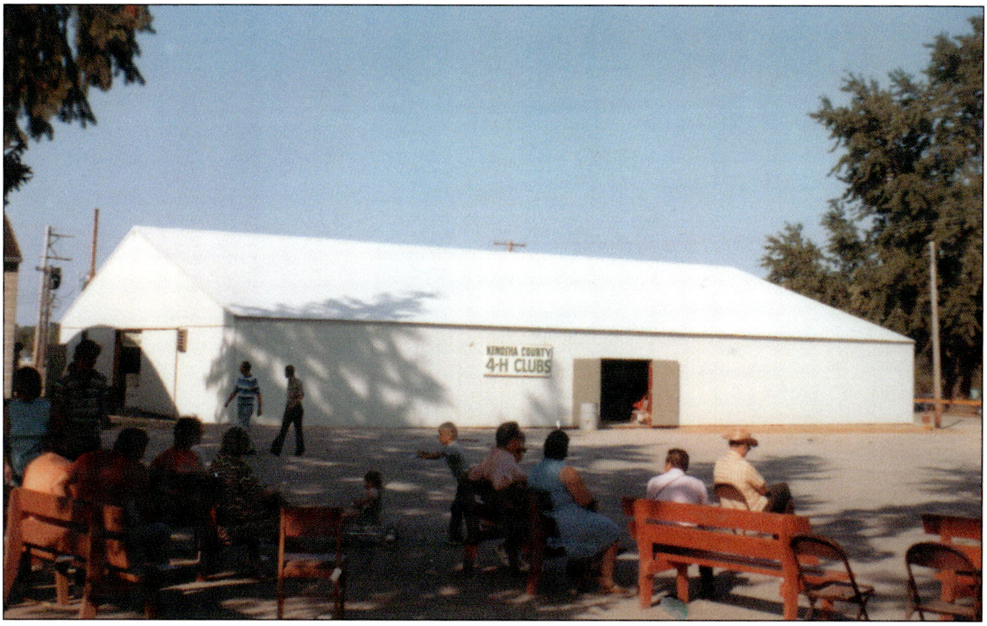

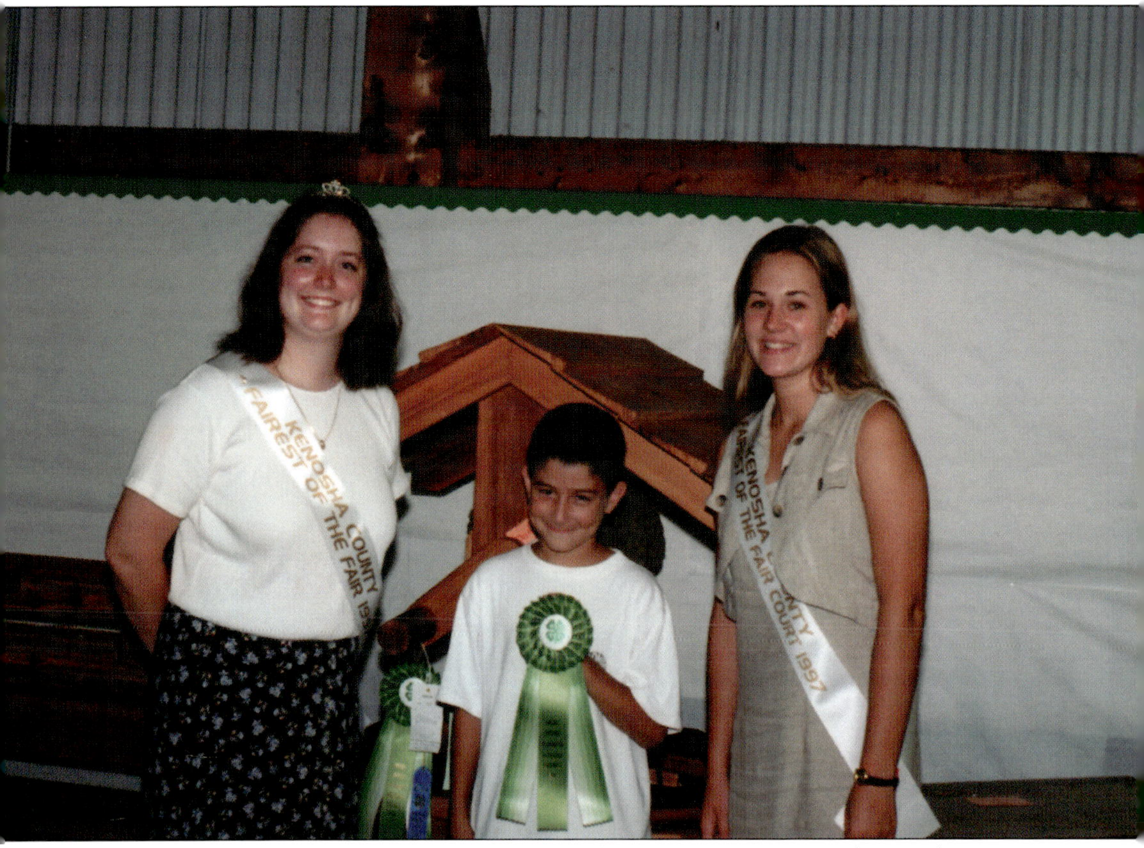

The Fairest of the Fair is a pageant held in each county in Wisconsin during their respective county fairs. Contestants are judged on their personality and attitude, maturity and professionalism, speaking ability, poise and appearance, involvement and activities, and overall impression. They go on to make special appearances throughout the county for community events, agricultural and livestock competitions, and more. Winners at the county level go on to compete at the Wisconsin State Fair. In Kenosha, the winner also receives a lifetime membership to the Kenosha County Fair and has a court of three girls who also receives prizes. At the state level, contestants are required to bring a county-related item that can be auctioned off during the competition. This 1997 picture shows the Kenosha Fairest of the Fair flanking a young boy who won a merit award. (Courtesy of the Kenosha County University of Wisconsin-Extension.)

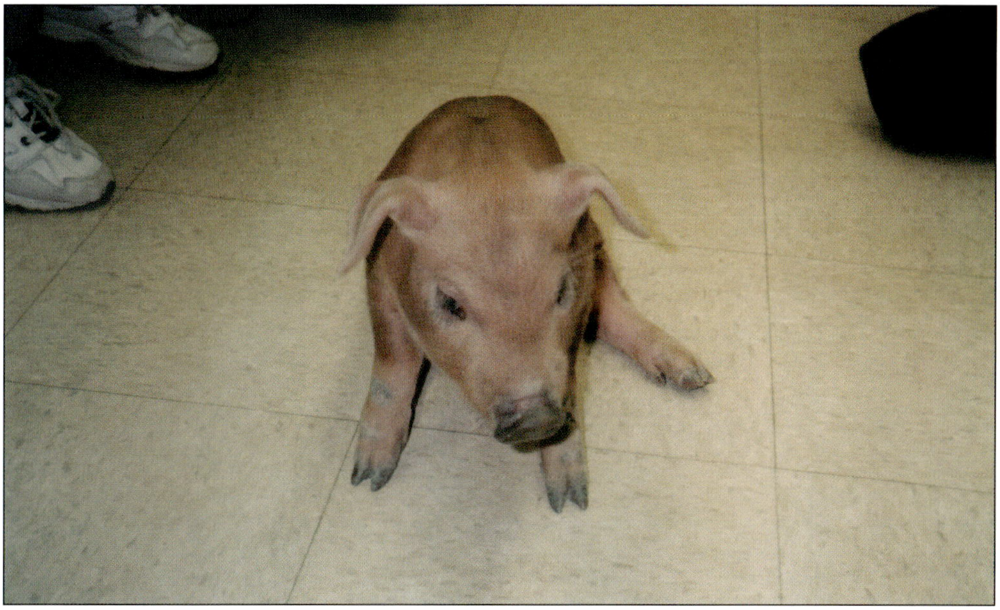

Safe Night USA was an annual program that emphasized the need for safer communities for children. Schools across the country would hold parties where kids could come learn about healthy eating, hygiene, and safety. This photograph is from the Bain School Safe Night—the guest of honor was this adorable piglet. (Courtesy of the Kenosha County University of Wisconsin-Extension.)

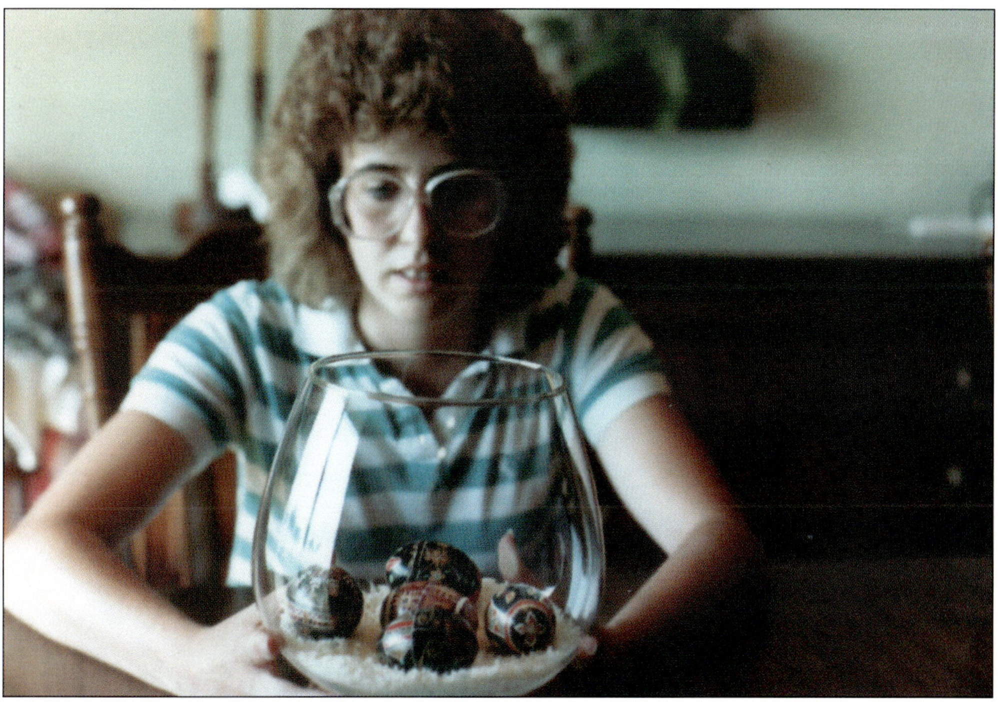

A *pysanka* is an Easter egg decorated in traditional Ukrainian folk patterns. *Pysanka* has long been an activity for 4-H kids, and a competition category at the county fair. Here, a young girl is preparing to display her eggs at the fair. (Courtesy of the Kenosha County University of Wisconsin-Extension.)

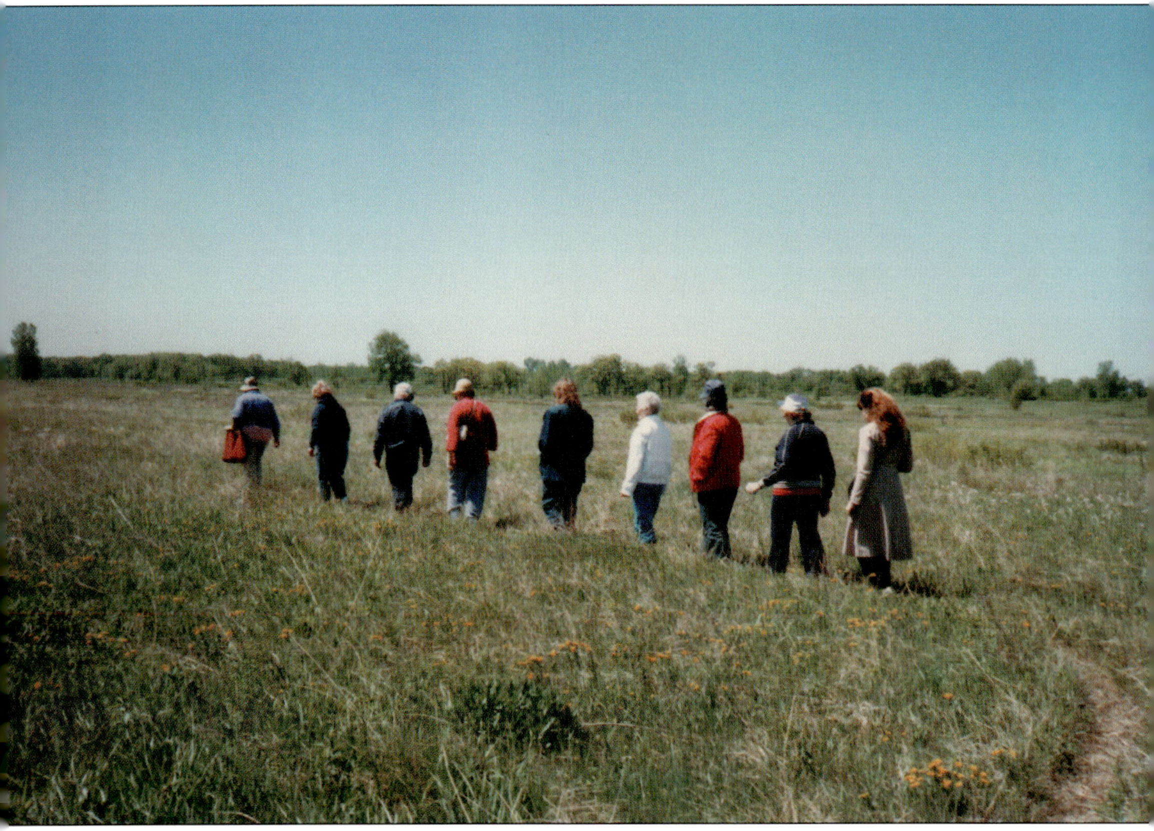

The Chiwaukee Prairie is a 410-acre natural area that spreads from Kenosha down to the Illinois state line along the lakefront. The prairie is one of the largest in the state and the most intact coastal wetland in southeast Wisconsin. More than 400 species of plants grow at Chiwaukee, 26 of which are rare and 10 of which are endangered or threatened. There are also several rare animals, like the Blanding's turtle and Franklin's ground squirrel. The land is used year round for photography, birding, hiking, and nature study. During the breeding season, more than 75 species of birds make their way through the prairie. The Kenosha Dunes, an area of sand dunes at the southern edge of Southport Park, are part of Chiwaukee as well. Here, a group of Kenosha Public Museum volunteers are being led through the prairie in the early 1990s. (Courtesy of the Kenosha Public Museum.)

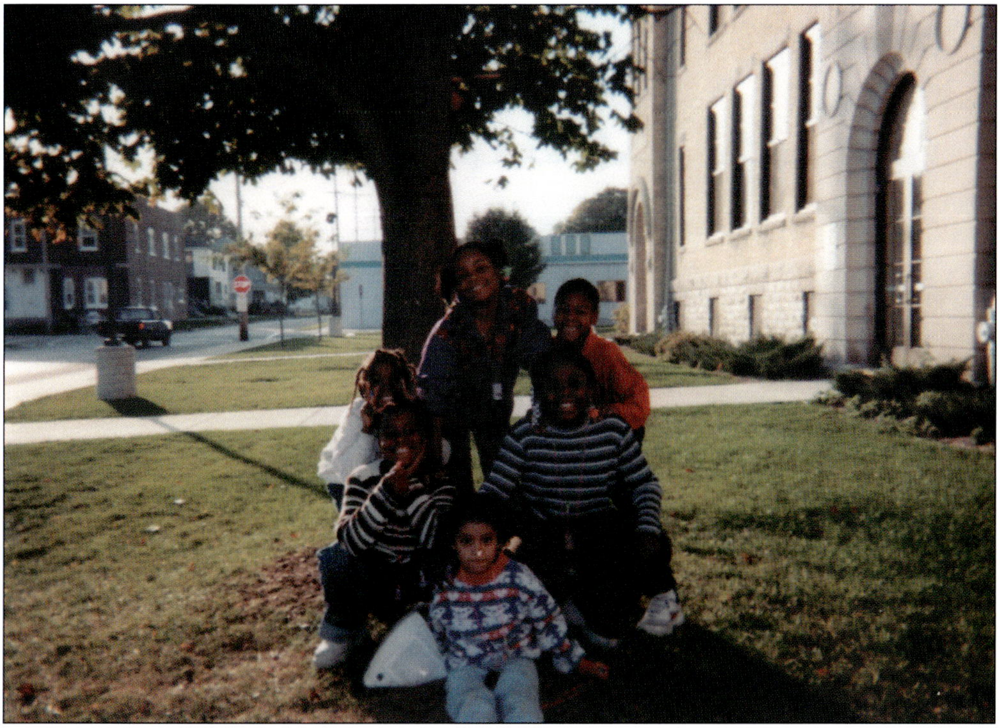

The Kenosha Extension and 4-H programs work hard to ensure the success of area children. To do so, they often host and sponsor events at local schools. These six girls were the main helpers for the day's events at Frank Elementary School. (Courtesy of the Kenosha County University of Wisconsin-Extension.)

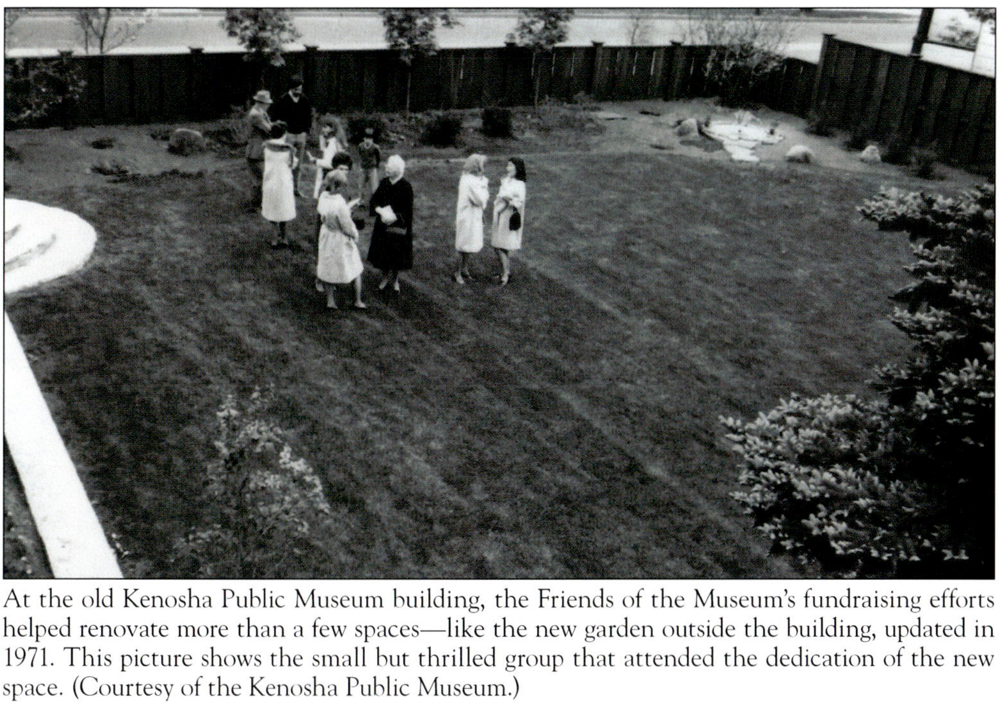

At the old Kenosha Public Museum building, the Friends of the Museum's fundraising efforts helped renovate more than a few spaces—like the new garden outside the building, updated in 1971. This picture shows the small but thrilled group that attended the dedication of the new space. (Courtesy of the Kenosha Public Museum.)

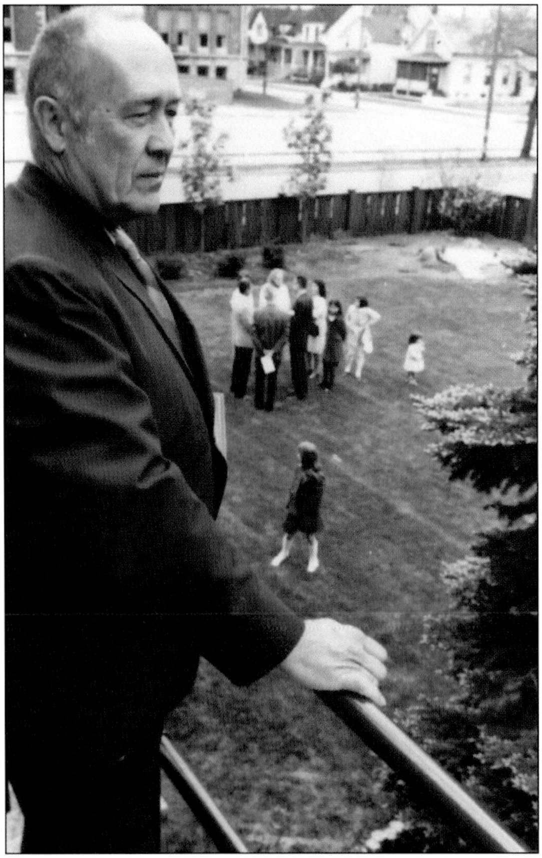

In the 1960s and 1970s, Kenneth Dearolf was the director of the Kenosha Public Museum. Dearolf worked hard to make all the museum exhibits something to be proud of—like the time he spent researching nearly 300 pieces of 19th-century pottery to determine artist names and could only find 20. He was also an avid photographer, specifically of wild mushrooms; he had a collection of more than 2,000 color slides of the fungi. At left, Dearolf stands on a balcony overlooking the renovated garden at the Kenosha Public Museum. Below, a group of museum employees and Friends of the Museum cut the ribbon, welcoming everyone into the new space. (Both, courtesy of the Kenosha Public Museum.)

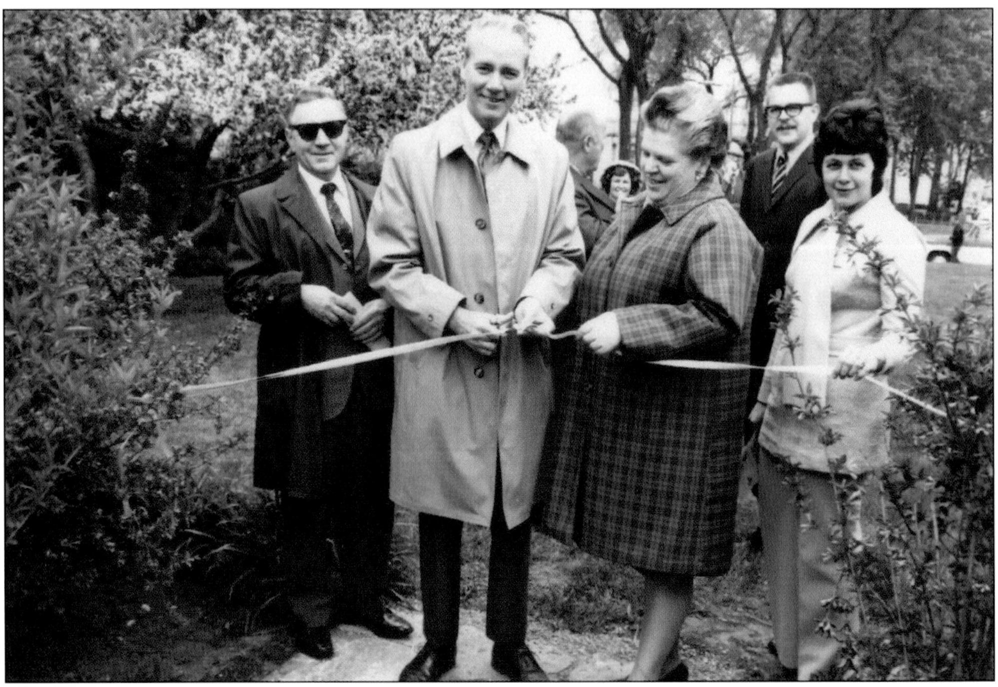

The Kenosha Public Museum Friends Garden was an open space for children to play in as well. There was ample space and plenty of grass for them to enjoy. Here, a young girl stands by her parents, making a kissy face for the camera. (Courtesy of the Kenosha Public Museum.)

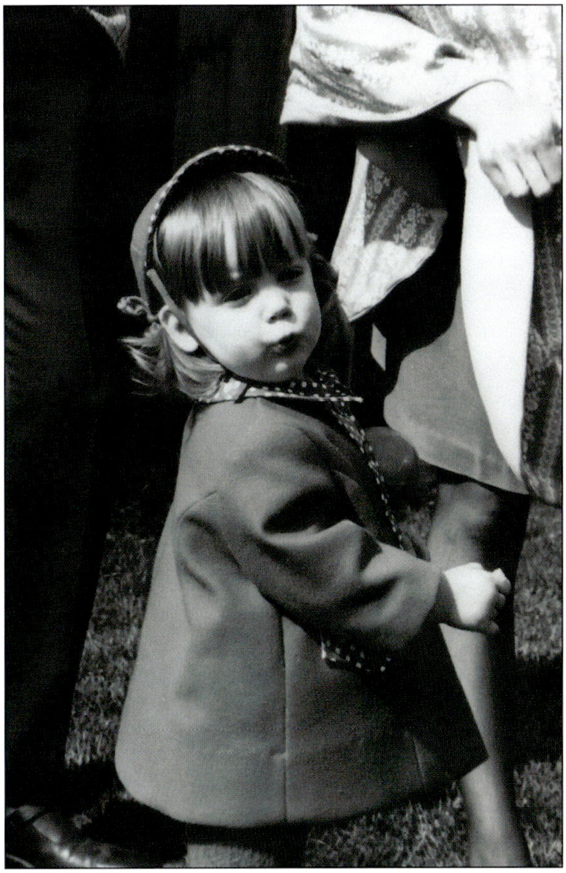

In 2002, Carthage College's men's basketball team made it to the national championships in Salem, Virginia. The series lasted from March 15 to 16. This photograph shows the enthusiastic crowd clad in red and white cheering on their team. Carthage took a third place finish that year. (Courtesy of the Carthage College Archives.)

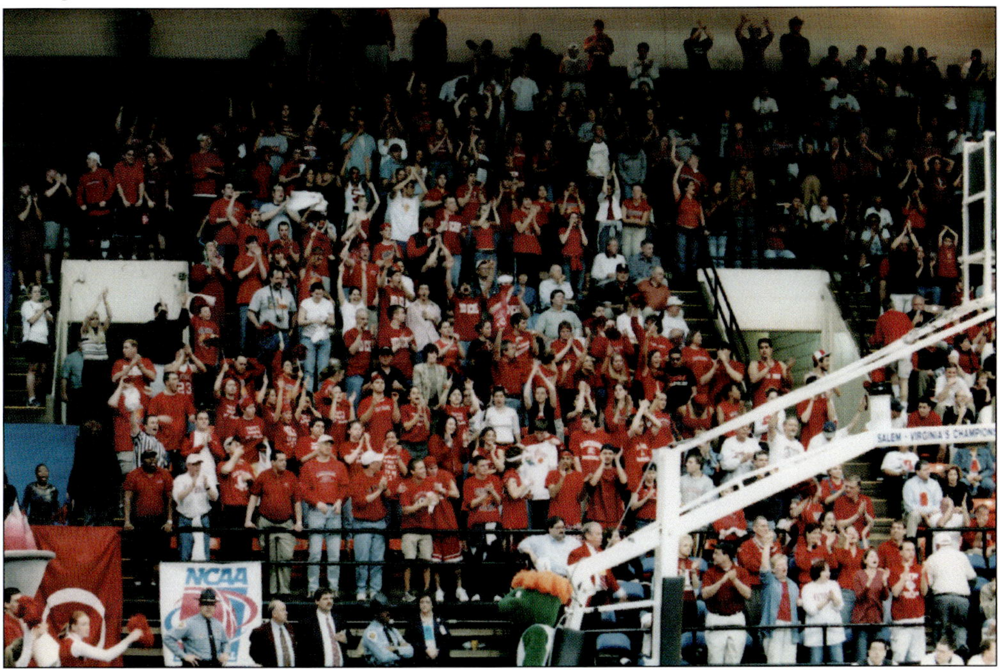

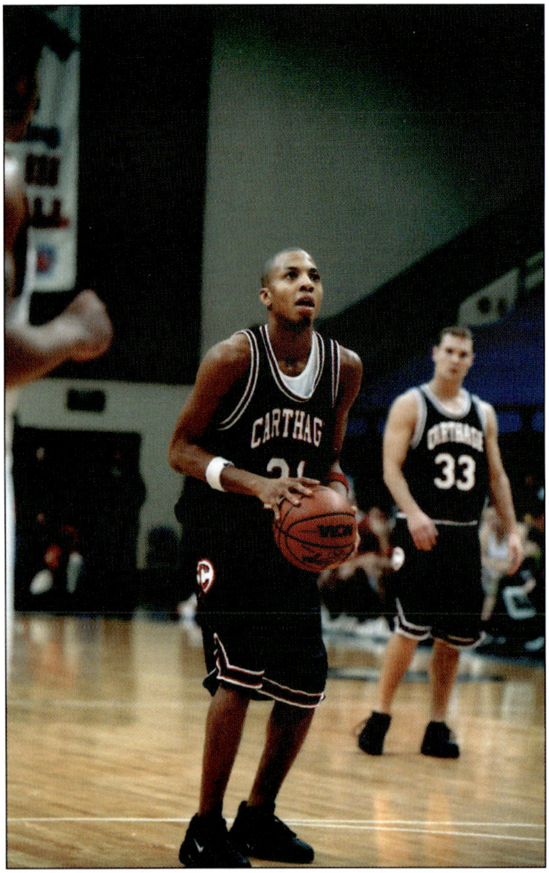

Pictured here is Rob Garnes in action on the Carthage basketball team. He was one of the only players to be named first-team All-CCIW all four years he was at the school. He also received high honors from a college basketball website. (Courtesy of the Carthage College Archives.)

Carthage sports are a big deal among area basketball fans, and the school only hires the best. Bosko Djurickovic is Carthage's head men's basketball coach, a position he's held for 20 years. His winning percentage is the sixth best in the 67 years of the league's existence. (Courtesy of the Carthage College Archives.)

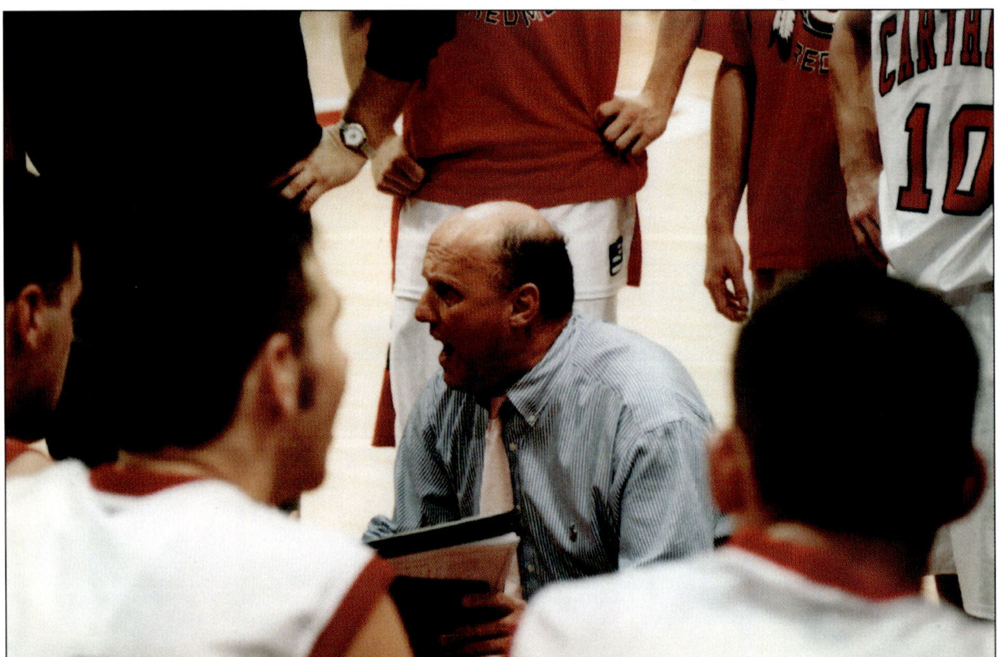

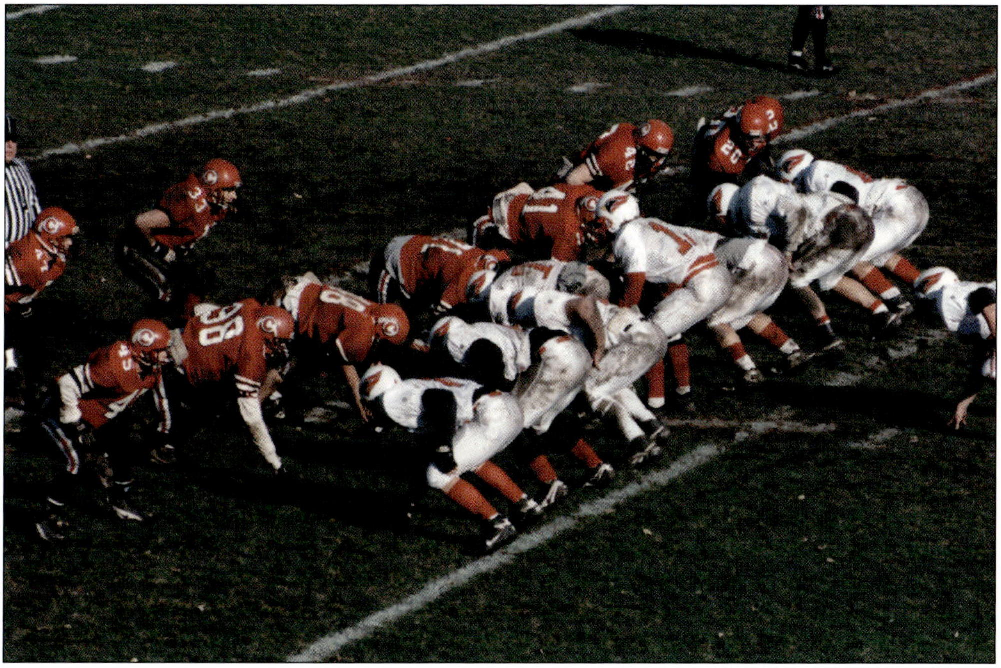

Carthage joined the National Collegiate Athletic Association in 1976. Along the way, the football team has consistently been ranked among the top in the nation and has set a number of school records, including most wins in one season. The team's original 1920s name, the Redmen, based on the team's red jerseys, sparked a controversy, later forcing a change to Red Men because the original name was considered offensive. Above, the Carthage team squares off against North Central College from Naperville, Illinois. Below, a Carthage player runs into the end zone for a touchdown. (Both, courtesy of the Carthage College Archives.)

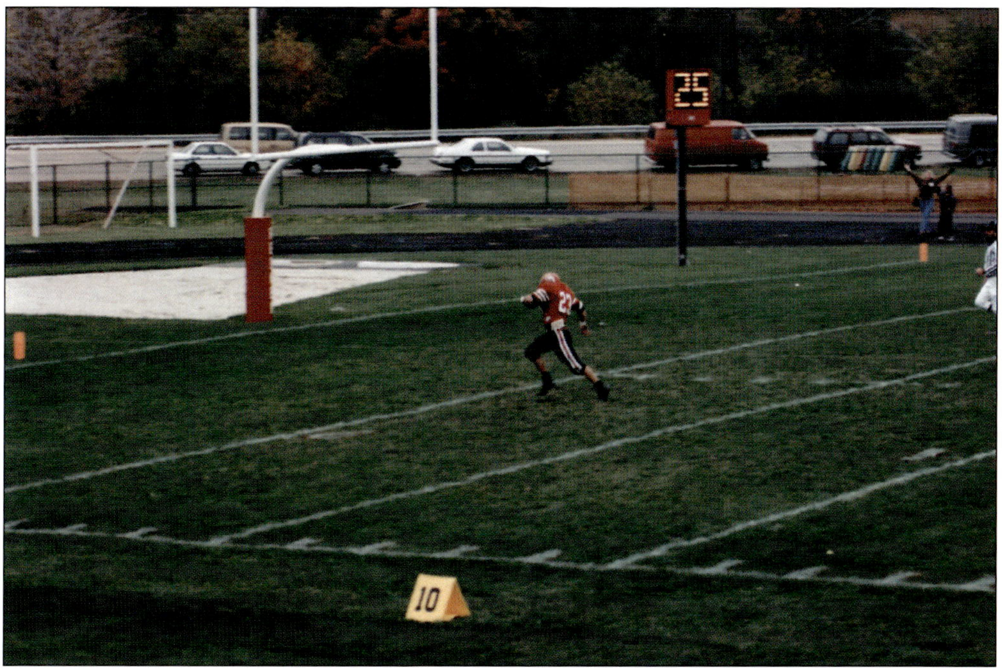

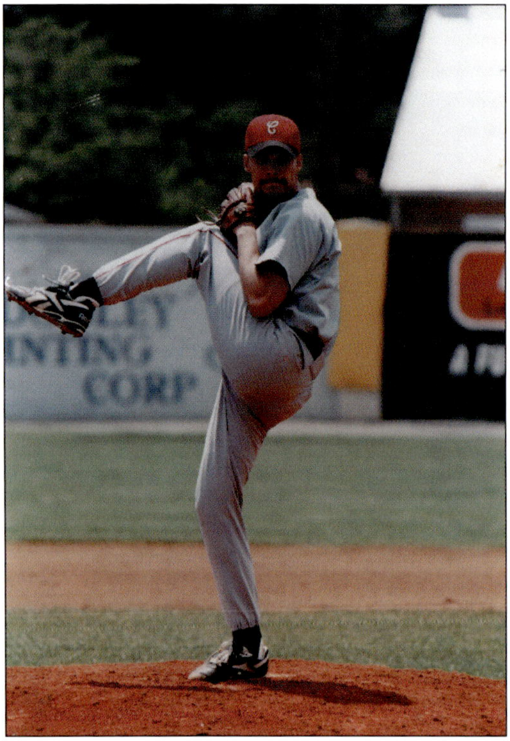

The baseball team at Carthage has an even more sterling reputation than football. The team averages 35 wins per season and was invited to the NCAA Division III World Series a number of times. Other accolades include eight divisional titles, one divisional title tie, nine conference crowns, sixteen regional berths, six regional titles, two third-place championship wins, and two fourth-place championship wins. At left, Brent Sagedal readies to release a pitch. He was named to the 1995 American Baseball Coaches Association All-American Team. Below, a player powers through a swing during a 1970s game. (Both, courtesy of the Carthage College Archives.)

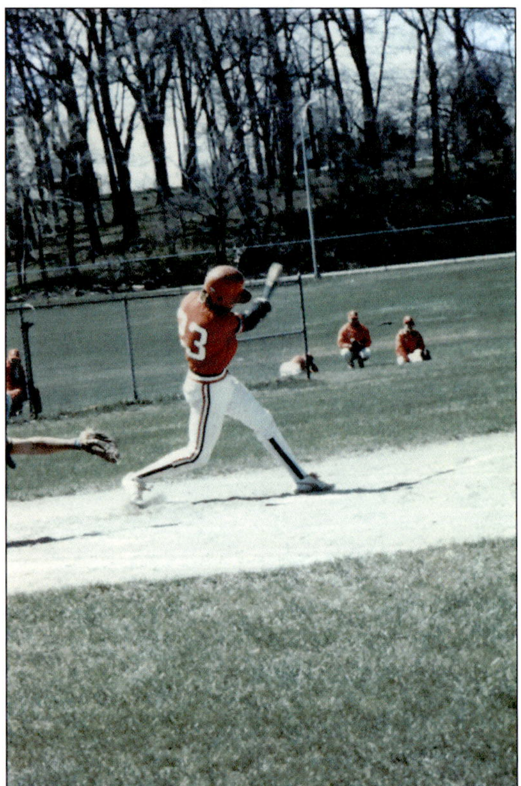

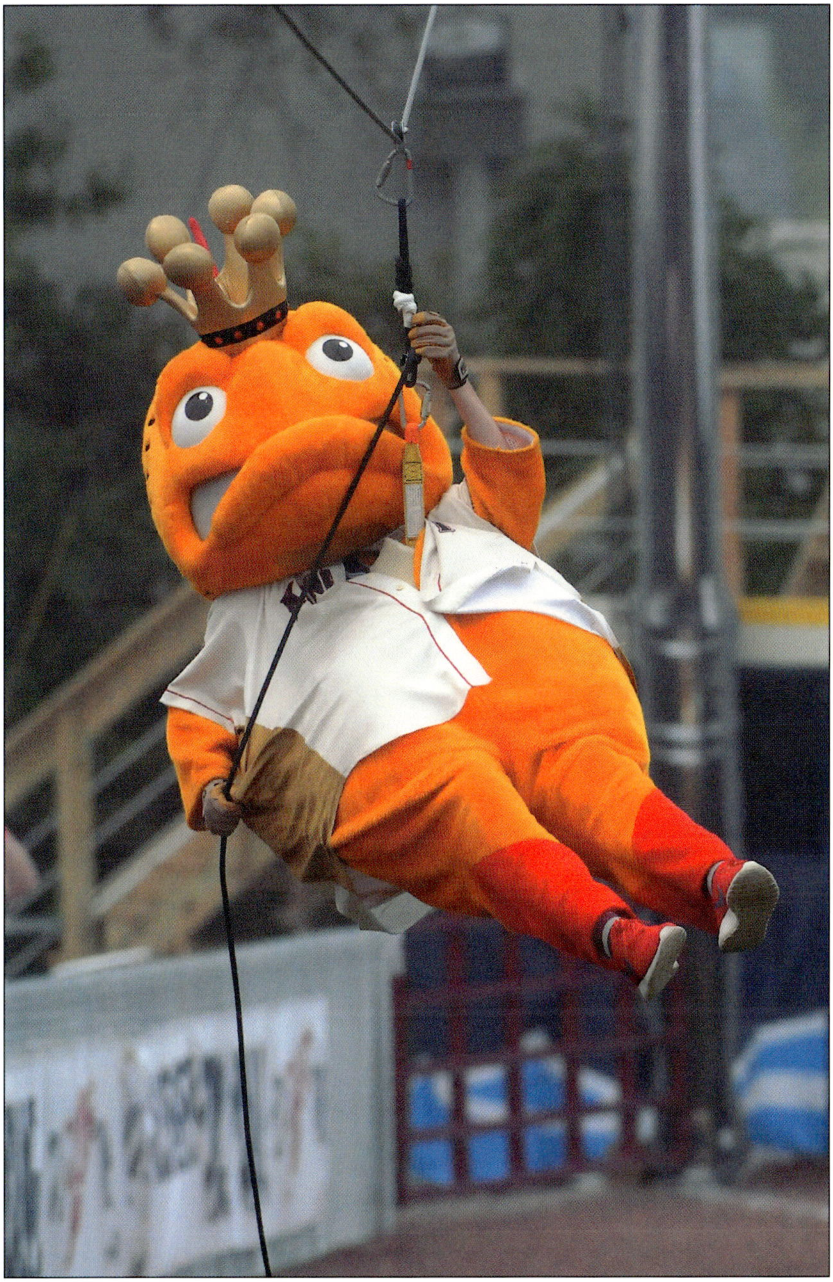

The Kenosha Kingfish are the city's newest baseball team in a long history of ball playing. King Elvis the First is the Kingfish's mascot. At every home game, King Elvis uses a zip line attached to the left field foul pole, which is part of the Bambino boat, to deliver the ball for the first pitch to the pitcher's mound. The Kingfish are dedicated to having a unique ballgame experience at every home game throughout the season. The opening season had a theme for each of the 36 home games, including fireworks shows, dancing, races, toy giveaways, and human cannonballs. The team involves the community as much as possible and has even sponsored and hosted a 5K run and a fall festival inside Simmons Field. The Kingfish play a 72-game season every year. (Courtesy of the Kenosha Kingfish Baseball Club.)

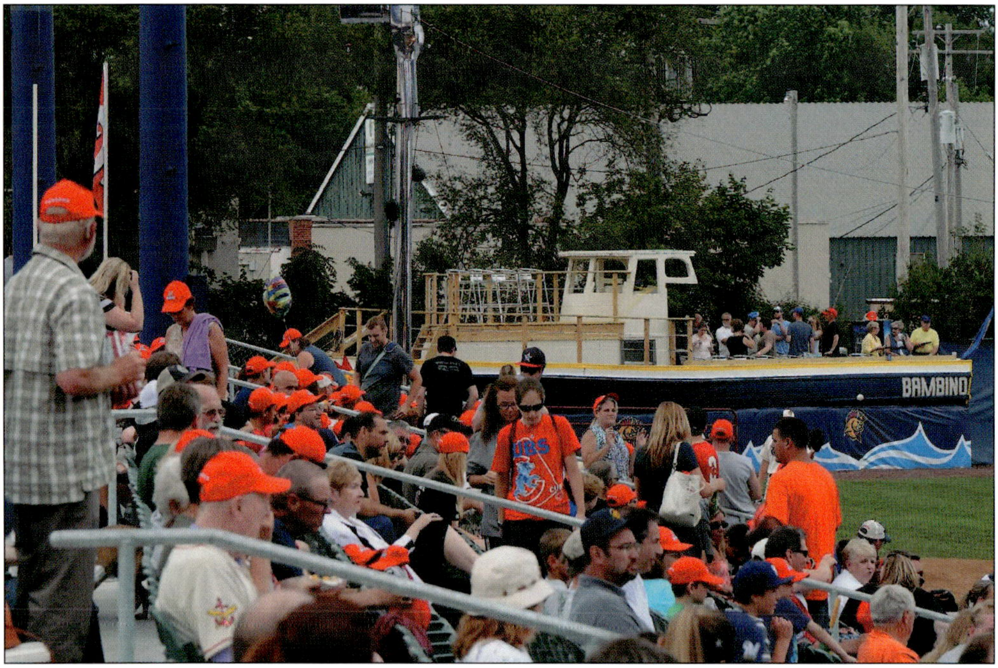

The *Bambino* is a fishing boat that is part of the outfield wall at the stadium. The boat was built in the 1930s and used as a commercial vessel on Chesapeake Bay. It took four permits and an entire day of travel for the boat to make it to Simmons Field. (Courtesy of the Kenosha Kingfish Baseball Club.)

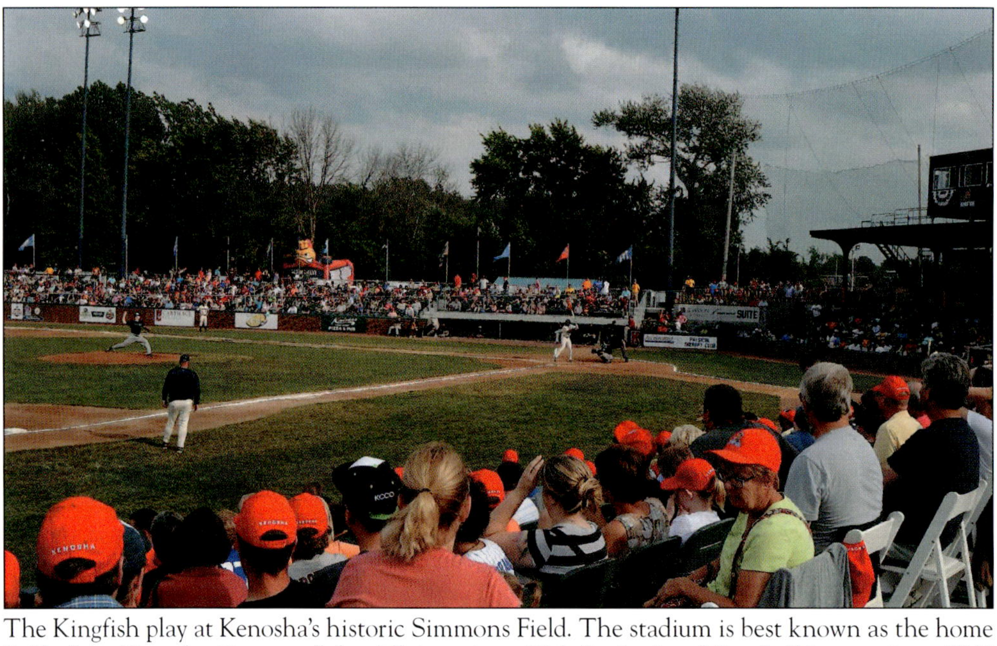

The Kingfish play at Kenosha's historic Simmons Field. The stadium is best known as the home field of the Kenosha Comets of the All-American Girls Professional Baseball League from 1948 until 1951. Although the stadium has been renovated, it still maintains the old-time feel of the past with a historic grandstand behind home plate and the original stadium configuration. (Courtesy of the Kenosha Kingfish Baseball Club.)

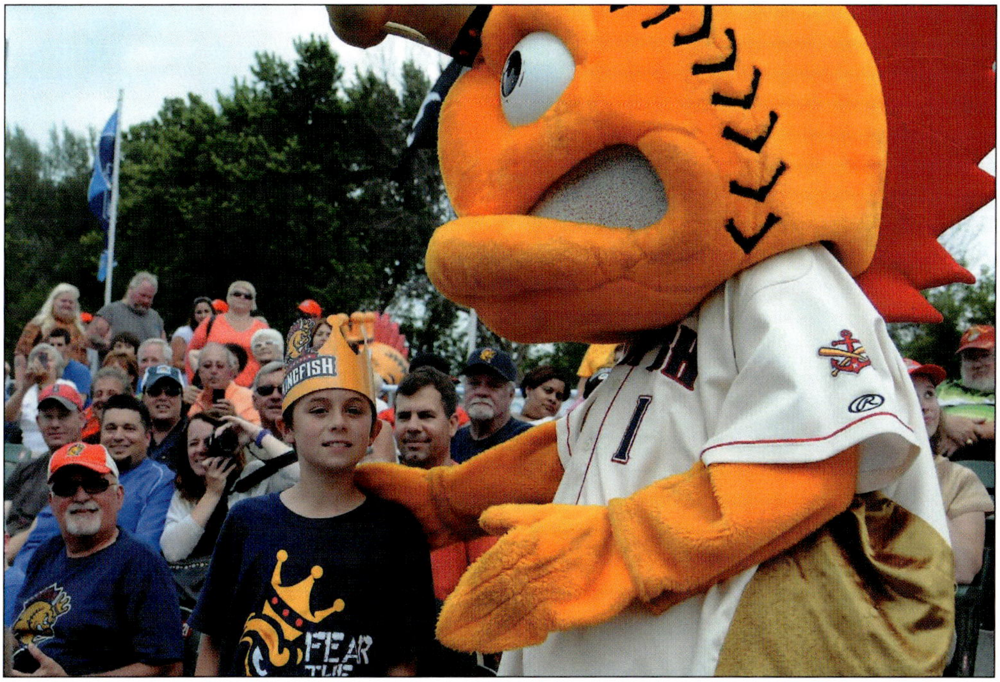

Simmons Field has a robust Kid Zone that families can use at any time during the games. It has a bounce house, bobblehead ring toss, and sandbox, in addition to a variety of games. The Kid Zone is part of the Kingfish commitment to bring a massive level of fun to every game with themes and inning-break entertainment. (Courtesy of the Kenosha Kingfish Baseball Club.)

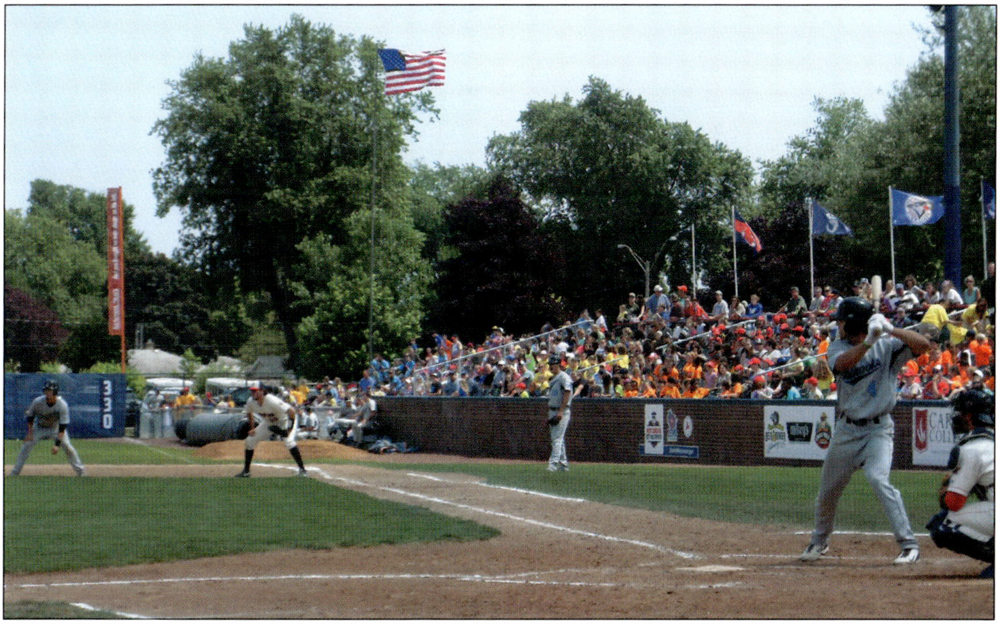

The Kingfish team is part of an elite collegiate summer baseball league called the Northwoods League. The team's first season was in 2014, and the group worked together with the city on a $1 million-plus renovation of the stadium, which was built in 1920. (Courtesy of the Kenosha Kingfish Baseball Club.)

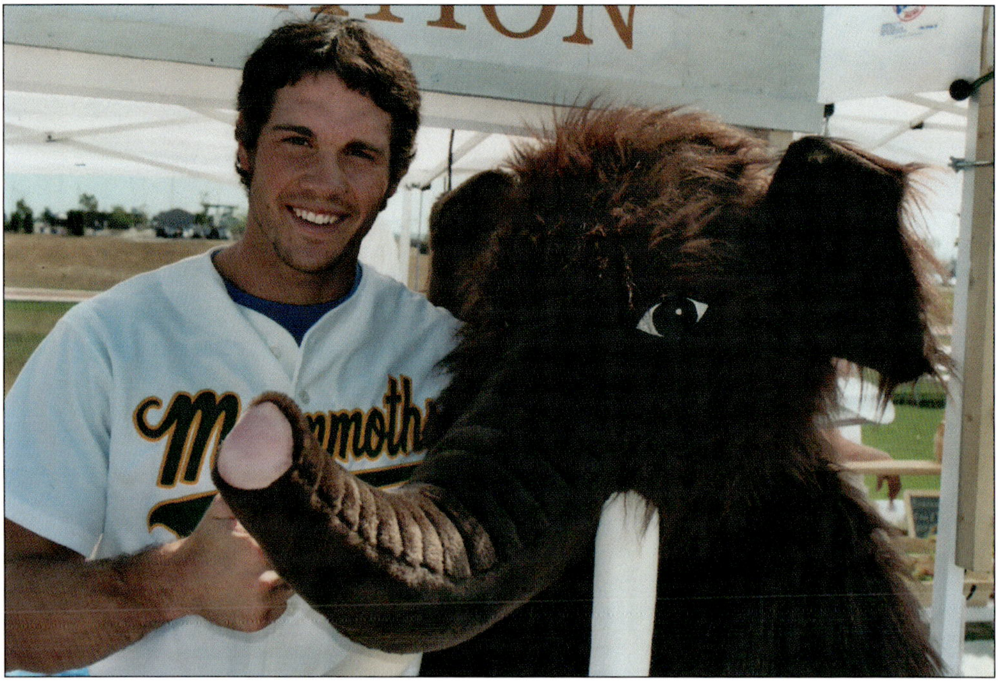

One of Kenosha's previous short-lived baseball teams was the Kenosha Mammoths. The team played only one year as part of the Frontier League, an independent minor league. Pictured is one of the players with the team's mascot, Woolly. Their home field, like the Kingfish, was Simmons Field. (Courtesy of the Kenosha Public Museum.)

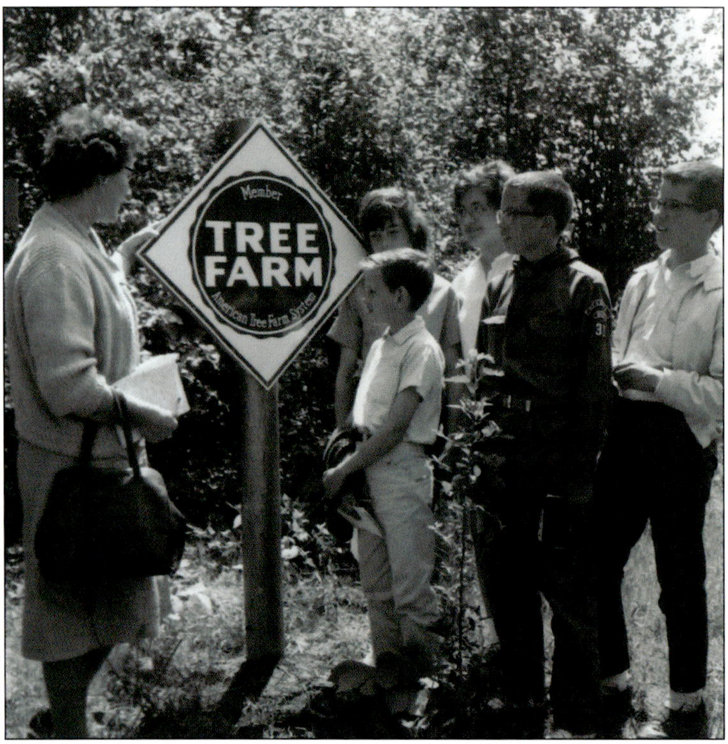

The American Tree Farm System is a network of tree farmers managing 24 million acres of forest. Here, the 1964 Roosevelt Elementary School sixth-grade class is investigating one of the forests. The teacher on the left is Miss Heide, and the students are, from left to right, Melinda Higgins, James Rasch, Gail Dubaniewicz, Roy Hanson, and Robert Router. (Courtesy of the Kenosha County University of Wisconsin-Extension.)

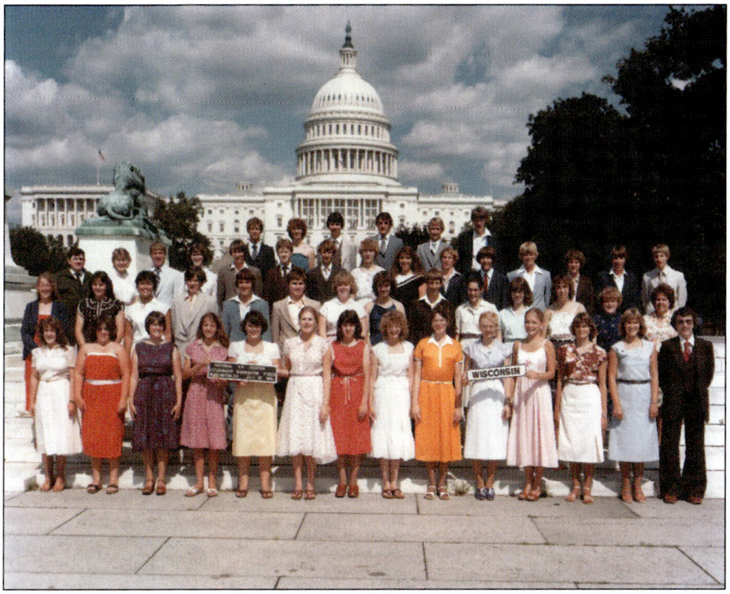

This 1981 picture shows the Wisconsin 4-H high school students who attended that year's Citizenship Washington Focus (CWF). The CWF is an annual conference that allows attendees to get a behind-the-scenes look at what is happening in Washington, DC. The program has been in place for more than 50 years. (Courtesy of the Kenosha County University of Wisconsin-Extension.)

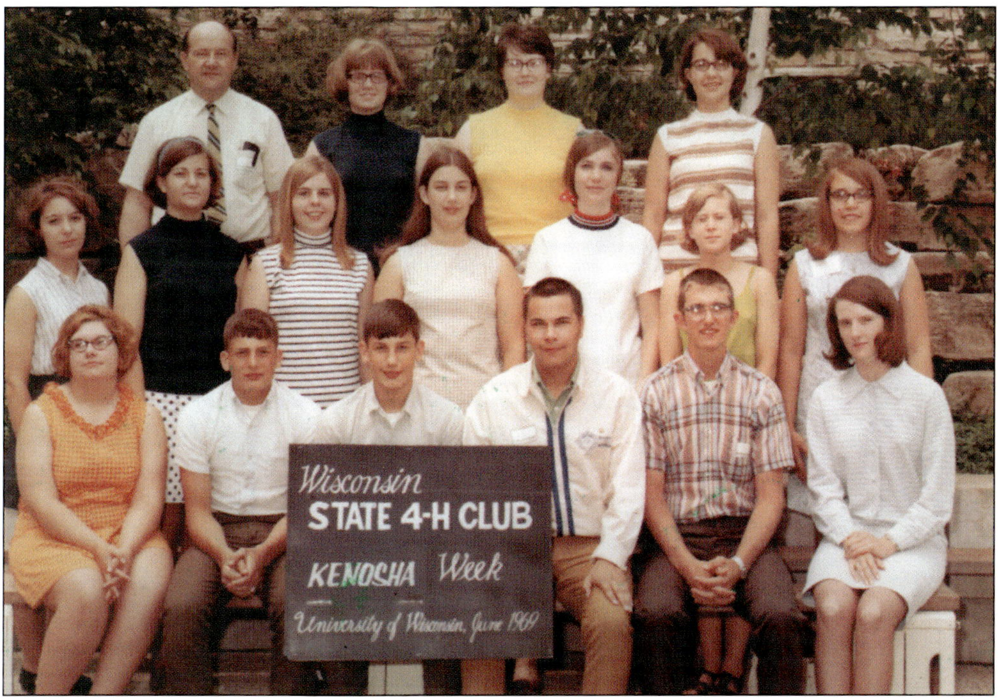

In June 1969, the Kenosha 4-H Club members headed to the University of Wisconsin-Madison to celebrate Kenosha Week at the state 4-H and youth conference. About 600 club members attend the conference every year, where they participate in educational seminars and assemblies. (Courtesy of the Kenosha County University of Wisconsin-Extension.)

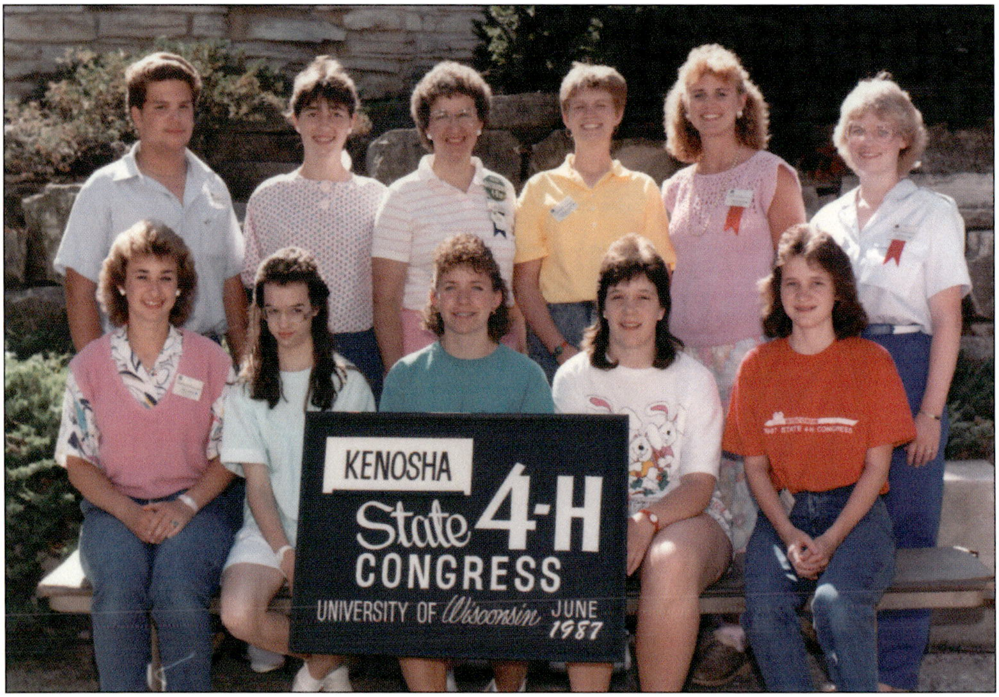

The National 4-H State Congress has been a part of the 4-H program for more than 90 years. Every club selects delegates through an interview and application process to attend the conference, where they learn leadership, community service, and multicultural integration skills. Above is the 1987 group. From left to right are (first row) Heidi Harris, Debbie Boehon, Dodi Daniels, Teresa Skora, and Jamie Weiss; (second row) Mark Glas, Kristin Weiss, Nadine Harris, Ann Sporenburg, Heidi Schultz, and Karen Nelson. The 1991 group is pictured below, with Ellen Reinge (left) and Kristen. (Both, courtesy of the Kenosha County University of Wisconsin-Extension.)

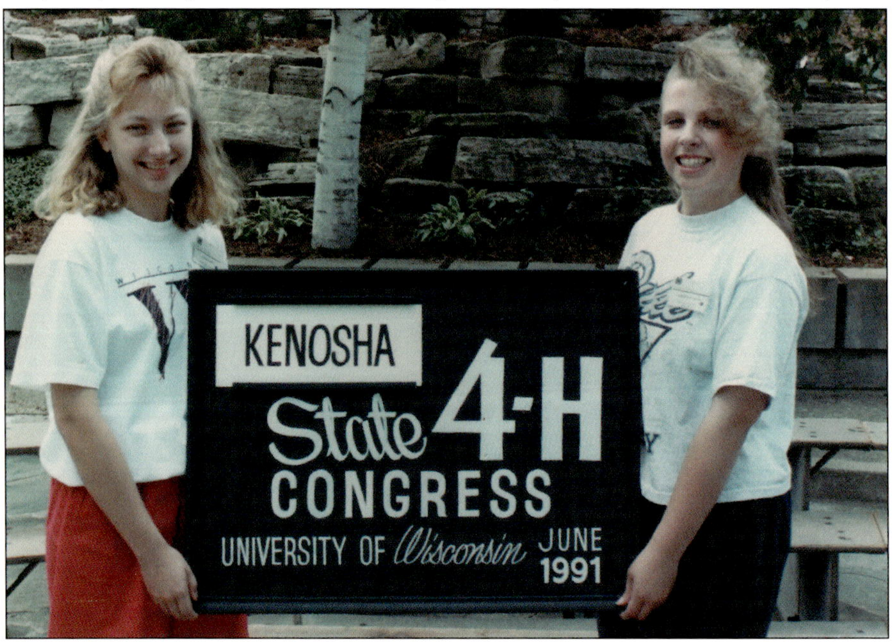

Four

College Life

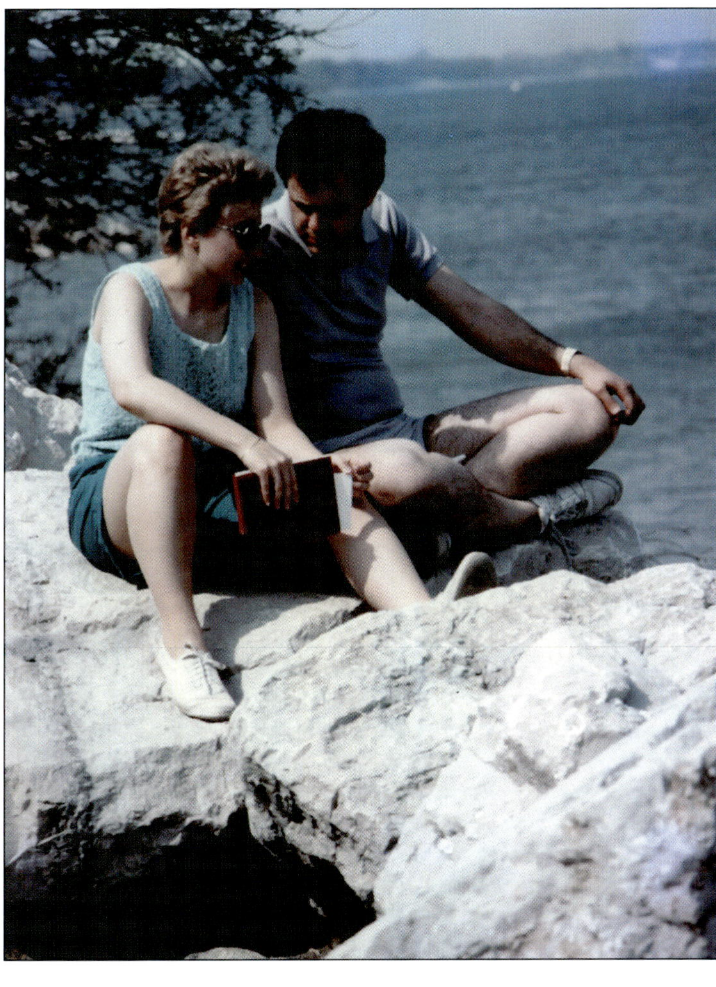

Students at Carthage College have always sat on these boulders, overlooking the lake, to hang out with friends, sit and think, or study. The liberal arts and sciences school strives to provide an environment of self-discovery and reflection—something the lake itself provides in spades. (Courtesy of the Carthage College Archives.)

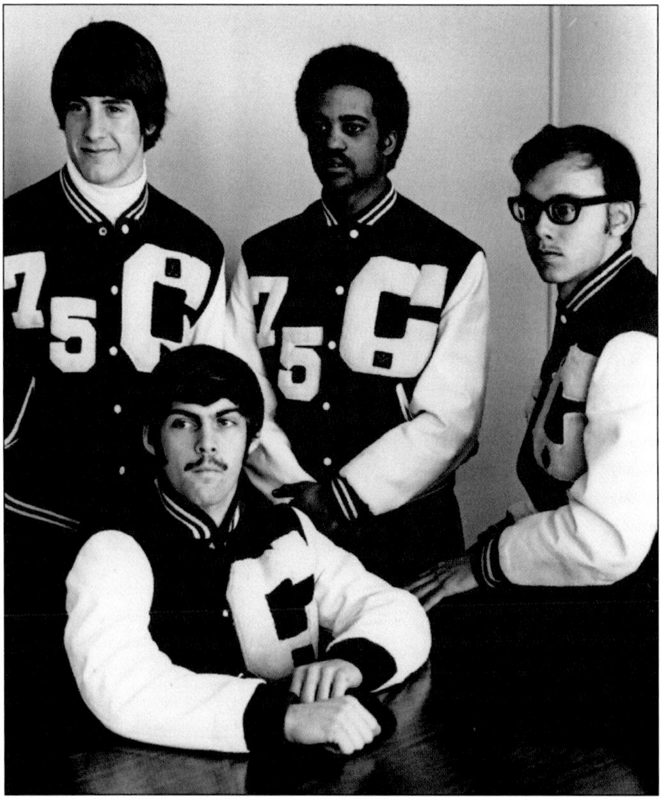

Carthage is ranked as one of the best colleges in the Midwest. It was founded in 1847 and now has around 2,600 full-time students. This photograph shows a group of students from 1973. Bob Heinkel is seated, and standing behind him from left to right are Ross Anderson, Murray Dennison, and Mike Ulrichsen. The four boys were all letter winners in school sports. (Courtesy of the Carthage College Archives.)

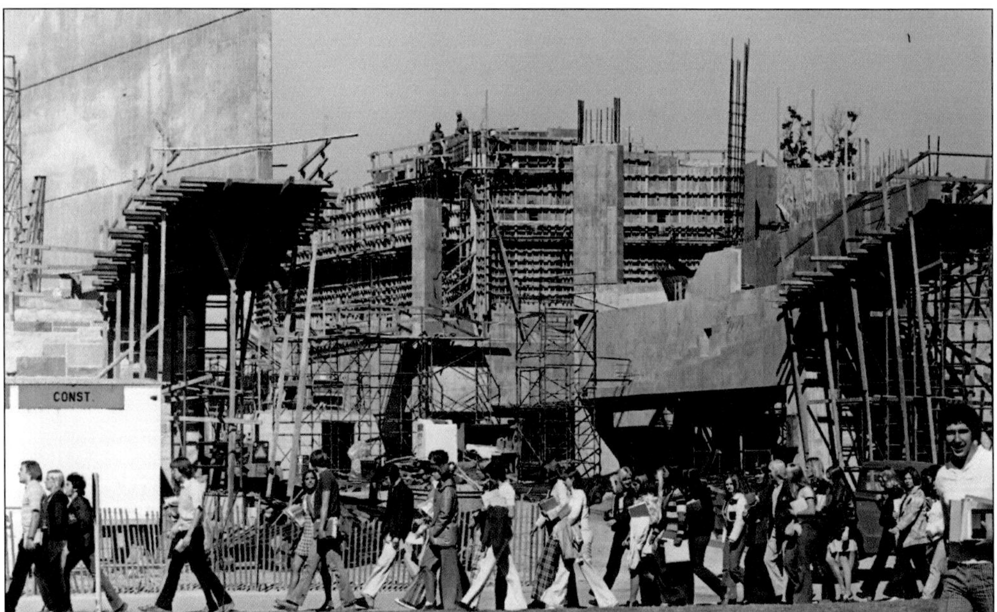

Carthage is an evangelical Lutheran college. This image shows the construction of the Siebert Chapel, which opened in 1975. The chapel seats 1,400 and is right in the middle of campus; it is the main location of almost every event that pulls the student body together. (Courtesy of the Carthage College Archives.)

Kenosha instills a love of sports and recreation in the community beginning at a young age. This is driven home in the college years, as Carthage College has many highly ranked teams. This image shows the Carthage majorette from 1994, Cyndi Kuba. She performed baton twirling during Carthage's games. (Courtesy of the Carthage College Archives.)

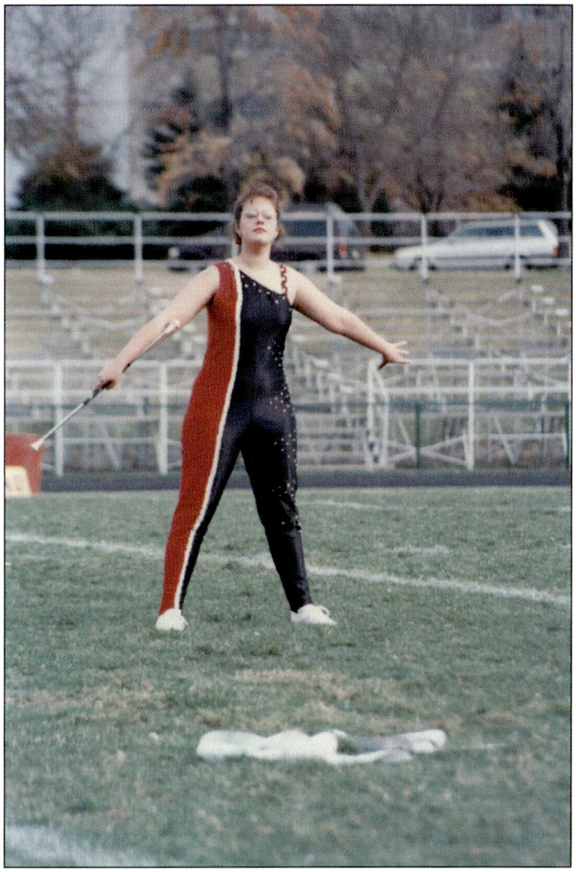

Music is another major part of the sports experience at Carthage. Here, the pep band plays a set from the stands of the homecoming football game. The pep band also performs at basketball games and campus events. The students receive a stipend for participating. (Courtesy of the Carthage College Archives.)

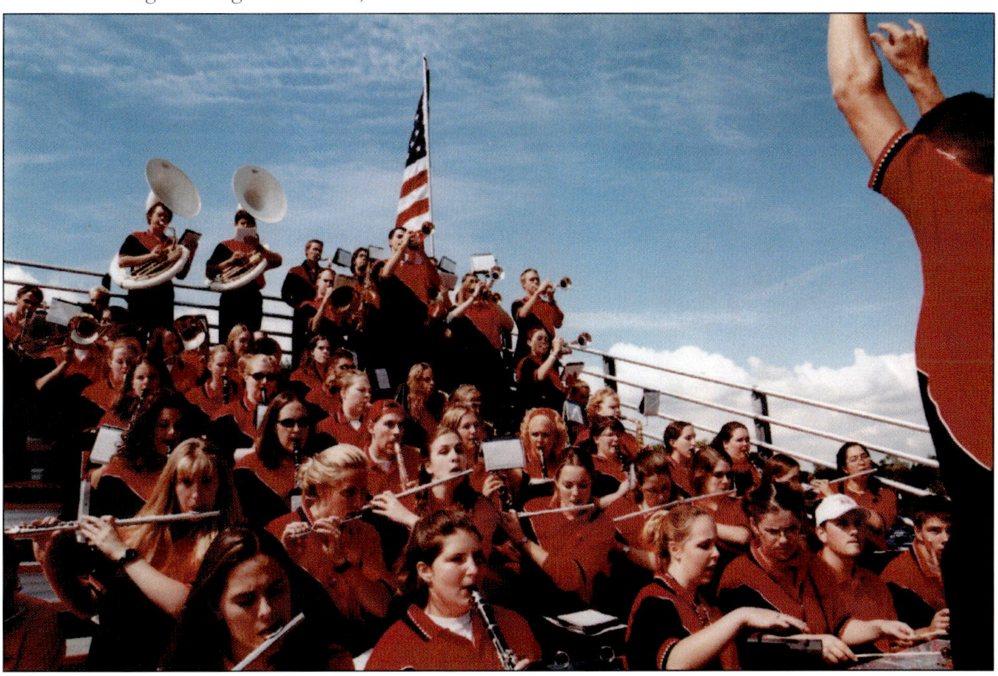

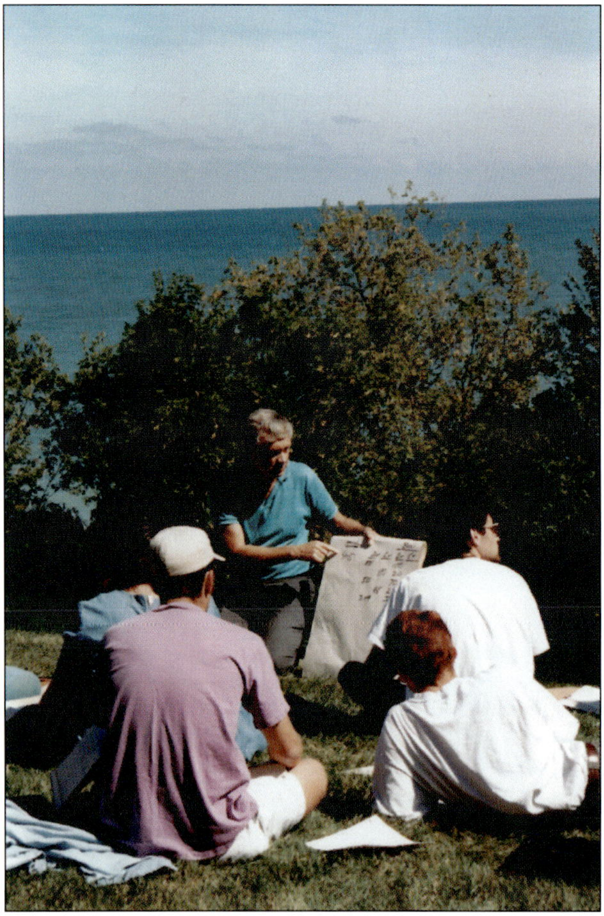

Carthage's campus is an 80-acre arboretum right on Lake Michigan's shores. The school has some of the best views in the area, along with a rocky beach and walking trails throughout the property. When it is nice out, generous teachers take their students outside to hold class on the lawn, like this accounting class. (Courtesy of the Carthage College Archives.)

In the 1960s, Carthage participated in the *College Quiz Bowl* television show. The school played against Drury University in a competition of trivia. Sadly, Carthage lost, with a score of 350 to 50. The show has since been taken off the air, but Carthage still has yearly quiz bowls between school organizations. (Courtesy of the Carthage College Archives.)

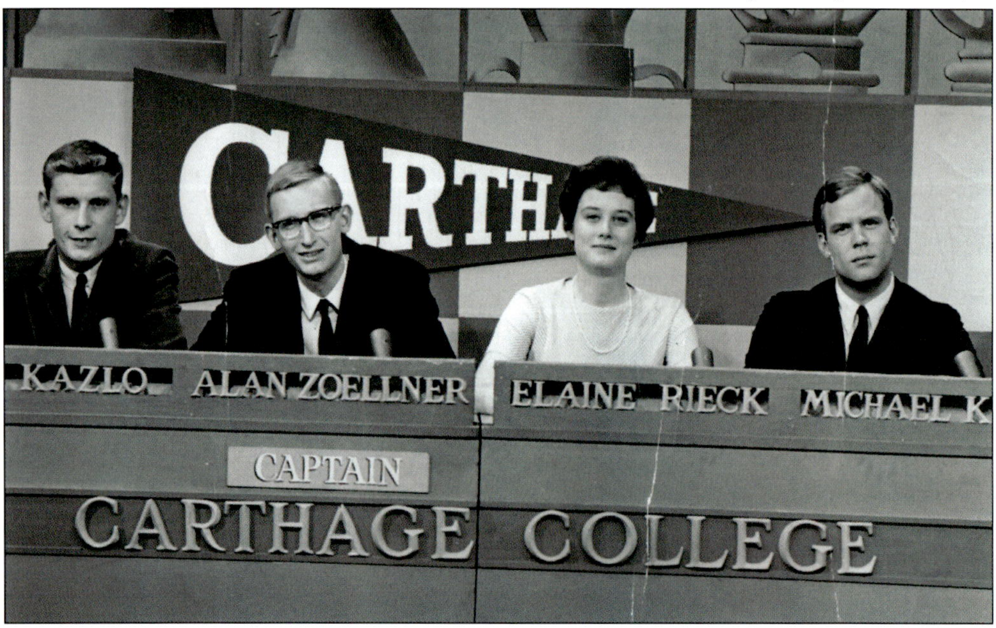

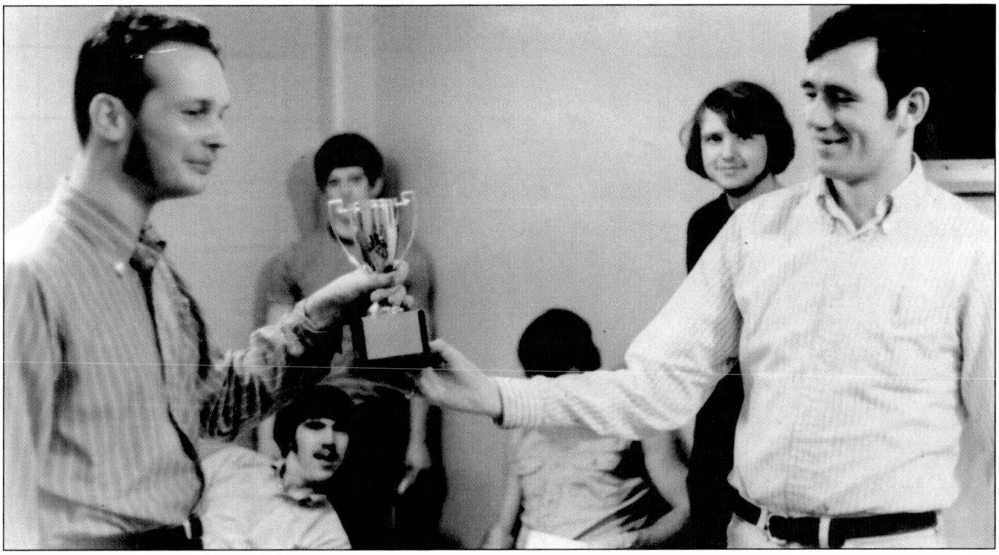

In this photograph from February 1971, the president of the Men's Dorm Council, Kim Efird (left) presents an award to Carl Bristelow. Bristelow is accepting the honor for his entire dorm floor—they won the trophy for best Christmas decorations. (Courtesy of the Carthage College Archives.)

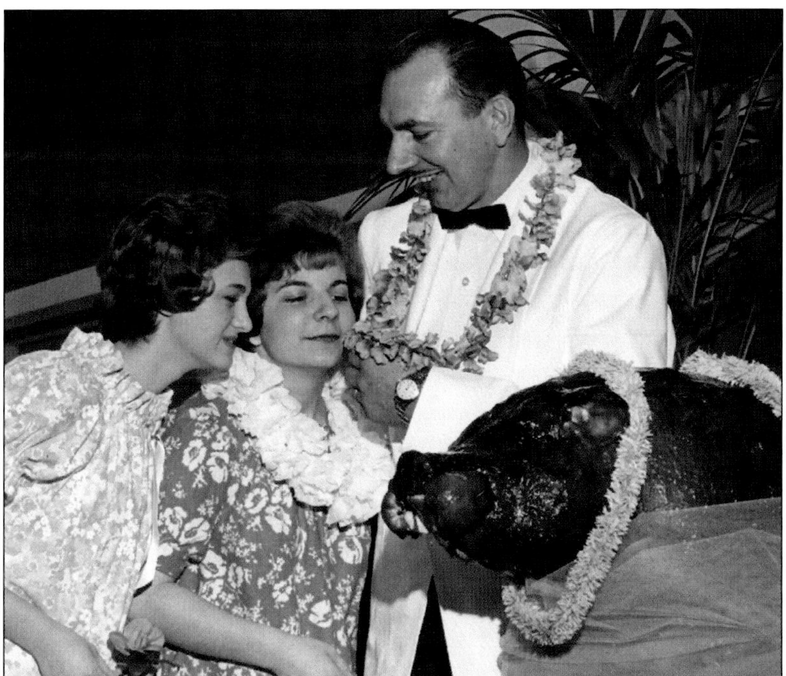

Faculty, staff, and students are encouraged to participate in all of Carthage's campus events, whether it is the yearly senior luncheon, a school parade, a sporting event, a concert in the chapel, or a more unique event like this 1963 luau, complete with roasted pig. (Courtesy of the Carthage College Archives.)

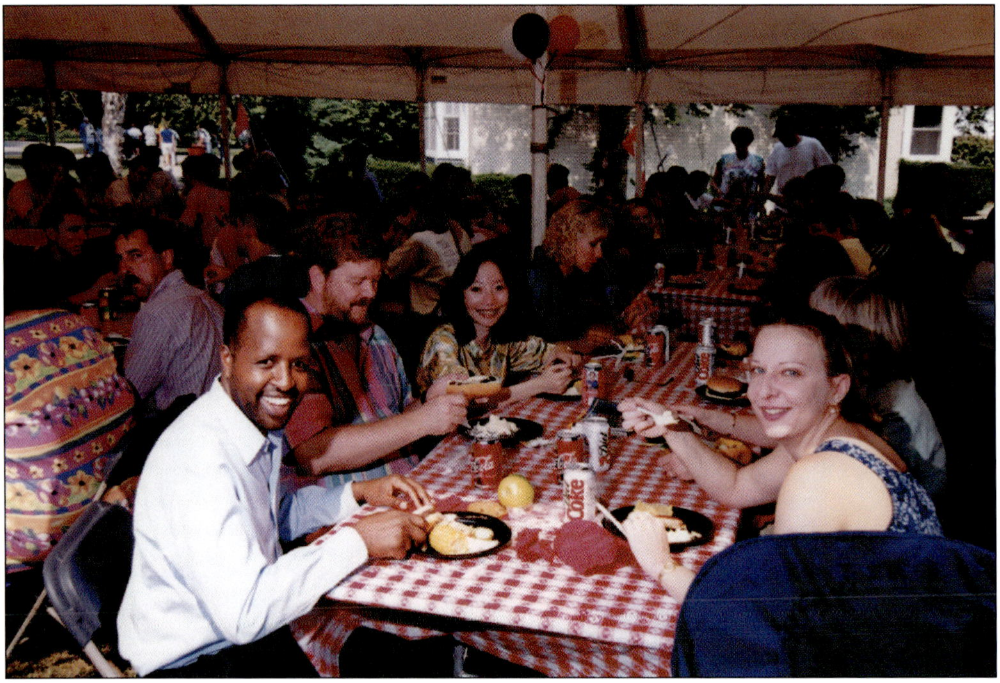

Every year, Carthage admits about 700 new students. The college welcomes these students with open arms—and with a three-day celebration to introduce them to the school. Above, the new 1999 students enjoy a picnic. Below, a group of students from the 1993 freshman class take time out of orientation in Lake Geneva, Wisconsin, to roast marshmallows. (Both, courtesy of the Carthage College Archives.)

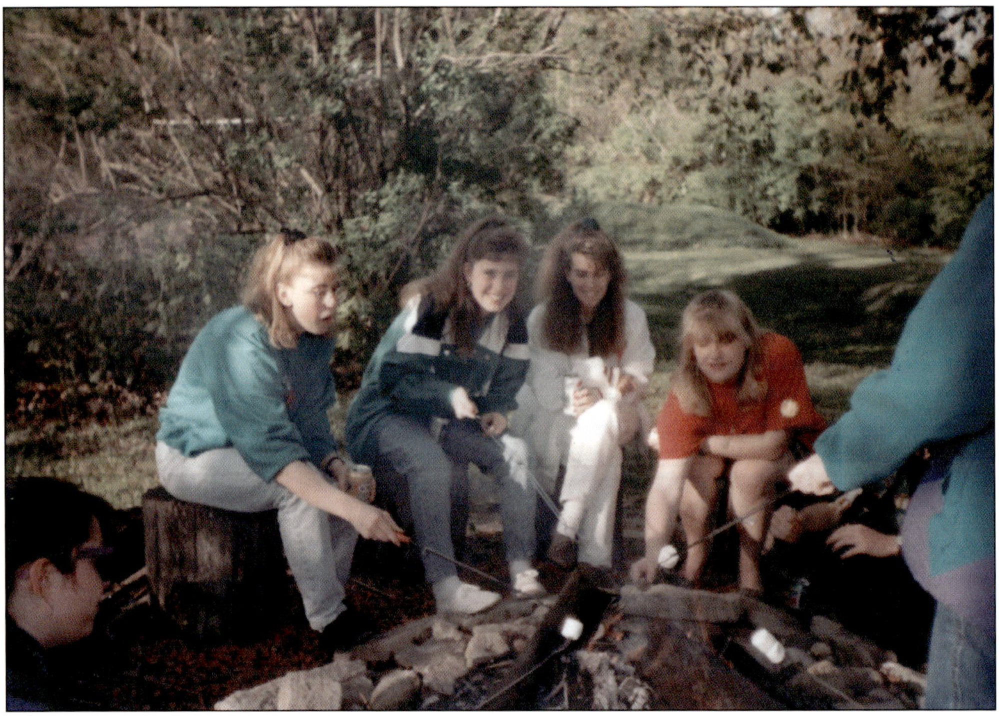

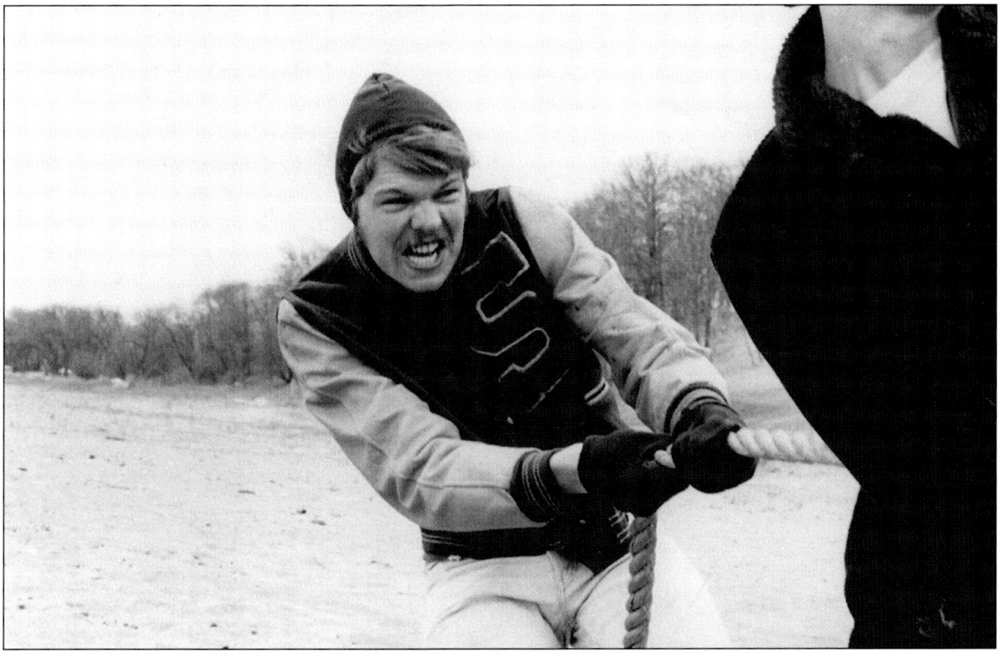

Twenty percent of Carthage's students are involved in Greek life. The school has 17 fraternities and sororities with a shared purpose of enhancing leadership skills and promoting a respectful community. Here, Paul Kostelny is giving it his all in the 1970 Greek Olympics tug-of-war competition. (Courtesy of the Carthage College Archives.)

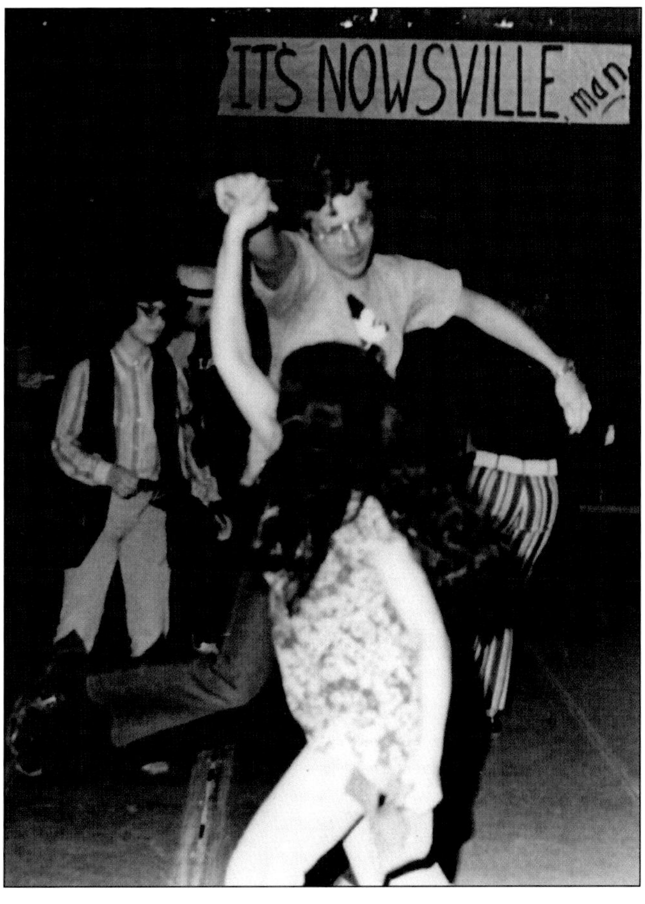

This 1970s photograph shows a dance hosted by Carthage's On Campus Club. The slogan in the back, "It's Nowsville, Man," comes from a poem by Mona Van Duyn called *What the Motorcycle Said.* Basically, the poem is told by a motorcycle and speaks about his lifestyle, which is all based in the present moment, or "Nowsville." (Courtesy of the Carthage College Archives.)

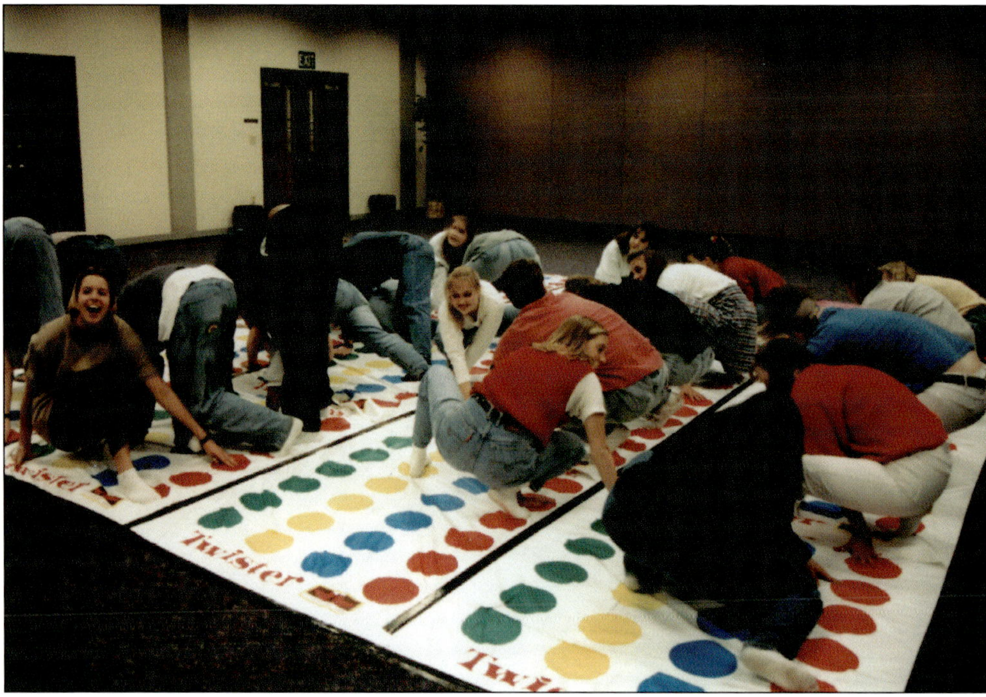

Seventy percent of Carthage's students live on campus in 11 residence halls and student apartment buildings. That is more than 1,800 students living in close quarters. In an effort to loosen the squeeze a little bit, this group of students in the 1990s got even closer with a giant game of Twister. (Courtesy of the Carthage College Archives.)

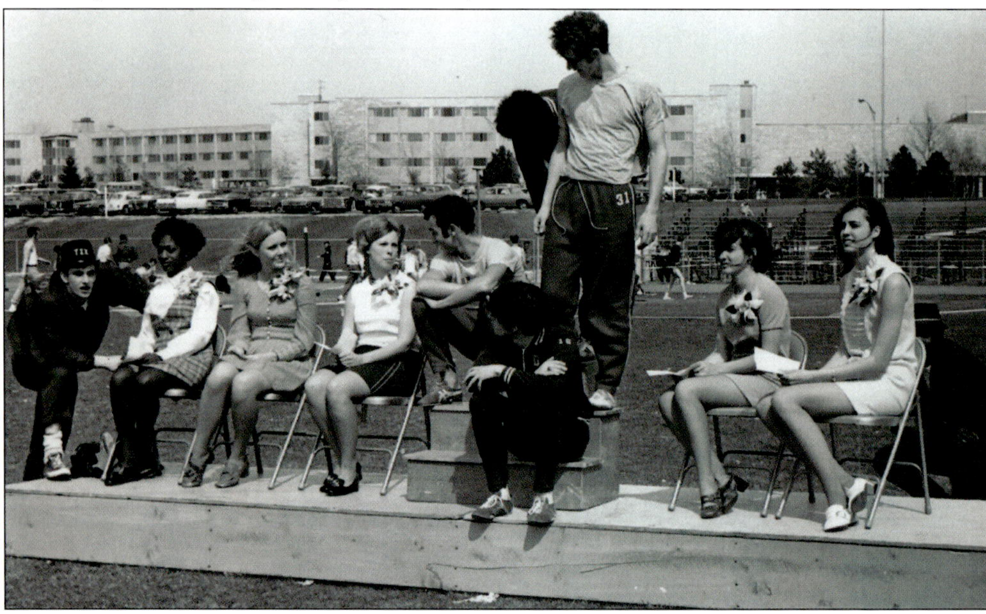

Athletics have played a big role in Carthage's history. The college has 22 NCAA Division III sports for both men and women. One third of the student population is on varsity teams, and another third participates in intramurals. This spring 1970 photograph shows the homecoming court attending a track meet. (Courtesy of the Carthage College Archives.)

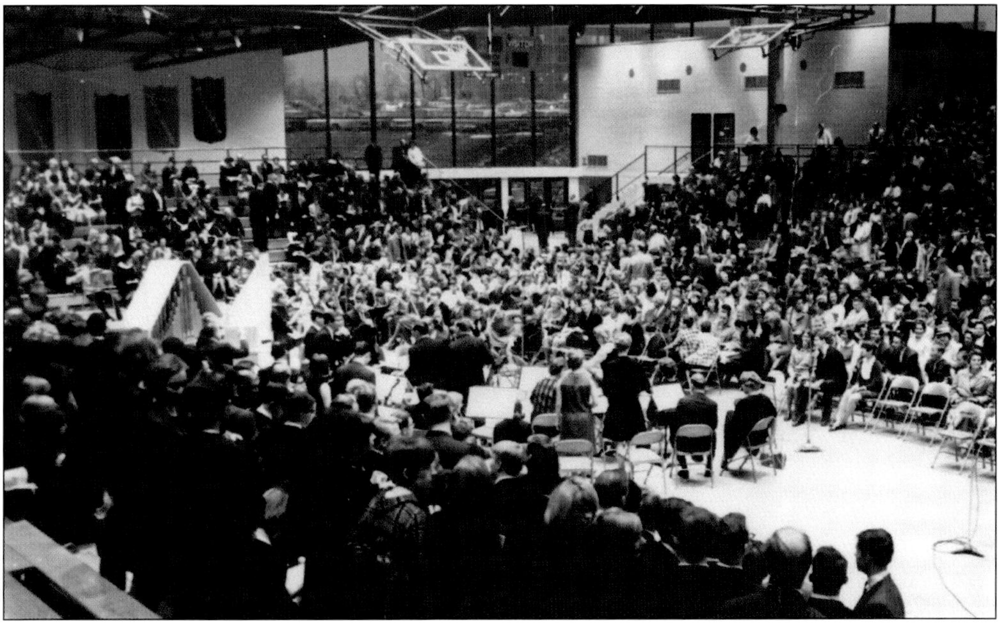

This December 1966 image shows a performance of the *Messiah* oratorio, a musical composition composed by Handel in 1741 that incorporates scriptures from the *King James Bible* and *Book of Common Prayer*. At the left of the performers sits a pipe organ built for this event. (Courtesy of the Carthage College Archives.)

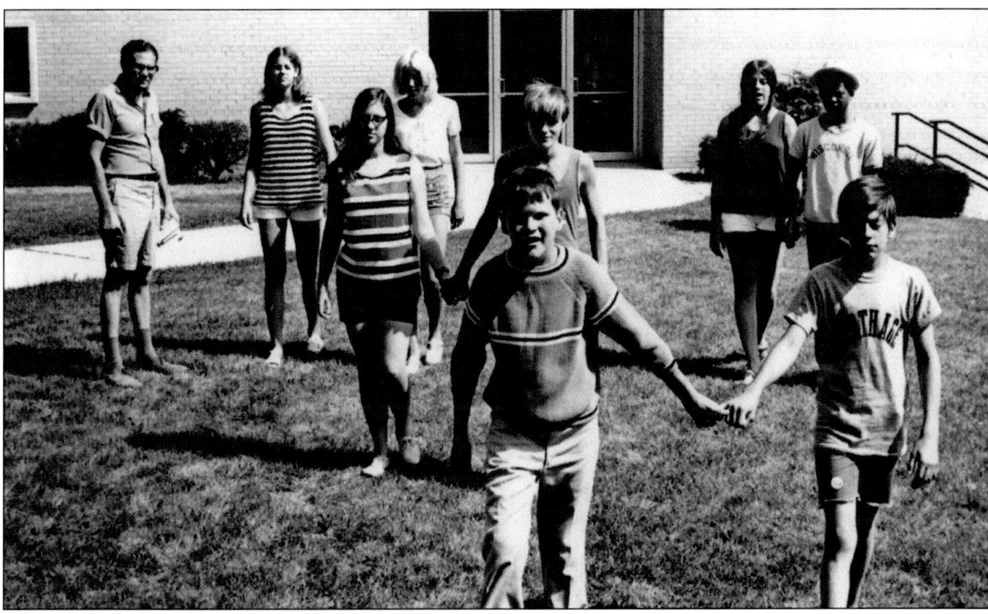

Carthage is a Lutheran school, and the college seeks to uphold those values in the community as well. This 1971 photograph is from a Lutheran camp that was held on campus. Participants are doing a trust exercise, where one person leads another around who has closed eyes. (Courtesy of the Carthage College Archives.)

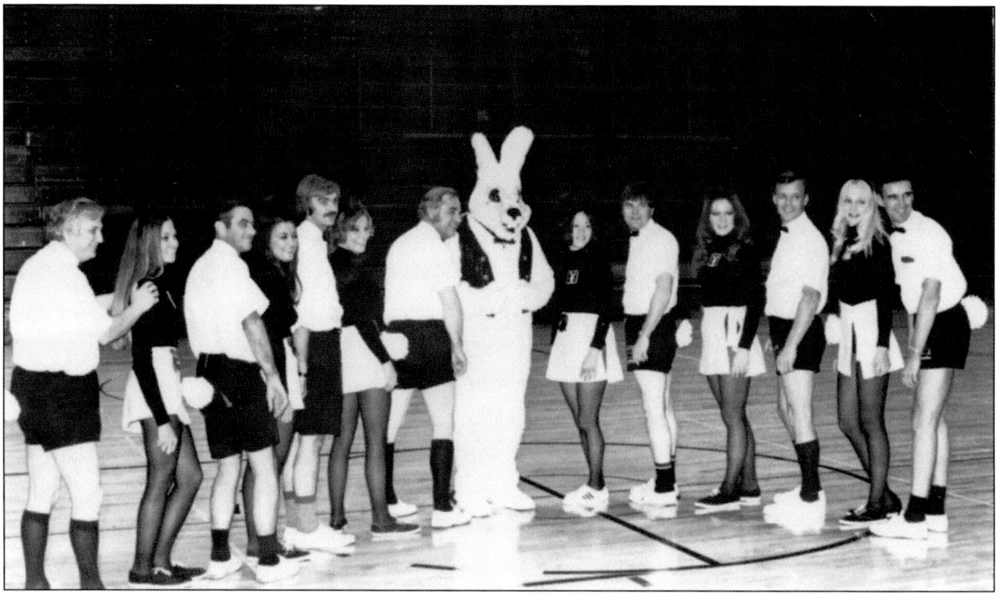

On October 17, 1972, bunnies and hares battled it out in the Carthage College Fieldhouse. The basketball game was a benefit for the Kenosha County Drug Abuse Inc. Switchboard, a nonprofit that helped with youth problems. The bunnies were the Lake Geneva Playboy Bunnies, and the hares were 50 Kenosha men who played in rotating squads. (Courtesy of the Carthage College Archives.)

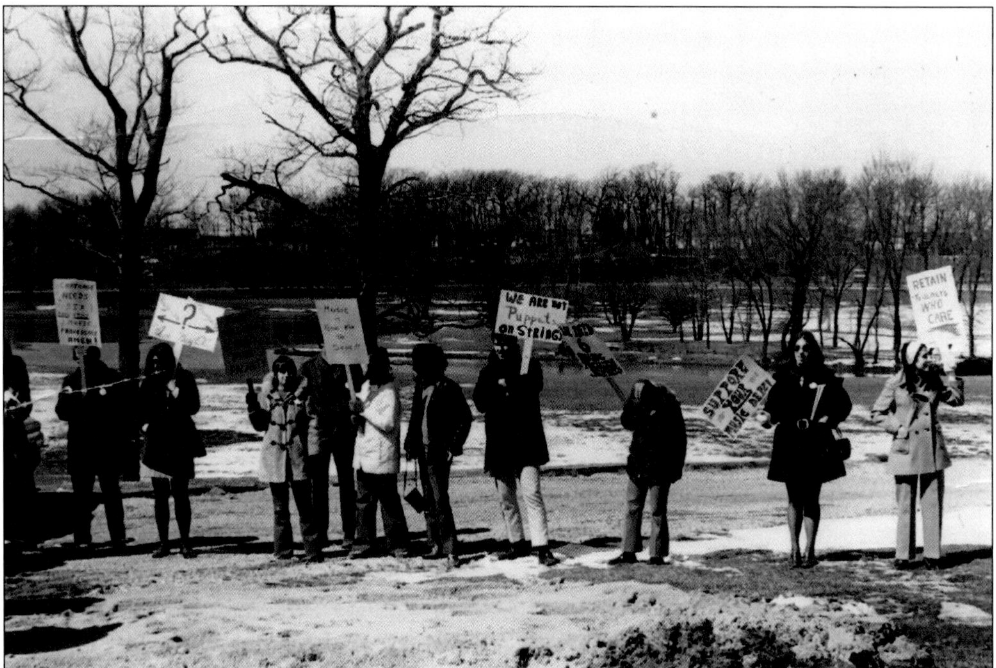

Carthage College may be a religious institution, but that has never kept the students from exercising their freedom of speech. In this March 24, 1971, photograph, students protest the unfair treatment of a music teacher based on the tenure process at the school. (Courtesy of the Carthage College Archives.)

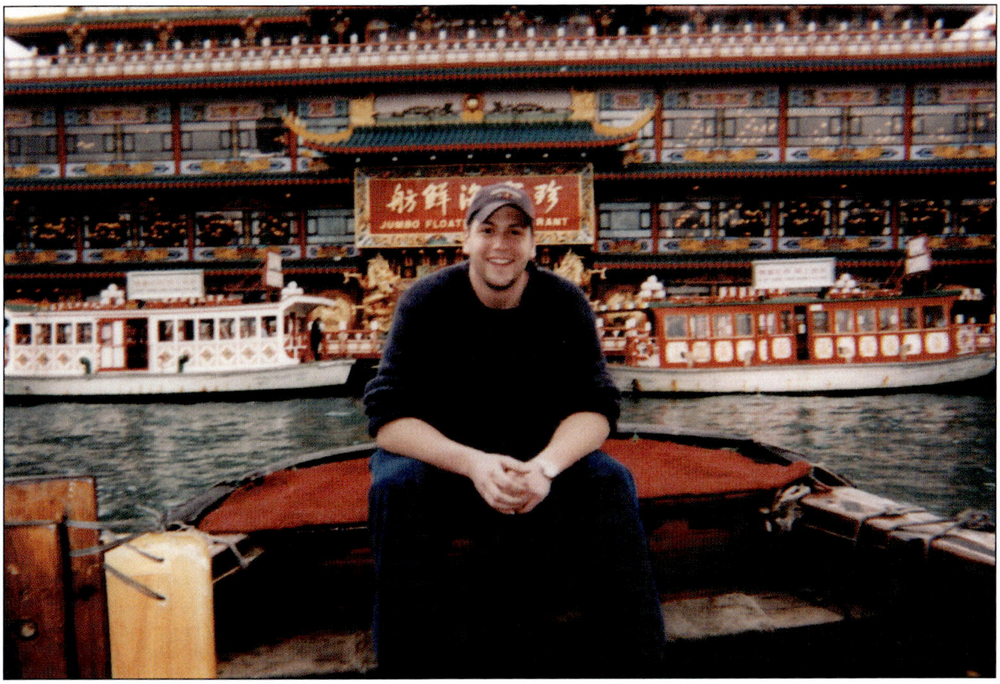

Carthage offers a unique program called J-Term, or January Term, where students can elect to take a month of classes outside their major. These classes are held in various countries throughout the world. This photograph shows a J-Term student visiting the Jumbo Kingdom Floating Restaurant in Hong Kong. (Courtesy of the Carthage College Archives.)

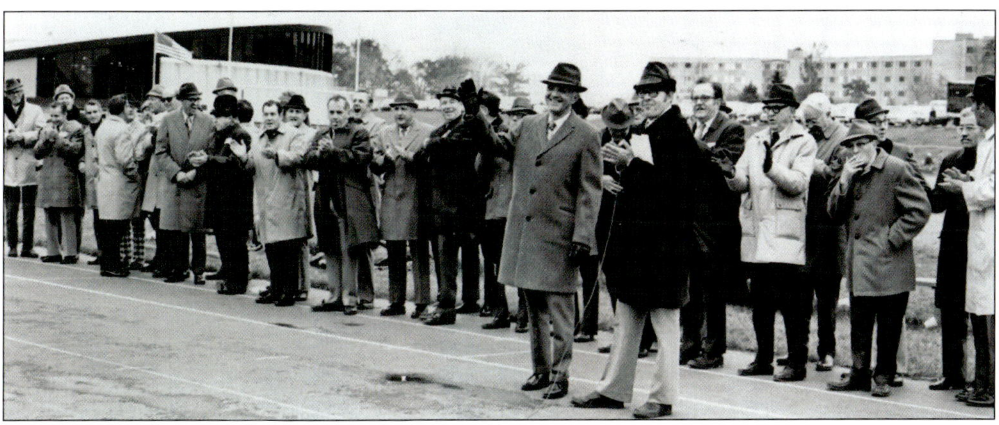

This October 16, 1971, photograph shows George Halas, a founding father and owner of the Chicago Bears, being honored for his contributions to football during Carthage's homecoming game's half-time show. More than 3,500 fans were in the stands that day to watch Carthage slaughter Millikin, with a final score of 34-7. (Courtesy of the Carthage College Archives.)

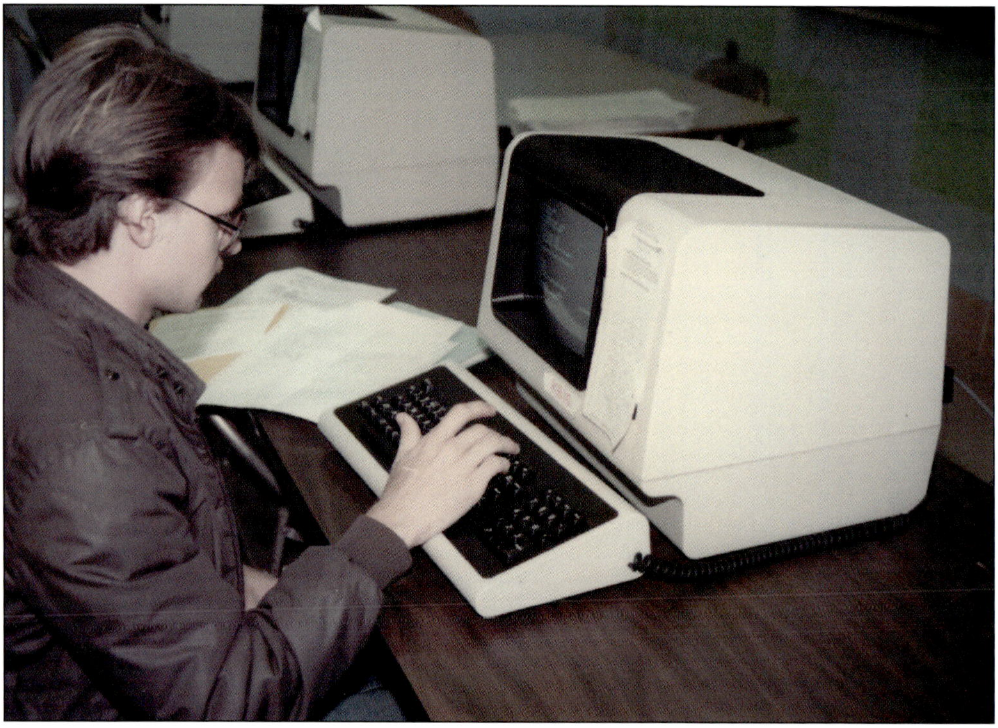

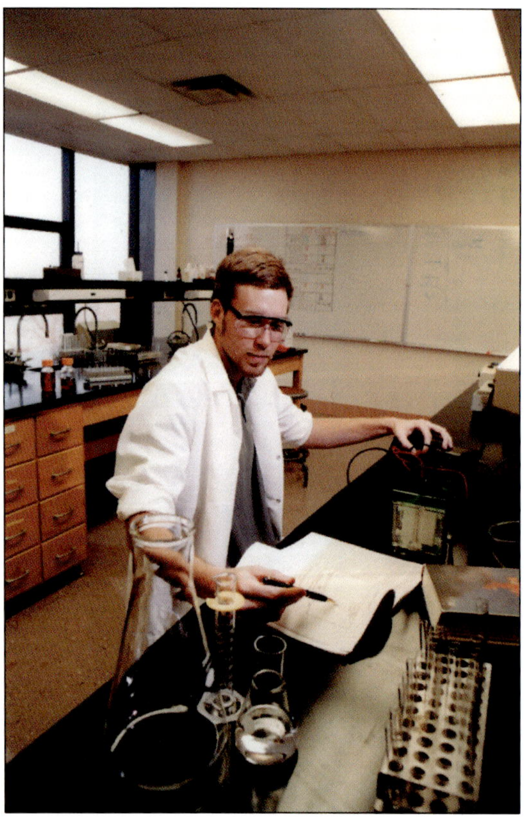

Carthage does its best to be on the leading edge of technology for all its classes. Above, a student in the late 1970s works on a DEC VT100 computer. These machines were produced beginning in 1978. At left, a student working on a chemistry experiment utilizes modern wiring tools. With the college's focused curriculum (every one of its 50-plus areas of study requires hands-on projects and writing intensive courses), these up-to-date tools are necessary to stay in line with some of the school's core values: to develop the skills necessary to not only do well in life and work, but to excel. (Both, courtesy of the Carthage College Archives.)

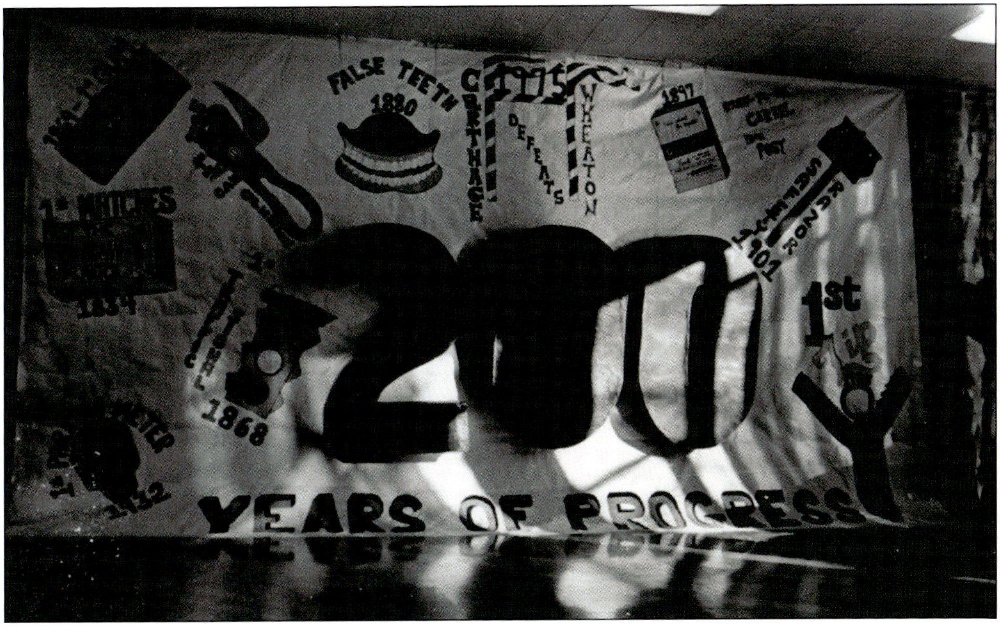

In 1976, Carthage students created a mural to celebrate the bicentennial of the Declaration of Independence. The mural highlighted some of the United States' greatest achievements—like invention of traffic lights in 1868, matches in 1834, the safety razor in 1901, and the all-important false teeth in 1880. (Courtesy of the Carthage College Archives.)

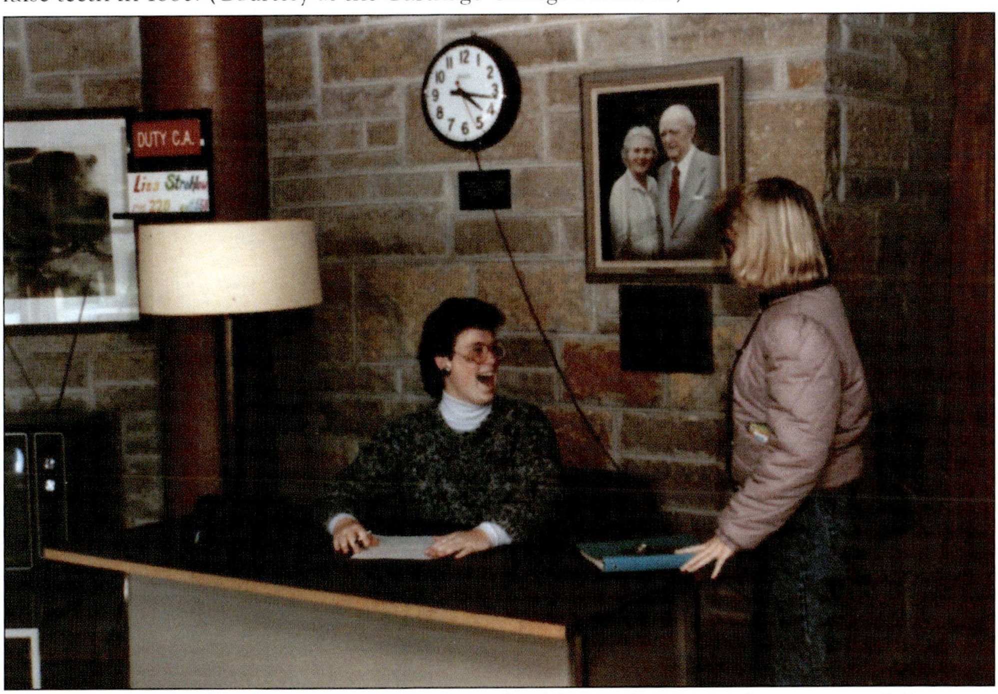

This 1980s image shows campus assistant Lisa Strehlow helping a student in one of the many campus buildings. On the college's sprawling campus, Carthage currently has about 18 facilities available for classes, religious study, sports, and student use, as well as 11 residence halls. (Courtesy of the Carthage College Archives.)

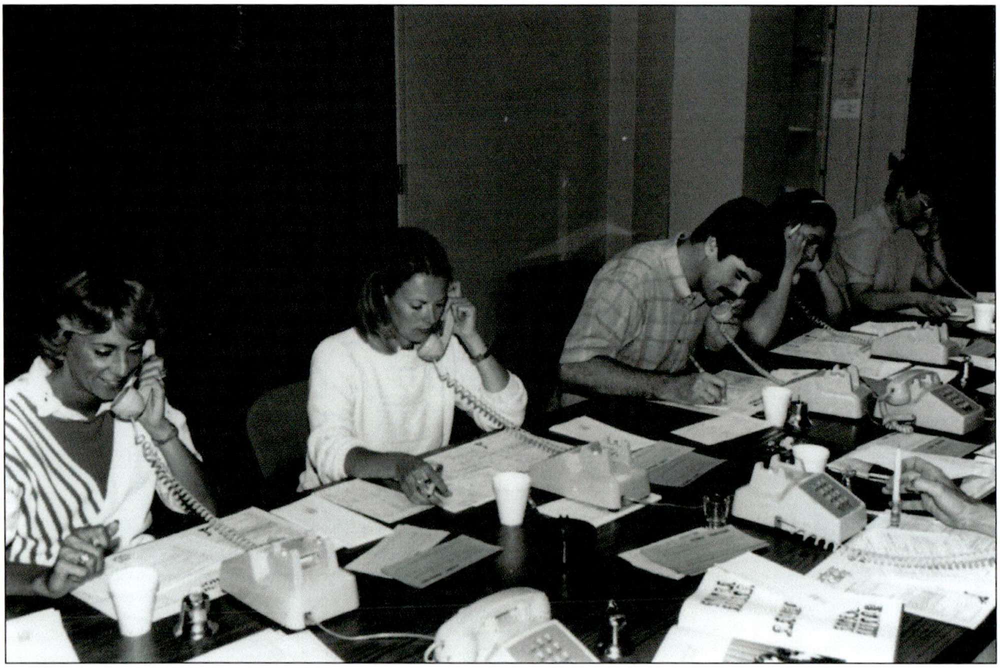

Carthage has a long history of holding fundraising drives, such as this one staffed by faculty and students in the late 1970s, to obtain money for needed campus enhancements and to fund college organizations. The yearly events can include everything from telethons to interactive sports events and live concerts. (Courtesy of the Carthage College Archives.)

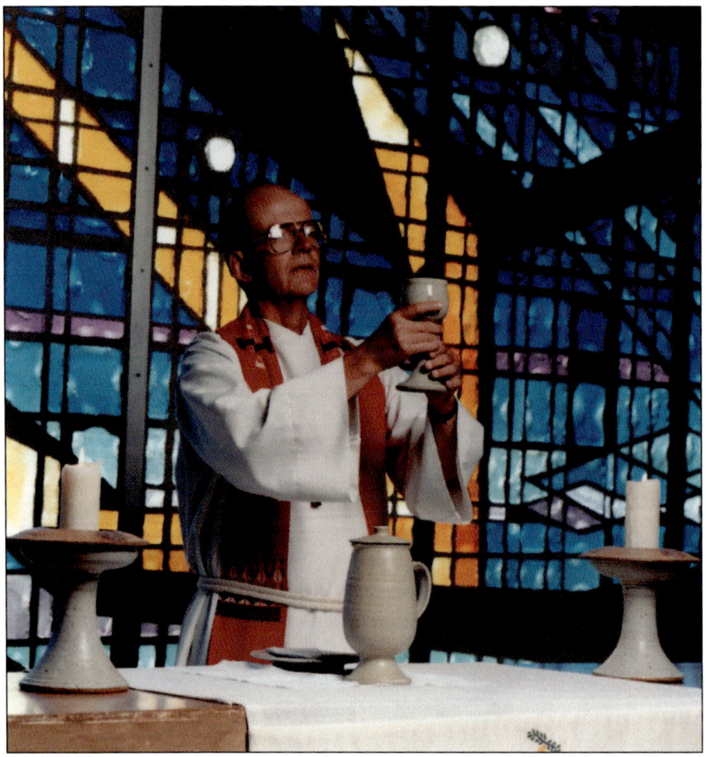

Ross Larson has been teaching classes at Carthage since 1991, and spent several of those years acting as campus pastor. Carthage awarded him an honorary doctorate in divinity in May 2013. Larson is seen here leading a service in the Siebert chapel in 1995. (Courtesy of the Carthage College Archives.)

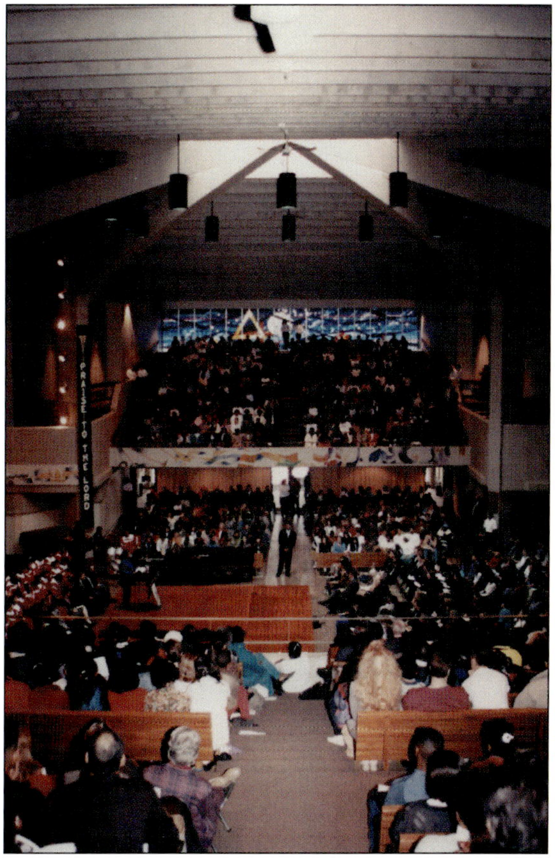

On February 26, 1992, Coretta Scott King came to speak at Carthage. More than 1,800 people attended the speech, during which she discussed using non-violence as a tool against social injustice. She was Martin Luther King Jr.'s wife and was invited as part of Black History Month celebrations. (Courtesy of the Carthage College Archives.)

At that same visit, student Arthur Foy directed a performance by the Gospel Messengers, a gospel choir composed of students, faculty, staff, and friends of the college. The choir was, and continues to be, known for its welcoming attitude to people of all traditions and backgrounds. (Courtesy of the Carthage College Archives.)

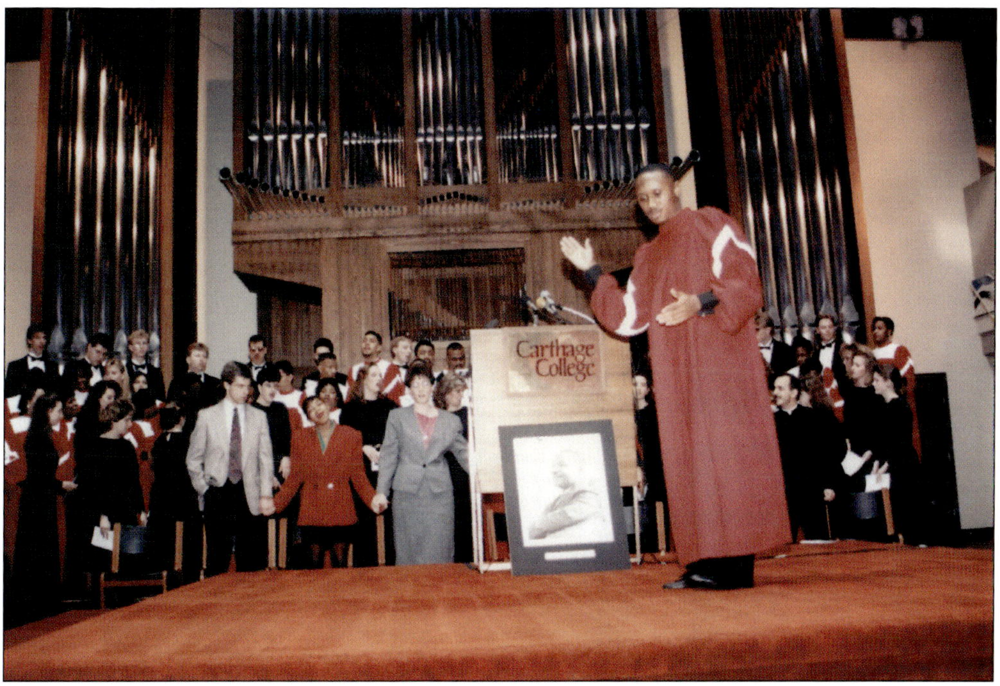

Discover Thousands of Local History Books Featuring Millions of Vintage Images

Arcadia Publishing, the leading local history publisher in the United States, is committed to making history accessible and meaningful through publishing books that celebrate and preserve the heritage of America's people and places.

Find more books like this at
www.arcadiapublishing.com

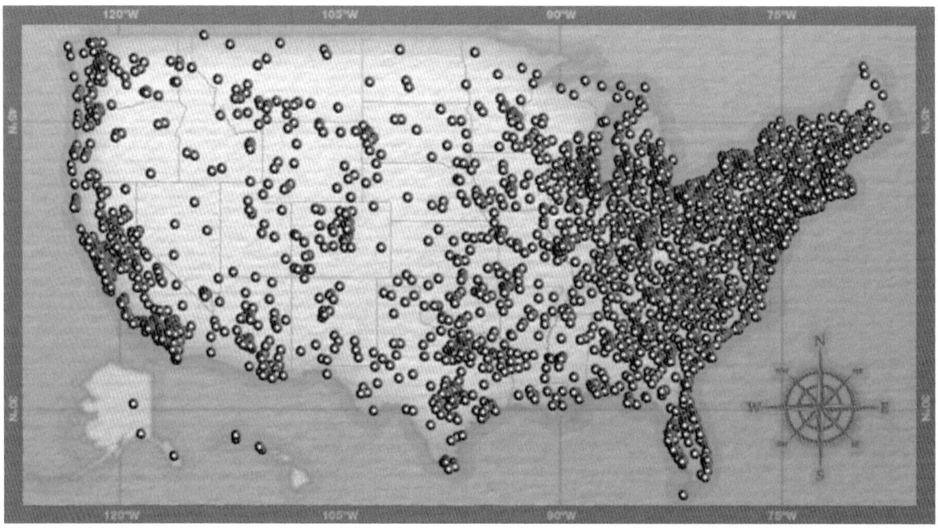

Search for your hometown history, your old stomping grounds, and even your favorite sports team.

Consistent with our mission to preserve history on a local level, this book was printed in South Carolina on American-made paper and manufactured entirely in the United States. Products carrying the accredited Forest Stewardship Council (FSC) label are printed on 100 percent FSC-certified paper.

MADE IN THE USA